To Les,

a friend and ⌐⌐⌐ ⌐⌐⌐

in the development of ⌐⌐

transnational world, with

best wishes —

Henk

March 1993

GLOBAL EMBRACE

GLOBAL EMBRACE

CORPORATE CHALLENGES IN
A TRANSNATIONAL WORLD

HENRY WENDT

HarperBusiness
A Division of HarperCollins*Publishers*

HarperCollins books may be purchased for educational, business, or sales promotional use. For information please write Special Markets Department, HarperCollins Publishers, Inc., 10 East 53rd Street, New York, NY 10022.

FIRST EDITION

Designed by George J. McKeon

Library of Congress Cataloging-in-Publication Data

Wendt, Henry.
    Global embrace : corporate challenges in a transnational world / Henry Wendt. — 1st ed.
        p.   cm.
    Includes bibliographical references and index.

    ISBN 0-88730-591-1
    1. International business enterprises—Management. I. Title.
HD62.4.W45   1993
658'.049—dc20   92-53336

93 94 95 96 97 ❖/HC 10 9 8 7 6 5 4 3 2 1

To Chip and Laura, the next generation

CONTENTS

ACKNOWLEDGMENTS

THE TERM *TRANSNATIONAL CORPORATION* was first uttered in my hearing by Howard Perlmutter of the Wharton School of Business at a conference for senior managers conducted in Geneva, Switzerland, in October 1971. For years I have thought it ironic that I traveled to Geneva to attend a seminar led by a professor who normally taught students less than a mile from my office in Philadelphia. On reflection and with the passage of time, it now seems appropriate that in such an international city as Geneva and in company with a group of businessmen drawn from Europe and around the world, I should first have been exposed directly to Howard's views. By then I had lived and worked in Philadelphia, Honolulu, Montreal, Tokyo, and Palo Alto. Howard's stimulating observations and thinking about the conduct of global business fell on fertile ground. I had experienced directly much of what he discussed and since then have lived much of what he projected.

Many others contributed directly to the ideas and endeavors that are described in this book. My early teachers at Smith Kline & French Laboratories included such serious and able international businessmen of their day as Koey Rivinus, Kurt Solmssen, Peter Howsam, Kurt Reiss, Frank Hodson, and Francis Grant. Jim Abbegglen taught me much about Japan, but even more important he set an admirable personal example for learning about the Japanese people. Ray Kutsunai, as companion and friend, provided valuable insights each day we worked together. Subsequently, in the forum of the U.S.–Japan Business Council, my sights were lifted from company strategy to national and global welfare under the tutelage of Ed Spenser and Roger Swanson.

Louis Allen and his colleagues taught me how to think about the work of management. Authoritative observers and writers on global corporations, including especially Kenichi Ohmae, Michael Porter, Christopher Bartlett, and Sumantra Ghoshal, with whom I met while contemplating what this book might contain, exerted profound influences on my thinking. Many of their ideas and approaches manifest themselves in the pages that follow.

Morris Cheston, Sam Ballam, Carter Burgess, Roy Anderson, Chauncey Medberry, and other members of boards on which I have been privileged to serve showed me the best corporate governance in action during good times and bad. I owe a special debt to Bill Grant, who has not only served as a splendid example of corporate governance but has been a friend and mentor for twenty years. Bill's personal interest in this book and his guidance on this and many other matters have helped me immensely.

But perhaps most of all, it is the many men and women, employees and managers, of SmithKline Beecham working on the front lines of building a truly global company, transnational in nature, who have taught me the most and to whom I am most indebted for their contributions to my busy career and to this book. Under the firm and energetic direction of Bob Bauman and the management team of SmithKline Beecham, they are accomplishing great things and in many important respects are showing the way.

The project of writing this book was first discussed with Tod Hullin and Myles Martel. Although the ideas were no doubt rattling around in my head at the time, it was their challenge to me and their encouragement that brought them forth. Tod and Myles were very much present at the launching. My able and resourceful literary agent Sue Katz provided the practical advice and expert guidance that set me firmly on course toward completion and, together with my able editor at Harper Business, Virginia Smith, managed to keep me from going too far off course.

Without the help of my collaborating writer Bruce Tucker, I am certain this book would still be languishing in a hopeless muddle of ideas and words. Bruce contributed much to all that is contained between these two covers. His expert interviewing and friendly interrogation of me brought vague ideas and concepts to practical expression. His management of our data base brought organization and order. His mastery of the language facilitated expression, and his responsiveness greatly aided our mutual efficiency. Above all, Bruce brought to our working relationship not only his vast arsenal of writing skills and experience, but, more important, great patience, unfailing courtesy of the old school, and a wonderfully dry and ironic sense of humor. If the reader finds good things in this book, they are at least as much a product of Bruce's manifold contributions as of mine.

Throughout the time in which this work was in preparation, many other pressing duties and obligations competed for my time and energy. Only with the good work of my executive assistant in Philadelphia, Chris Burlaga, and her companion in arms Daphne Carter in London was I able to keep at least some of the balls in the air. I owe them both a tremendous vote of thanks for the many ways in which they help and support me every hour of every day, seven days a week.

Writing is always challenging in that it requires one to clarify continually thoughts and opinions previously kept safely from view in the cupboards of the mind. Often the act of writing provokes introspection and self-examination. In the process of working on this book, I was brought face to face once again with the realization of how much I rely on Holly, my wife and companion of thirty-six years. She continually sacrifices most of her priorities to help me pursue all of mine. She not only accomplishes it without ever mentioning that it is occurring, but she is always there with love, good cheer, and a helping hand. And she is a counselor, sounding board, and a wonderful copy editor. Holly is responsible, in large measure, for all the good things that have happened in my life, including the concentrated effort that went into this book.

As readers encounter errors and omissions, not to mention opinions and points of view with which they disagree, I hope they will remember that I, and I alone, am responsible for them. In return, I thank them for their indulgence.

INTRODUCTION

THE TRANSNATIONAL CHALLENGE

AT A ROADBLOCK SOMEWHERE outside Beijing, the policeman stopped our van and told us we had to turn back. It was the fall of 1989, and I was traveling with the local manager of a factory my company, SmithKline Beecham, had opened in Tianjin. As chairman of one of the few foreign pharmaceutical companies allowed to operate in the People's Republic of China following the overthrow of the Gang of Four, I was eager, as I had been on my previous trips there, to see firsthand how things were progressing. But I was making this visit only a few months after the turbulent events in Tiananmen Square, which I suspected might account for the policeman's behavior.

As the policeman stood impatiently beside our vehicle, I expected my Chinese manager to offer a lengthy explanation of our reasons for traveling outside Beijing and perhaps to produce some documents that might persuade the guard to let us pass. My manager did neither. Instead, he pointed at me and spoke a few animated words in Chinese. The guard smiled broadly and ceremoniously waved us through.

I asked the manager what magic words he had uttered. "Oh," he replied, "I told him you had come from a very long way and, what's more, that we are the 'Two Tablets' company."

I had to laugh. The television ad we had produced for the first product we introduced in China — a remedy for intestinal parasites, which are widespread there — featured a doctor in a white lab coat saying emphatically, "Remember, two tablets a day — *two tablets a day* — kills worms!" And the doctor drove home the point by holding up two fingers and thrusting them forward as he spoke the tag line.

In a country where few people own television sets and the state broadcasting service airs only a few hours each evening, it is sometimes difficult to know with any accuracy whether these glossy, Western-style commercials are effective. But in this case we at SmithKline Beecham already had a fair idea that we had made our product widely known. The evidence came from a surprising source — the Tiananmen Square demonstrations themselves. Anyone among the millions of people around the world who watched those extraordinary events unfold on their television screens will recall the students holding up two fingers in what looked like the Victory sign (or the Peace sign) and chanting in unison. In fact, they were mimicking the doctor in the television ad and were chanting, "Two tablets for Li Peng!" The implication, of course, was that the premier was a parasite.

I was amused by the response of the policeman at the roadblock, but I was also moved to reflect on the impact such companies as SmithKline Beecham, operating in markets around the globe, were having in a world shrunk by electronic communications and the universal desire for global products. Moreover, the novel use to which the students put the ad offered a powerful reminder that although companies may operate globally, the individual countries and cultures in which they do so are decidedly local, each with its unique purposes, prospects, and problems. This is a dual recognition that has been slow to dawn, even on many of us who have been deeply involved in international commerce, but it is at the heart of a profound transformation in the nature of global business and international affairs.

Large-scale international business enterprises have, of course, existed at least since the days of the Dutch, French, and British East India trading companies. As their names suggested and their actions confirmed, they were tied to the interests of a particular country and radiated their power outward from centers of imperial might. In many respects, that early model still colors the way many people think of corporations that operate globally, whether they are classic international companies exporting to foreign countries or more recent multinational companies establishing overseas operations around the world. Yet in the past decade, almost everything about that long-standing model has been rendered obsolete by a new kind of corporate entity that is rapidly pushing its way into the global reality: the transnational corporation.

Each passing day brings more news of cross-border business ventures, from strategic alliances and joint ventures to international mergers of companies that were already enormous. Similarly, many other large corporations that once seemed inextricably associated with their countries of origin have shed their national identities to become truly global companies that are equally at home in markets around the world. Transnational in operation, ownership, and often in origins, all these enterprises seek a global presence while respecting local differences. Yet, despite the accelerating pace at which these corporate giants are forming, they are barely understood, even by people who are most directly affected by them — from ordinary citizens to corporate managers to heads of state.

The emergence of transnational corporations is one of the most far-reaching and, to many, controversial transformations under way in our rapidly changing world. Indeed, it is fair to say that through the remainder of this century and well into the next, transnationals are likely to be decisive not only for the way individuals live and work, but for the way in which the politics and economies of the world are bound together. Whether we work for transnationals, lead them, compete against them, regulate them, buy their products, or act as citizens to deal with them, transnationals present a unique set of challenges to all of us, throughout the world.

In the pages that follow, I hope to lay out those challenges and come to grips with them. As I do so, I will rely most heavily on concrete, contemporary examples from companies, both familiar and not so familiar. But I will also draw on my experiences from more than thirty-five years spent in international business. Those experiences run the gamut from fateful multi-million-dollar business decisions to amusing, and not so amusing, cultural misunderstandings. My purpose in detailing some of the more significant events is not to produce yet another overbearing business autobiography, but to offer a firsthand look at the transnational world and, most important, to communicate the sense of urgency and importance I think these issues merit.

My fascination with issues of internationalism long predates my business career. As a sixteen-year-old high school student spending a summer in Cuba, I avidly followed reports of the Korean War in Spanish-language newspapers. I marveled that the world's great powers, which had so recently cooperated to defeat the Axis countries in World War II, were unable to cooperate on the geopolitical issues in what was then considered a remote part of the world. Perhaps in a belated effort to understand, I majored in American diplomatic history as an undergraduate at Princeton University. I vividly recall Eric Goldman, the renowned scholar of the liberal progressive tradition, advising me on my senior thesis. "Why don't you write on Senator Robert Taft's foreign policy," he suggested, "because, Mr. Wendt, many people don't think he had one." So I laboriously pored over newspapers, starting with the 1930s, and followed Taft's career as he went from being the prototypical midwestern isolationist, reluctant to be drawn into World War II by the perfidious British, to something of an internationalist, grudgingly recognizing the interdependence of nations. After graduation I eyed a career in the foreign service, where I thought I might play a part in a world moving toward integration and understanding despite the Cold War. But a State Department interviewer kindly informed me that high-level political appointees, not career diplomats, made the real difference, so I decided to go into international business, where I have been ever since.

I have never regretted the choice. As chairman of SmithKline Beecham, a transnational pharmaceutical company, I have been afforded an international perspective that is perhaps broader than any I would have gained in the foreign service, tied as it is to the interests of a single country at any point in time. A two-year stint as chairman of the U.S.–Japan Business Council put me in the trenches on issues of protectionism and free trade. And I have been able to live in Japan, the United States, Canada, and Europe and to travel to most of the rest of the world. Today I spend about 40 percent of my time in London, 40 percent in Philadelphia, and the remainder traveling or handling the affairs of a winery that my wife and I have in the Dry Creek Valley of Sonoma County, California—an enterprise that has given me yet another perspective on localism and globalism.

The initial challenge presented by transnational corporations lies in understanding what they are and how they differ from previous forms of corporate operation. Transnationals are not to be confused with the multinationals of the 1950s–70s that reproduced corporate versions of themselves in many countries. Nor do transnationals resemble international companies, which manufacture core products, with minor adaptations, for export and sale in foreign countries. Transnationals, such as Sony, IBM, and Nestlé, exceed national boundaries, transcend definitions of national identity, and regard the entire globe as a single theater of operations. These corporations locate factories, office staff, and research where they make the most sense for the global market they serve. They are often companies of enormous scale and competitive power, yet they act quickly and often sensitively on a local basis. And their ranks continue to grow, as many already large corporations, from diverse countries, are joining forces across borders to survive in the global marketplace.

For chief executive officers (CEOs), the transnational challenge lies in the familiar domain of competition, but of a fierce kind, different from that of the days when companies operated comfortably from secure home markets and simply exported to willing agents. Today competition comes in relentless waves from all directions. And CEOs, in rare moments of quiet reflection, must examine the place of their corporations in a world where national boundaries are blurring and the global market is becoming integrated at a dizzying pace.

Not all the questions the CEOs ask themselves are easy or pleasant: What new products will be offered and at what price from Thailand and Korea, as well as from Japan and more traditional sources of competition? How can we get our prices down to challenge both new and old competitors and still make adequate returns for our shareholders? How can we compete against giant transnationals that enjoy huge economies of scale and offer worldwide responsiveness to local markets? Is our organizational structure adequate in this emerging transnational world? To keep pace, should we pursue joint ventures? Strategic alliances? International mergers?

These questions of external strategy lead to further questions about internal organization and management: Where can we find managers who understand the forces at work and can help us compete on a global basis? And once we find them, how do we keep them? Do we have time to train and develop from within while fending off global competitors? And how can we explain what's happening in global terms to our employees in Lincoln, Nebraska; Lincolnshire, England; Ostend, Belgium; and Osaka, Japan?

CEOs are not the only ones asking tough questions about the emerging transnational world. Governmental policymakers in the gray office buildings of Washington, London, and Tokyo want to know why their ability to influence the course of their national economies seems to be slipping from their hands. Why do more and more decisions require consultation with other governments and international organizations like the Group of Seven (Britain, Canada, France, Germany, Italy, Japan, and the United States) on financial matters or the European Commission for seemingly simple regulatory and economic matters? Is national sovereignty giving way to some anonymous and unaccountable collectivism as the new world order takes shape? On the other hand, what happens when the machinery for collective international rule making breaks down, as exemplified by the perilous condition of the GATT (General Agreement on Tariffs and Trade) talks?

In the treasuries of the major capitals around the world, other questions are raised. What are the implications of cross-border acquisitions and mergers for the tax base and national revenue? Is research and development that is carried out in one country a legitimate deduction against income in another country? How about the transfer of production to locations with tax-advantages, such as Singapore and Puerto Rico, at a time when corporate taxes are increasingly relied upon to fund national governments?

In the meantime, concerned citizens from all walks of life, including employees and investors in large global corporations, grow puzzled and anxious at the changing face of industrial competition. After all, what has happened to the fine old companies that underpinned our communities and proudly flew the national flag? Some, like Pan Am, have vanished. Many are declining, and others seem to be flying more than one flag. When IBM moved its telecommunications division from New York to Surrey, was that a defeat for the United States and a victory for Britain? Or did it portend a stronger position in the dynamic European market for a company that is already global?

When Honda exports more autos from its Marysville, Ohio, plant to markets around the world than all the U.S. exports of General Motors, Ford, and Chrysler combined, does that make Honda something of an American company? If Honda were to take the next step and locate its world headquarters in the United States, would it become an American company? Or if Honda becomes something of an American company, will it automatically become less of a Japanese company, or will it acquire an added dimension of competitive strategy?

These questions and the answers to them challenge traditional views of national identity. They also raise new questions of corporate governance and accountability. As transnational corporations increase their market share around the world, their economic power not only will grow, but many people fear that they will move beyond the regulatory authority of properly constituted national governments. As the national identity of many of these companies becomes blurred, how can we be sure that they will serve the national interest? At a more fundamental level, how can we be sure that they will have the larger interests of society at heart? What is their system of governance and to whom is their top management really accountable?

The answers to these difficult questions are important for consumers, citizens, managers, employees, and shareholders of these large global corporations — and for the world at large. As the global market takes shape in the post–Cold War world and becomes an overwhelming fact of life, our destiny is increasingly being driven by large global companies. Some of them, such as Sony, Honda, and IBM, are household names. Others, such as Asea Brown Boveri, Arjo Wiggins Appleton, and Roche/Genentech, we may know only vaguely, if at all. Nevertheless, these transnationals and many others like them unite the world through their technology, their continuing capital investment, their products, their employees, and the wealth they create all around the world. Yet, as illustrated by the many questions posed here, their very success and global evolution challenge many traditional concepts of corporate identity, ownership, accountability, governance, and regulation.

Having worked almost all my adult life in international business, I found that the transnational challenge was posed most starkly soon after I became chairman of SmithKline in 1987, when the corporation's very survival in the new global environment was in doubt. Though SmithKline had operated internationally for decades, it was still a distinctly American company, based in Philadelphia, in the mid-eighties. Organized in worldwide product divisions, it was a typical multinational corporation.

Consumers perhaps know it best through a wide variety of over-the-counter products—Contac, Sine-Off, Ecotrin, and many others. Health care professionals and their patients know it from, among many prescription drugs, Tagamet for ulcers and Dyazide for hypertension. It was also then in eye care, toiletries, and analytic instruments, and it remains in the animal health and clinical laboratories businesses.

I use SmithKline's situation as an example not to justify the strategy I ultimately pursued, but because pharmaceutical companies like SmithKline offer particularly telling examples of the transnational challenge. More to the point, the white heat of competitive pressure forced me, the management, and the board of directors to do intensive thinking and strategic soul-searching about many of the issues explored in this book.

As producers of products in universal demand—people the world over fall ill and seek relief—pharmaceutical companies have long operated globally. And today, more than ever, it is necessary to win a large share of the global market to recover the enormous investment of time and money required to develop a new drug and bring it to market, which now means an average of about twelve years and $230 million. Moreover, the very nature of the business demands that drug companies must stay on the cutting edge of globalization. As science-based, knowledge-driven enterprises producing high value-added products, they must look all around the world for the ideas and innovations that are the lifeblood of all such industries—and good ideas know neither borders nor nationalities.

The dilemma SmithKline faced in the rapidly integrating global market of the eighties had, in large measure, been brought on by its success. The engine of that success was the remarkable anti-ulcer medication Tagamet, which we had launched around the world in the late 1970s. The first of the so-called designer drugs and now routinely cited among the greatest scientific innovations of the twentieth century, Tagamet was truly a miracle drug. Not only did it help win a Nobel Prize for James Black, the brilliant company scientist responsible for it, but, more important, it ended the suffering of an untold number of ulcer victims around the world. People who had borne unremitting pain for years, many of them facing the possibility of gastrectomies, found their ulcers cleared up in a matter of weeks.

Knowing SmithKline had a drug that was safe and effective and that would revolutionize the treatment of ulcers, we moved quickly to introduce it around the world. Though previous experience told us it took as long as ten years to roll out a global product, Tagamet was well established in more than fifty countries within two years. Two years later it was winning a consistent share of the market in more than 100 countries. Before the introduction of Tagamet, most pharmaceutical companies had enjoyed the bulk of their sales in only one or two markets.

Though the company was prepared for the global success of the product, it was not prepared for the sheer scale of that success. Tagamet was the first pharmaceutical to achieve $1 billion in sales and to penetrate all world markets quickly and consistently. The value of the company's shares quintupled. SmithKline greatly expanded its personnel and its presence internationally. With the resulting profits, it acquired — in a final act of diversification — Beckman Instruments, an analytical instruments company, and in the early eighties it belatedly began to rebuild its research and development, which had been allowed to languish during the years it had pursued the typical multinational's strategy of diversification into unrelated businesses.

In the meantime, however, an international competitor had launched a similar anti-ulcer drug and captured a significant share of the market. Suddenly, SmithKline found itself overextended and exposed in the rapidly globalizing environment of the 1980s. To maintain its new position in the global market it needed another success on the scale of Tagamet. But given the lead time required to develop new drugs and because its research and development had not caught up to its new global scale, it gradually became apparent that no such breakthrough was imminent. Moreover, cross-border joint ventures and mergers among formerly competing pharmaceutical companies were transforming the industry.

SmithKline had partially prepared for the new competitive environment by returning to its roots in the life sciences and health care fields. Determined to concentrate on what it did best, it abandoned the path of the diversified multinational and turned toward becoming a more focused international health care company. But it became dramatically evident that this strategy of comparative advantage would not suffice. The industry was rapidly evolving toward a structure that would soon be dominated by a few global giants, leaving only niche strategies for small companies and a dangerous middle ground for companies like SmithKline, which, although large, was not truly global.

The alternatives that were available to me in this dilemma are becoming painfully familiar to other beleaguered CEOs in rapidly globalizing industries: At one extreme, you can simply give up and sell off the company in whole or in pieces; at the other, you can acquire a competitor through a highly leveraged transaction. In between, lie such possibilities as joint ventures and strategic alliances across borders. For companies with immense resources, there is the additional possibility of organic growth toward a global scale, but the speed with which many industries are globalizing often forecloses that time-consuming approach.

I rejected the extreme solutions, both of which are easy—and usually wrong. Selling off the company greatly benefits the shareholders, but it sells out the employees and the community. Wildly leveraging the company's assets to acquire another company greatly benefits the employees, especially the top management, but it shortchanges the shareholders. I also explored various other options for acquiring companies, but in each case the premium required to consummate an acquisition of scale would have diluted the stock so much that it was hard to see how the shareholders would ever realize a return. As for organic growth into a global company, there simply was no time.

So I was left with the prospect of joint ventures and strategic alliances. Such ventures result in the low-cost, fast access to new markets, and there have been some notable successes. But having tried joint ventures and found them less than satisfactory—for reasons I will detail in Chapter Two—I had come to believe that they are an inadequate response to the challenges of the global market. Instead, I concluded that to protect the human and scientific assets of the company, I would have to engineer an international merger, on equal terms, with another pharmaceutical company.

Without overdramatizing, it is fair to say that the plan met with widespread skepticism. The business press was dubious. Some of my closest financial advisers reckoned the odds of success to be incredibly long. And there was speculation that news of the impending merger would put SmithKline in play and lead to precisely the kind of breakup and sale of the company I most wanted to avoid. Nevertheless, after several years of exploring all the possible permutations and combinations, I found that the British company Beecham offered the best fit with SmithKline. Equally important, Beecham saw the world in much the same way as did SmithKline.

Discussions with Beecham's management began in 1988, and despite the enormous difficulties of such unions, we soon focused on a merger of equals, including a 50–50 division of key management positions and of places on the board of directors. These initial discussions revealed the possibility of agreement and led to intensive negotiations, which stopped and restarted over the winter months. In April 1989 we reached the final agreement. The company that resulted—now called SmithKline Beecham—comes close to meeting the definition of a true transnational corporation, the first test of which is its ability to generate sales and profits that are proportional to the worldwide distribution of the markets it serves. In the case of SmithKline Beecham, roughly 40 percent of the sales and profits are from North America, 40 percent are from Europe, and the remainder are from Japan and other countries around the world—a distribution that comes closer than that of any other company in the business to reflecting the proportions of the global market.

Neither company could have acquired the other in a takeover, and the merger certainly created a more exciting contender for the twenty-first century. But, as I have said, my purpose in telling this story is not to engage in self-justification or autobiography, but to take a hard look at the reality of global competition. Even today, the truth is that nearly every industrial company, large or small, is already competing against global products in most markets. In many industries only those companies with huge economies of scale and clout in the global market will be able to lower the costs and improve the quality of their products while investing in the breakthrough innovations in products and processes that are necessary to remain competitive.

Moreover, rapid and striking political and economic developments are continuously creating new conditions that demand a transnational response. The pace and magnitude of these developments is staggering, as was demonstrated by the events of November 9, 1989, when the entire global village watched mesmerized as a scene unfolded on its television screens that had been unthinkable a few months before: The Berlin Wall—the symbol of the bipolar postwar world—was breached and soon came tumbling down. The widespread acceptance of market economics that those startling images confirmed has suddenly drawn many countries closer together economically and created vast opportunities that will require a global scale and sensitivity to local conditions to be realized.

Events everywhere point to similar conclusions. The rise of global capital markets has already led to the internationalization of financial markets and corporate ownership. The determination of the European Community to become a unified, barrier-free market alone demands that companies achieve insider status if they are not to be left outside looking in at a market of 340 million people or more—the largest single market in the world. The emergence of other regional trading blocs, such as the North American partners, and the continuing form of self-centered neomercantilism practiced by countries such as Japan will likewise require companies to achieve insider status in those vital markets.

SmithKline Beecham is by no means alone in pursuing the transnational strategy demanded by these new global realities, nor was it the first. Shell Oil, Unilever, Volvo/Renault, Asea Brown Boveri, and Arjo Wiggins Appleton all achieved a global scale through cross-border mergers. And there are, of course, companies that have grown to transnational status on their own: Sony, IBM, and Nestlé come quickly to mind. It is the example of these and many other companies, along with my own experience, that convinces me that the transnational solution promises the best chance for competing in the global market.

I recognize that this claim flies in the face of current wisdom, which holds that strategic alliances—the cooperation of international competitors on a defined project—are the wave of the future. I argue, on the contrary, that the best strategy generally lies along the path of the truly committed transnational enterprise, rather than that of the tentative joint ventures and strategic alliances being promoted by many consultants, academics, and corporate strategists today.

Many companies face the kind of dilemma that confronted SmithKline in the mid-1980s, and they will ponder similar choices. But as the quickening pace with which the global market is integrating gives companies less and less room to maneuver, those choices will increasingly narrow to cross-border joint ventures and strategic alliances or international mergers and acquisitions. Although highly focused joint ventures and strategic alliances often achieve limited success, I believe that for many companies they merely postpone the moment of truth. Moreover, because joint ventures are narrowly contractual and time limited, they are often inflexible and unresponsive to fast-changing market conditions. Limited by definition and tentative by nature, they are also likely to be plagued by the partners' cross-purposes, different levels of participation, and sometimes mutual suspicion. In contrast, an international merger entails an irrevocable and wholehearted commitment that is unconstrained by contractual limits and is highly responsive to changing conditions. But whether achieved through mergers, acquisitions, or organic growth, only transnational status provides the economies of scale, the global reach, and the sensitivity to local conditions that are required by today's global market. Less tangible perhaps, but no less important, a genuine transnational creates cross-cultural synergies among diverse nationalities within the company and harnesses these strengths for the long haul.

The transnational solution is not for everyone. Niche marketers will always find their places in the interstices of the transnational world. And companies in low-tech or service industries can safely remain regional, national, or international and continue to thrive. But the transnational challenge will be acute for large companies operating in industries that depend upon high technology, knowledge, or information and that offer high value-added products or services: computers, consumer electronics, aviation, heavy machinery, pharmaceuticals, biotechnology products, automobiles, appliances, office machines, telecommunications, and on and on. Though precise conditions may vary from industry to industry and from company to company, the nature of the challenge remains the same: how to survive in the radically changing global environment.

If the transnational solution is not for everyone, neither is it easy. Whether the strategy is merger or growth, the business logic must be sound. It makes no sense to become transnational merely for its own sake, just as wild diversification for diversification's sake made no sense during the heyday of multinationals. In the case of cross-border mergers in particular, the obstacles to be overcome are enormous. Cultural and semantic differences greatly confound understanding. It is difficult to reach agreement on the relative value of each company; it is even harder to win the consent of both boards of directors and both companies' key managers. Personnel decisions are doubly difficult. In addition, the companies must satisfy diverse groups of shareholders and conform to all the securities laws in the various countries involved.

Once transnational status has been achieved, the hard work really begins. The companies must then merge not only their different corporate cultures, but the different national cultures as well. In the case of SmithKline Beecham, those cultures are primarily those of Britain and the United States, two countries, as Mark Twain wryly observed, that are divided by a common language. Moreover, the management must work hard to understand not only the national cultures in which the companies do business, but the many local communities and subcultures within them. This does not mean a facile ecumenism, but a strenuous effort to enter into the spirit of other cultures, which is a particularly difficult task for Westerners, whose chief cultural characteristic is, paradoxically, a cultural absolutism.

Once a company makes the transnational commitment, it must live with that decision for many years. Troubles do not magically disappear, and on the much larger stage of global competition mistakes are often magnified. The dictates of geography alone add whole new sets of complications, which are compounded, in turn, by distance, difficulties in communicating, and cultural mismatches, as well as nagging differences in time zones. The nature of transnationals requires executives to be adaptable, but should not demand superhuman investments of time or risk emotional overload. The human dimension requires, if anything, more careful nurturing and consideration in a transnational environment than elsewhere. Thriving as a transnational requires hard work, an intelligent strategy, and ever faster responsiveness, and I would not want to minimize the difficulties.

Neither would I want to minimize the difficult issues raised by the emergence of these corporate behemoths. Though I argue in favor of the transnational solution for many kinds of companies and explore the best strategies for achieving it, I do not intend this book to be a kind of value-free, how-to handbook. The notion that these trends are invariably benign, self-regulating, and capable of automatically eliminating problems of governance, accountability, and national sovereignty is, to say the least, naively utopian.

The social and political challenges that transnationals present are complex, and their resolution requires hard thought. Those social and political challenges are at least as daunting as the competitive business challenges with which they are intertwined. My aim in writing this book was to deal forthrightly with both. Thus I mean *Global Embrace* to serve as a guide for the perplexed—inside and outside the international business community—for citizens as well as CEOs, for consumers as well as members of Congress, for students as well as shareholders, for managers as well as ministers of finance. It is a guide to the transnational world by someone who has been actively engaged in bringing it into being, a player for whom strategic choices have more than theoretical consequences.

The book is in three parts. Part One explores the nature and impact of transnationals: the conditions that have stimulated their growth, their effects on consumers, and the challenges they pose for companies that have yet to come to terms with the emerging transnational world. It begins by examining the essential realities and effects of global interdependence on corporations and their ability to compete in a wide variety of markets and conditions. This discussion sets the stage for a discussion of corporate strategies that includes illustrations of the responses of a variety of companies and the effects, for good or ill, of top managers' decisions in the face of global interdependence.

Part Two describes the hard work that faces companies once they have decided to take the fateful transnational step. It lays out what I believe are the essential elements of global strategies. It details the requirements for creating a corporate culture that can work across borders. And it develops a model of the appropriate organizational structure for channeling organizational behavior into a global strategy. Part Two also looks at the peculiar demands that transnationals make on employees across the board—senior managers, middle managers, knowledge workers, and production workers—and on people who do not work for transnationals but who must nevertheless come to terms with them: suppliers, service providers, local competitors, business educators, and students who aspire to enter business careers.

Part Three takes a hard look at the perplexing issues raised by these vastly influential and little-understood transnationals. What form should their internal governance take? How should governments, many of which are less powerful than the companies themselves, regulate these global giants? And what is the impact of these transnationals on issues that are of concern to citizens everywhere:

environmental integrity, quality of life, and political freedom. Part Three concludes with a discussion of the resurgence of local and cultural identities as the reverse side of the coin of global interdependence. These two dominant trends of our times—transnationalism and tribalism—are mutually dependent and, in turn, define the need to apply corporate strategies with exquisite sensitivity to local conditions.

Ironically, the questions of governance and accountability arise at a time of growing conflict between the managers of huge corporations and the large, professionally managed institutional funds that own most of their shares. In the United States and Britain, the funds' investment horizons seem short, their buy and sell decisions are often embodied in anonymous computer programs, and they do little to inspire allegiance from the managers of the companies they own. And these large institutional investors definitely feel estranged from the top management. CEOs and boards of directors seem to hide behind poison pills (financial maneuvers that render the stock of a takeover target less attractive) and other defensive barricades, denying shareholders their rights as owners. Between the two camps is an atmosphere charged with suspicion and frustration, a condition to which large transnationals can be particularly susceptible. Yet the institutional shareholders vote the majority of the shares, elect the directors, and represent the concept of "owners" for which the top managers profess to be working. Where does this leave the other stakeholders in the corporation—the employees, customers, debt holders, and communities in which these global giants reside? Or are the top executives, who sometimes even sit on each other's boards, really accountable only to each other?

In the political sphere, transnationals raise complex issues of taxation, governmental regulation, and—perhaps most important—national sovereignty. Contrary to the views of those who are fond of elegant laissez faire theory or prone to blame their business troubles on regulators, I do not believe that all governmental officials everywhere are benighted or that regulation in itself is evil. Policymakers have legitimate cause to wonder whether transnationals are good for their countries and their people. Indeed, they have a responsibility to ask tough questions—and to produce good policies.

What is perhaps most unsettling for policymakers, and citizens, is the loss of sovereignty that governments around the world, including the most powerful, are undergoing. International trade is so important, the integration of world financial markets is such an established reality, and world communications are so ubiquitous that the authority of governments to make unilateral decisions has been decidedly reduced. Ministers of finance, unable to act on their own, meet collectively (and in secret) to plot the courses of monetary policy, interest rates, currency fluctuations, and the like. The United States and Japan perform a love-hate minuet over trade issues because together they account for 40 percent of the world's gross national product (GNP)—a responsibility so great that they must dance with each other. Increasingly, countries must cede authority in trade issues to supranational bodies like the European Commission and GATT. The rise of great regional trading blocs, such as the European Community, the North American partners, and the member countries of the Association of South Asian Nations (ASEAN) is fast rendering the notion of the single, mercantilist nation-state obsolete. Indeed, the free-trade agreement between the United States and Canada has made the breakup of Canada a topic of serious discussion because secessionist provinces, such as Quebec, would face little in the way of adverse economic consequences for leaving.

The collapse of the Soviet empire and the Soviet Union itself represents the most striking loss of governmental authority in our time (and the most striking restoration of self-determination for millions of people). The collapse was hastened in general by the rapid integration of world trade, from which it is impossible to secede, and in particular by the coming of European economic union, which acted like a magnet to pull apart the Iron Curtain. In the United States, a debate currently rages over fast-track procedures that prohibit Congress from amending trade bills and permit only a yes or no vote on the bills in their entirety. Many people argue that such a restriction erodes democracy by ceding authority to the executive branch and thus to the trade representatives of the foreign countries with whom the bills are negotiated.

But what looks like the erosion of sovereignty may, from another point of view, appear to be a remarkably enlightened governmental policy. The privatization of enterprises; deregulation; the reduction of tariffs; and the international protection of intellectual property, such as patents and copyrights, are all trends that have been accepted by governments almost unanimously and strengthened by governmental initiatives. Rather than resist this tide, governments around the world have encouraged it, creating, for example, conditions for universal capital markets. Enlightened policy has often meant considerable national sacrifice, as when countries agree to strengthen GATT, in the process administering some economic pain to their people in the interest of long-term real growth around the world.

As the capacity for action by individual nations diminishes, the bipolar military alliances disappear, and market economics gains universal acceptance, the world is becoming more and more united by the great global corporations. Just as policymakers have legitimate cause to worry about the loss of national sovereignty, citizens have legitimate cause to worry about a transnational world that is increasingly dominated by corporations elected by no one.

Though corporate apologists sometimes conflate consumers and citizens, the two are not identical. As consumers, we may live in a global market, but as citizens, we live in local societies. Consumers want good products at low prices, but citizens want clean air and water, fair labor practices, good government, and ethical corporate behavior. As consumers, we focus on our standard of living, but as citizens, we are more apt to focus on the quality of our lives. Yes, we want the fantastic array of goods and services that global companies produce, from life-saving drugs to advanced technology to expensive toys, but do we want them at the price of neocolonialism, exploited labor, complicity with repellent political regimes, and the disappearance of regional and ethnic identities in favor of an anonymous global collectivism? What is to prevent transnational corporations, operating beyond the capacity of any single government to call them to account, from behaving in any fashion they please?

There is no question that private corporations, as opposed to state institutions, are the primary source of innovation and the creation of wealth. And it is transnational corporations that spread those innovations, from superconductors to new consumer products, around the world. I remember vividly and poignantly my company's international introduction of the first psychotropic drugs—Thorazine, in Hawaii, and Stelazine, in Canada. I saw mental institutions transformed almost overnight from twentieth-century versions of Bedlam—with naked, anguished patients soiling themselves—into places where these same people could lead lives of dignity and from which they could finally be released after years of institutionalization.

But transnationals do more than disseminate products. They are also the primary source of the transfer of technology from country to country, giving people everywhere greater possibilities for competition and creativity. By raising the level of competition worldwide, transnationals have also been the stimulus for improved productivity—the essential ingredient in the creation of wealth. They have stimulated improved productivity not only among themselves, but among the many local companies that must live in the transnational environment. All three—technology transfer, increased competition, and greater productivity—in turn, stimulate the need for higher standards of education, a phenomenon now taking place everywhere, including—to our great surprise and embarrassment—the United States.

The great economic and even social benefits of transnational activity aside, however, the question remains whether global companies, by virtue of their transnational status, are free to engage in unethical practices, especially in poorer countries that desperately need direct foreign investments. Of course, unethical corporate behavior is simply wrong, and as a reasonably ethical human being, I will not engage in it. But I recognize that critics of corporate behavior are certainly not going to accept pious assurances of personal goodness. They want some guarantee that ethical standards will be upheld and some mechanism that compels ethical behavior by the corporation as an institution.

That mechanism is the globality of business itself. Global competition compels companies to perform to the highest standards in quality, product-cycle time, productivity, and service to win their market share, especially in the crucial triad of the United States, Europe, and Japan. It also compels them to perform to the highest ethical standards. This is not to suggest that transnational managements are endowed with superior moral values; quite the contrary. Transnational companies perform to the highest ethical standards because the stakes are so high in the major markets. They cannot afford to be embarrassed, much less prosecuted, in their major markets for infractions committed elsewhere.

My larger point is that the transnational, far from being "stateless," as some of the present commentary has it, is "many stated," tethered in myriad ways to the nations and the local communities in which it operates. As corporations become globalized, they assume more responsibility, not less. The same forces of world competition that produce higher and increasingly common standards of quality and performance produce higher and increasingly common standards of ethical behavior.

But as we move toward global standards of quality, performance, and behavior, as national sovereignty slips, and as supranational bodies thrive, do we also move toward a thoroughly homogeneous world, bereft of ethnic, regional, and national differences among peoples? Just as we used to worry about the "Los Angelesizing" of the United States and the Americanizing of Europe, must we now worry about the "transnationalizing" of the entire world? It would seem inevitable that we must, but even a cursory look at world events presents a bewildering paradox: Even as the world is increasingly knit by supranational bodies, transnational corporations, and borderless communications, there is a vast upsurge in ethnic, regional, and national assertiveness around the world. The breakup of the Soviet Union is only the most visible instance. Examples abound in the West, as well: the rise of Scottish nationalism, the resurgence of Welsh culture, the newfound respectability of Quebecois separatism, and the acrimonious debate over multiculturalism on American campuses.

It is with these apparently contradictory phenomena—supranational institutions and resurgent tribalism—that the book concludes. It is in this great, but little-understood paradox that we finally glimpse the real contours of the new world coming into being. And it is here that I attempt to lay out my view of how markets and societies, transnationals and tribes, companies and countries will be held together in a transnational grip that is neither a vise nor a stranglehold, but a global embrace.

As we set out toward that final picture of the emerging transnational world, I forewarn the reader that I am a committed internationalist. In offering this guide to the transnational world, therefore, I am hardly a disinterested spectator. But I hope that whatever bias the reader detects will be more than offset by the value of hearing from someone for whom these issues have been a matter of lifelong engagement and remain a matter of daily struggle.

PART ONE

GLOBAL IMPERATIVE

CHAPTER ONE

THE GLOBAL MALL

WE HAVE BECOME SO ACCUSTOMED to hearing revolutions proclaimed that we often ignore them until they envelop us. For years we heard about the information revolution. It was always just around the corner, yet never seemed to arrive. Then one day we awoke to find that sophisticated telecommunications, satellite transmission, computers, faxes, modems, and data bases had reached a critical mass, erupting into our personal lives, as well as our work lives. So it is with the rise of the global marketplace.

Imagine for a moment a representative American using some common products that apparently originated in Europe or Japan. He may, for example, drive home in a Honda automobile, go for a jog in his Reebok sneakers, prepare dinner in a Sharp microwave oven, and eat a dessert of Häagen-Dazs ice cream. After dinner, when he flicks on his Sony television to watch the news, the commentator gravely informs him that the U.S. trade deficit is the largest since such deficits first started showing up. Depressed by the news, and perhaps feeling a slight twinge of guilt, he may pop a videocassette into his VCR or a compact disc into his CD player. The VCR and the CD player may carry Japanese nameplates, but the movie is *Hook,* starring Robin Williams, or the disc is Bruce Springsteen's *Born in the U.S.A.* Some things, at least, like Hollywood movies and rock and roll — those two quintessentially American cultural forms — remain. Recall, however, that Sony recently purchased Columbia Pictures, which produced *Hook*. And Spring-steen records on the CBS label. That means *Born in the U.S.A.* isn't owned in the U.S.A. Robin Williams and the Boss work for Sony — for *them*.

But who are *they*, and what are they doing? A typical Japanese, for example, may work diligently at her Apple computer all day. In the evening she may decide to attend a movie with her family. Before going out, she may apply some Estee Lauder cosmetics, pur-chased in a large urban department store. The movie she sees is *Beauty and the Beast*, produced by the Walt Disney Company. While viewing it, her entire family drinks that longtime symbol of Ameri-canization, Coca-Cola. Meanwhile, the members of a typical Ger-man family may wash with Procter & Gamble soap, shop with an American Express credit card, and watch Cable News Network on their Sony television.

All these products being used by these typical Americans, Japanese, and Germans are representative of the global proliferation of brands and services that are recognizable by a great many people everywhere in the world. In effect, these products and services exist in a great global mall, accessible to nearly everyone around the world. Perhaps some Americans feel a little guilty when they pur-chase foreign products, thinking in the back of their minds that they are contributing to their country's trade deficit. In contrast, the Ger-man and Japanese families may feel a little smug because their countries seem to be running a trade surplus at the moment. But it's not quite as simple as that. Consider the following:

- The largest single automobile factory in the United States is the Honda plant in Marysville, Ohio. Honda employs 6,500 people and exports more autos from the United States than do Ford, Chrysler, and General Motors (GM) combined. The Hondas made in the United States also contain more American content than many cars sold by the Big Three.
- Reebok started as a British company, but is now American owned and operated. In 1990 the company shipped 75 million pairs of athletic shoes around the world.[1] About 60 percent of the shoes were made in South Korea, 20 percent in Taiwan, and the remainder in other countries. Operating in 120 countries, Reebok is the number one brand in Canada, Hong Kong, New Zealand, and Singapore.

• Procter & Gamble has built a huge business in Europe — running at about $7 billion in annual sales — and almost all its production is local.

• Sony also manufactures in plants around the world; in fact, less than half Sony's volume is manufactured in Japan. The television that the typical German family was watching is almost certainly made in Wales. And the typical American's television was probably made in San Diego at a factory established by Sony more than twenty years ago.

• About half Apple's computers are made in Japan and assembled in California. The computers are then exported, in this case to Japan. Even more interesting, most of the software originates in the United States, but more and more is being produced locally in many countries around the world, so that the flexibility and ease of the MacIntosh operating system are adapted to the specific local languages and needs of the users.

• The Clinique line of high-quality cosmetics marketed by Estee Lauder has displaced Shiseido as the leading brand of cosmetics sold in Japanese department stores. This extraordinary marketing success was accomplished by Japanese employees under the direction of a German general manager, who adapted an American marketing concept to the local situation with products made in the United States, Japan, and Europe.

• Coca-Cola, long thought of as the quintessential American company, now earns 80 percent of its operating profits outside the United States, up from 50 percent in 1985.[2] In Japan, Coca-Cola commands a whopping 85 percent of the market share, a 50 percent share in Spain, and an overseas market share of 46 percent overall.[3]

As these examples show, the national identities of products and corporations grow more ambiguous every day. We may ask, To what degree is Procter & Gamble, with sixty plants and almost 40 percent of its sales outside the United States, an American company? More accurately, we may ask, To what degree has Procter & Gamble become something *more* than an American company? Reebok, though American owned, still uses the Union Jack as its corporate symbol. The national identity of Häagen-Dazs ice cream has been artfully confused since its inception, when its American creators gave it a vaguely Scandinavian-sounding name. Häagen-Dazs was eventually acquired by Pillsbury, at the time an American company, which was itself acquired in 1989 by Grand Metropolitan, a British conglomerate. The ice cream is currently being introduced in Germany through thirteen carefully selected outlets. Is it less American as a consequence of these events?

Automobiles present an even more striking case of blurred national identity. The Honda Accords made by American workers in Ohio are the best-selling cars in the United States. Are they American or Japanese cars? The same plant recently began making Accord station wagons for export to Europe and Japan. When France, which has strongly resisted the import of Japanese cars, recently tried to bar the American-built station wagons, American trade officials went to bat for Honda, successfully arguing that the automobiles must be considered American products.[4] Yet for domestic consumption, the same Accords are classified as foreign cars by the U.S. Department of Transportation.

Nissan and Toyota have followed Honda's lead, building factories in the United States. As a result, the share of the American car market enjoyed by these "Japanese" automakers has increased even as imports from Japan have plummeted.[5] Increasingly, the cars are not only being built and adapted, but designed in the United States. Nissan, for example, is opening a new research facility in Farmington Hills, Michigan. Nevertheless, the national identity of these cars remains cloudy: All of the some 1.3 million cars and trucks built by Japanese automakers in the United States in 1990 were considered imports under one set of federal regulations and domestic products under another.[6]

The automakers cannot agree among themselves, either. In February 1992, Toyota introduced a U.S.-built Camry station wagon 75 percent of whose parts are made in the United States. At the same time, the company pointed to an in-house study that purported to show that 55 percent of Chrysler vehicles were built by foreign producers or had significant foreign content. Coming to Chrysler's defense, GM chairman Robert Stempel asserted that the Big Three American automakers do 97 percent of their business with American suppliers, while only 48 percent of the spending by the Japanese transplant factories goes to U.S. suppliers.[7] Chrysler also countered by pointing out that many of its vehicles and parts that were counted as foreign by the Toyota study were produced in Canada and are regarded by U.S. law as domestic under the terms of the free-trade agreement with Canada.[8]

In any case, in these and many other instances, it is increasingly difficult to know exactly what many products stand for in *national* terms. Most of the foregoing examples are more accurately described as *global* products and services. They are widely available in many countries, instantly recognizable by people of many nationalities, and almost universally desired by consumers. Many of those consumers may be confused or mistaken about the national identities of the products, but they know what those products and services stand for in terms of the image and quality of the brands the world over.

The revolution that the rise of this global marketplace represents has been building since the first round of free-trade talks in Geneva shortly after World War II and has been gaining momentum ever since. As long as five years ago, *Fortune* magazine told its corporate readers: "Thinking about going global? Friend, you're too late. The train has already left."[9]

Nevertheless, the emergence of a full-blown global marketplace in which goods, money, and people flow easily back and forth across national borders around the world comes as a shock. Suddenly, the volume of world trade has reached staggering proportions. Even in 1991, a year punctuated by war and recession, world trade grew three times faster than did the total economic output among the twenty-four member countries of the Organization for Economic Cooperation and Development (OECD).[10] The trade in merchandise reached $3.53 trillion in 1991, and the trade in commercial services added another $850 billion to the total. Trade and global economic issues dominate the news as never before. International diplomacy increasingly turns on issues of economics instead of ideology. So does politics. Tariffs, for example, used to be seen as a remote and technical issue with little political mileage. But today protectionism versus free trade stands at the center of elections all over the world.

The explosion of the global marketplace into general awareness is not, however, merely a matter of tariffs. We have all long been aware of the profusion of imported goods. Every time we bought a car, booted up a computer, or ducked under the headphones of a Walkman personal stereo we knew that older patterns of commerce had been shattered. Since World War II most attempts to liberalize world trade have been aimed at cutting tariffs. But after tariffs were greatly reduced, it soon became clear that there were many hidden barriers to freer trade among nations: Various countries provide different levels of government subsidies for their domestic industries. Some countries generously subsidize agriculture; others do not. Product-safety regulations, technical specifications, environmental standards, the observance of patents and copyrights, and rules for foreign investment vary widely from country to country. For example, a manufacturer operating in a country with lax environmental standards, other things being equal, enjoys lower production costs than does a competitor located in a country with tougher rules. Similarly, a domestic company operating in a country that permits the wholesale violation of international patents and copyrights needs no massive investment in research and development and can easily undercut the prices of the foreign companies that own the products being pirated. On still another front, different labor practices and levels of political enfranchisement raise human rights considerations that make some nations international pariahs with which many other nations find it distasteful to trade.

All these issues transcend technical matters, cutting right to the heart of important political, philosophical, and national policymaking considerations. And because they touch on so many sensitive issues, from unemployment to environmentalism to national sovereignty itself—issues that impinge on us all—we suddenly find ourselves swept up in a rapidly changing and controversial business environment. With the collapse of the world's bipolar political structure, we watch as the peoples of the world grow closer. It is as if we had gone to sleep and awakened to find ourselves in a new world—one that seems smaller and more tightly interconnected, yet simultaneously more fractious and disparate.

Is this globally integrated world really new, or was the world we previously knew a historical aberration? The concept—indeed the reality—of a globally integrated economy and a community of the world's people is neither new nor untried. Before World War I, goods, money, and people moved across borders with a freedom that would not be seen again for decades. John Maynard Keynes, writing in 1919, looked back wistfully at the world that the war to end all wars had destroyed:

> The inhabitant of London could order by telephone, sipping his morn-
> ing tea in bed, the various products of the whole earth, in such quan-
> tity as he might see fit, and reasonably expect their early delivery on

his doorstep; he could at the same moment and by the same means adventure his wealth in the natural resources and new enterprises of any quarter of the world, and share without exertion or even trouble, in their prospective fruits and advantages; or he could decide to couple the security of his fortunes with the good faith of the townspeople of any substantial municipality in any continent that fancy or information might recommend. He could secure forthwith, if he wished it, cheap and comfortable means of transit to any country and climate without passport or other formality, could dispatch his servant to the neighboring office of a bank for such supply of the precious metals as might seem convenient, and could then proceed abroad to foreign quarters, without knowledge of their religion, language or customs, bearing coined wealth upon his person, and would consider himself greatly aggrieved and much surprised at the least interference. But, most important of all, he regarded this state of affairs as normal, certain and permanent, except in the direction of further improvement, and any deviation from it as aberrant, scandalous and avoidable.[11]

The "various products of the whole earth" moved so freely, thanks largely to the liberal trade policies practiced by Great Britain during the last three quarters of the nineteenth century and in the early years of the twentieth. Successive British governments dropped restrictions on foreign shipping, lifted prohibitions against the export of gold, and lowered tariff barriers. The United States and other countries followed suit. International trade expanded at an unprecedented rate, with the value of all exports and imports increasing from £340 million in 1820 to £8.36 billion in 1913, a rate of growth that would not be seen again until the years following World War II.

Mobile capital provided the engine for this growth. The widespread adoption of the gold standard facilitated the convertibility of national currencies. Subsequent increases in the supply of gold from mines around the world financed the expansion of international trade and strengthened the reserves of British, French, and German central banks, which began branching abroad and serving as conduits for foreign investments. Much of this capital flowed into vast areas that were rich in natural resources like the United States, Russia, Brazil, Canada, and Africa. Initially, such areas exported raw materials and imported finished goods from Western Europe, but as more of the world industrialized, a lively international trade in manufactured goods also developed among industrialized countries.

People flowed across borders as well. Millions of European immigrants, seeking a better life, flocked to North and South America. Chinese and Japanese immigrants spread over eastern and southern Asia, Russians flocked to Siberia and central Asia, and Indians moved to southeastern Asia and South and East Africa. Encountering relatively few obstacles to migration, they were welcomed for the human energy they supplied and the resulting expansion of local economies that helped attract foreign investment. Individual travelers, like Keynes, faced even fewer impediments. Prior to World War I, passports were issued to travelers as an extension of national protection and identification, not as a means of regulating or preventing their travel. In fact, it was possible to journey from one end of Europe to the other without a passport. And the expanding foreign investment, much of which was channeled into the development of railways and other parts of the infrastructure of various countries, made travel and the transportation of goods easier than it had ever been.

But the steady integration of the world's economy and peoples expected by Keynes's Belle Epoque gentleman and regarded by him as a natural state of affairs was rudely interrupted. Global economic expansion often meant rapid colonization, exploitation, and the rise of virulent nationalism, usually followed by waves of protectionist trade legislation. Conflict among the three decaying Eastern empires—Turkey, Austria-Hungary, and Russia—and a destructive arms race among the great Western powers eroded the internationalist gains made during the long period of prosperity and peace that Europe had enjoyed during much of the last half of the nineteenth century. The consequence, of course, was two World Wars and the extended Cold War from which we are only now emerging.

As the Cold War ends, we find ourselves at a historic watershed: The "natural" state of affairs described by Keynes has returned. In fact, for the past 250 years, except for the disastrous period between 1914 and 1950, the annual growth in international trade has usually exceeded the annual growth of the GNPs in the industrialized countries. Today goods, capital, and people are once again beginning to move freely across national borders. Capital moves instantaneously from country to country at the touch of a computer key, and international investors eagerly snap up stocks in markets around the world, in effect trading in a global securities market that never closes. The Euromarket, based in London, sells debt to major corporations in an extremely efficient capital market made up of financial institutions operating in markets around the world and around the clock. The European Community is moving toward monetary union, and international economic bodies like the Group of Seven are seeking ways to stabilize rates of foreign exchange. The European Community plans to do away with passports within the borders of the community, greatly encouraging the free movement of travelers and workers alike. Free-trade zones that are emerging in North America and the Pacific Rim will similarly allow people greater freedom of movement across borders, while the liberation of Eastern Europe and the dissolution of the Soviet Union holds the promise, at least, that one day millions of formerly captive people will be able to travel and to learn for themselves about the rest of the world.

As people of different nationalities strive to know more about each other and to exchange goods and services around the world, international travel, communications, and investment have reached record levels. About 325 million people a year now travel outside their own countries, compared with about 25 million in 1950.[12] From 1960 to 1988 the real cost of international travel fell by almost 60 percent.[13] One equity trade in seven worldwide involves a foreign investor, one trade in five involves a foreign share, and in continental Europe it is one in three.[14] In the United States the trading of American Depository Receipts—certificates representing shares of foreign stocks issued by a depository bank—increased by almost 32 percent from 1985 to 1991.[15] And in just the two years from 1988 to 1990 net purchases of foreign stocks and bonds by Americans tripled.[16]

But the action is not confined to the triad of America, Europe, and Japan. Foreign investors are turning to the increasingly healthy financial markets of countries that were formerly thought to be hopelessly risky. Mexico's $42 billion stock market, largely fueled by foreign investors, has produced steady growth for the closed-end funds that invest in Mexican stocks and has begun to attract foreign institutional investors to its blue-chip stocks as well.[17] Meanwhile, cross-border mergers and acquisitions and equity flows are the fastest-growing part of international capital movements. Between 1983 and 1988 global direct foreign investments grew in real terms by more than 20 percent annually.[18] The world is integrating at a dizzying pace. National borders grow fuzzier and, in many cases, more irrelevant with each passing day.

Nevertheless, approximately eighty years of nationalistic strife have conditioned all of us to view the world through the lens of the nation-state. This conditioning begins with political matters, but carries over to economic, business, and financial affairs and even to the ways we keep score on national, regional, corporate, and sometimes even personal performance. Trade balances, current account flows, direct foreign investment, and national industrial policies are all expressed in terms of *us* versus *them*, of individual countries pitted against each other, and of nations winning and losing. Productivity figures are taken to measure the personal performance of one nation's workers against those of another nation. Discussions of direct foreign investment often draw on metaphors of combat against a hostile enemy: "Japan Invades Hollywood" screamed the headlines when Sony bought Columbia Pictures and Matsushita acquired MCA. Or there may be talk of selling your soul—presumably to the devil—as when Sony bought CBS Records and with it a great deal of America's indigenous music.

Governmental policies often turn the metaphors to reality: The European governments that subsidize the Airbus, a commercial jet-manufacturing enterprise, do so to thwart American domination of the industry. Airbus now enjoys 40 percent of the world market for commercial airliners and has overtaken McDonnell Douglas Aircraft to become the number two aircraft manufacturer in new orders.[19] In response, American trade officials have branded the European governments' subsidies unfair and threaten to retaliate by slapping higher import duties on key products from Britain, France, Germany, and Spain, which together have provided $26 billion to Airbus. As a consequence, a possible trade war looms. "Whoever starts a war," warned Jean Pierson, the president of Airbus, "will find himself in a war."[20]

Accustomed to score keeping on a national basis and perhaps conditioned by widely viewed international sporting events, such as the Olympics and World Cup Games, people seem to become more passionate flag-wavers and cheerleaders even as global interdependence becomes more obvious. In the United States, Lee Iacocca has become the chief economic cheerleader. An outspoken advocate of protection against Japanese competition, the chairman of Chrysler not only lobbies vigorously for protection, but frequently exhorts American consumers to "buy American." In the process he has become something of a folk hero. People seem to forget that while he has been giving anti-Japanese speeches, his company often ranks on the list of *all* companies — Japanese and American — as one of the biggest importers of Japanese goods into the United States. Much of the importing has been done through Diamond Star Motors, a recently abandoned joint venture of Chrysler and Mitsubishi Motors, which imports and sells models, such as the Colt. Chrysler also imports large quantities of engines and other components directly from Japan and other Asian countries.

Most countries have their outspoken, flag-waving cheerleaders, many of whom have gained widespread support. In Japan, Shintaro Ishihara, author of *The Japan That Can Say No,* accused the United States of deliberate anti-Japanese racism while arousing ethnic and national passion among his Japanese readers. Edith Cresson, the former prime minister of France, appealed to similar emotions in her attacks on both Japan and the United States. Patrick Buchanan, a newspaper columnist and television commentator, sought the 1992 Republican presidential nomination on an "America First" platform.

Although speeches and exhortations often inspire significant emotional support, the global economy continues to integrate, led, in most cases, by large transnational companies. People, despite their emotions, seem to understand that in an interdependent world economy companies, not societies or nations, compete. Societies can provide various levels of support, including capital, human resources, and appropriate regulations, but essentially the competition is corporate, unless we choose to revert to the dangerous world of protectionism and nationalist politics that characterized the first half of this century. Nor is the world economy a zero-sum game in which there is an equivalent loser for every winner. Most economic competition produces growth. Although some people may gain more from it than others, everyone usually benefits.

Despite the flag-waving and the rhetoric of combat and despite vast cultural differences, people the world over seem to behave in remarkably similar patterns. They travel more, they increasingly seek access to the same information, and they find their tastes and standards of quality converging. The common denominator appears to be a preference for global products and services. Nevertheless, it is hard for us to understand fully the new patterns of global economics, not only because our frame of reference is the nation-state, but because many global products and services carry familiar national labels that we associate with particular countries.

In the new environment of global products, companies are belatedly rediscovering the value of the image of brands and consumers' recognition of them. In the 1970s and 1980s many venerable companies, named after their lead product, adopted bewildering and abstract names that sounded like a kind of corporate Esperanto: United States Steel became USX; United Airlines became Allegis; Burroughs and Sperry merged to be reborn as Unisys.[21] Today many companies are reverting to homelier and far-more-recognizable names based on primary brands: Amstar is now known as Domino Sugar; Castle & Cooke has become Dole Food Company; United Brands has been renamed Chiquita Brands; Consolidated Food Corporation now goes by the far more familiar name of Sara Lee; and Allegis is once again United Airlines.[22]

But it is not merely a brand's image but the quality behind the image that wins the loyalty of consumers around the world. The howls of protest that greeted Coca-Cola's decision to change the formula of Coke virtually forced the company to reverse one of the great blunders in the history of marketing and bring back "the real thing" as Classic Coke.

Most companies are not as lucky as Coca-Cola. More often, disappointed consumers simply turn away in disgust. In the late 1960s and 1970s Schlitz beer was the number two brand in the United States. But in the midseventies, to cut costs, the company substituted corn syrup for barley malt in its formula and cut the fermentation process to four days from twelve, resulting in beer that grew cloudy after a short time on the shelf. Annual sales plummeted from 18 million barrels in 1974 to only 1.8 million barrels in 1984.[23]

Perhaps the most striking—and costly—loss of brand loyalty has occurred with automakers who neglected to provide the quality behind the image. And once squandered, the loyalty of consumers is hard to recapture. American automobile manufacturers discovered that many customers who were lost to Honda, Nissan, or Toyota in the 1980s are likely to be lost for good because the higher-quality Japanese cars generated superior brand loyalty. According to one recent study, the divergence in brand loyalty cost the Big Three about 7.2 million in car sales in the 1980s.[24] And even though

Detroit is now building many high-quality cars, the U.S. car companies face an uphill battle in winning back an entire generation of customers whose standards are based on world-class products and services they know they can depend on.

Such products and services are global in another sense as well. They are often manufactured in many countries and brought to market through a vast transnational network of plants, people, and capital. The enormous corporations that bring these products to consumers everywhere are, like the brands themselves, becoming increasingly transnational. That is, they operate on a vast global scale and tend to go beyond the usual boundaries of national definition. "IBM, to some degree," declared the senior vice president of IBM World Trade in 1990, "has successfully lost its American identity."[25]

The rise of transnationals that, like IBM, regard the creation of a global identity as a mark of success represents a new stage in the evolution of corporate strategies to develop world markets. Many, perhaps most, firms began as national—or regional—producers. After achieving domestic success, they found that the filling of a few orders from outside their national boundaries brought about the beginning of an interesting international business. Other firms deliberately sought international business to balance the capacity of their plants and smooth the peaks and valleys of the normal business cycle. Successful companies followed up by instituting international divisions that were generally based at their corporate headquarters and charged with developing profitable businesses in those overseas markets where the risks were low and they could rely on the convertibility of foreign currencies to the home currency.

It was just such an international division at Smith Kline & French Laboratories that I joined fresh out of college in 1955. In those days, operating in a world economy still defined by the Allied victory in World War II, the staff of the international division pursued a strategy that might best be described as constructively opportunistic. Our job was to build the overseas element of the corporation, which thought of itself as being an "international" company. SmithKline was happy to satisfy the demand for American medicines as long as it was paid promptly in dollars. In that sense the strategy was certainly opportunistic. But we also took a constructive view of the longer-term prospects and sought to establish local subsidiaries in countries where political stability, the strong demand for products, and the convertibility of currencies combined to persuade the top brass to make the necessary investments. Subsidiary companies developed quickly in Canada and Mexico, followed shortly by England and later the major markets of continental Europe.

The subsidiary companies were basically small cookie-cutter versions of the parent company, with all the major functions, such as manufacturing, product development, marketing, and sales, included in each one. With the passage of time and often helped by strong local managers, the overseas companies became relatively self-sufficient and semiautonomous in their relations with corporate headquarters. Sometimes they even designed and developed their own new products. In this way many international companies evolved into a corporate form usually labeled "multinational," a term intended to describe large, far-flung corporate operations in which the parent company essentially reproduces itself in a number of other countries.

My first direct experience with multinational management occurred when I was assigned to Montreal in 1958. I joined a small but aggressive and fast-moving Canadian subsidiary intent on showing that, as Annie Oakley once said, "we could do anything better." In our case, we wanted to best our colleagues south of the Canadian border. We developed and introduced Contac, the first sustained-release, over-the-counter cold capsule in the world, although the glory went to our American counterparts who successfully launched the product the following year. For the most part, we introduced products originally developed in the United States, and for good measure we added a few locally developed and locally adapted products. Like our colleagues in the States, we helped revolutionize the treatment of the mentally ill through the introduction of psychotropic medications. But in Canada we did it faster, won a greater market share, and accomplished it with a second-generation product, Stelazine. Of course, we had gained greatly from the experience of those in the home market and plagiarized as much as possible while avoiding the more obvious mistakes. In short, we considered ourselves to be accountable to our parent company but basically independent and fiercely proud of our successes.

A great many American companies went through similar evolutionary stages during the first three decades after World War II.

After all, they enjoyed an open field and were able to ride the rising tide of industrial and economic recovery in Europe and the Pacific Rim. Today this natural evolutionary pattern from an international company into a multinational organization remains the most common feature on the competitive terrain of the global economy. The automobile industry provides some particularly interesting and distinctive examples.

Ford and GM stand as early precedents for the multinational model. Both operated internationally before World War II. Ford enjoyed marked success in England through a wholly owned subsidiary that adapted Henry Ford's assembly line to designs that were well accepted by British customers. GM followed suit through its Vauxhall subsidiary. Both companies also exported profitably to Latin America and elsewhere. And in Australia, GM became the leading producer, again on a wholly owned basis, through its Holden subsidiary. After the war, Detroit concentrated internationally on rebuilding its former position in Europe. GM developed Opel as a strong subsidiary for the German market by patterning it after the parent company and building models specifically designed for German car buyers. Both Ford and GM were so successful in giving their major overseas subsidiaries autonomy over design and production that the term *multidomestic* was coined as a variant of the term *multinational*.

In 1991, GM won a 12.1 percent share of the Western European car market, now the largest car market in the world and the one with the greatest potential for growth. Among all GM's European competitors only Volkswagen, at 16.4 percent, and Fiat, at 12.8 percent, had larger shares. Ford, with a market share of 11.9 percent, was topped only by Volkswagen, Fiat, and Peugeot (at 12.1 percent).[26] By any measure the two American auto companies have performed well in Europe, creating strong competitive companies in Britain and Germany through early positioning and an adroit use of the multinational model.

Mercedes-Benz, in contrast, has remained with the basic international model by exporting its products from Stuttgart to a world that is hungry for premium-priced luxury cars that carry the cachet of German production and engineering. This strategy worked well when the deutsche mark was low relative to the dollar, when American cars were of poor quality, and when Japanese car companies concentrated on low-priced models. But these three conditions have now changed, and consequently German export sales are down. To compound the situation, fluctuations in currency can negate even modest gains in sales overseas, as happened in 1990 when the dollar's weakness against the deutsche mark effectively wiped out the 3.5 percent increase in the sales of Mercedes in the United States.[27] The limitations of the international strategy are becoming more apparent in a low-growth market with highly charged global competition.

Nevertheless, for companies with enormous economies of scale, localized production skills, or the need for particular raw materials, the international strategic model continues to make good sense. Commercial aircraft and jet engines come readily to mind as examples of industries that require huge economies of scale. Boeing, with 60 percent of the world's airframe market and a backlog of orders that will keep it busy until the year 2010, is just such a company. Meanwhile, General Electric, Pratt and Whitney, and Rolls Royce divide up the production of the world's commercial jet engines. Caterpillar Tractor continues to manufacture primarily in Peoria, Illinois, from which huge earth-moving machines are dispatched throughout the world.

But conditions are changing even in industries where international strategies still work. Boeing's share of the airframe market was 80 percent just a few years ago, but the advent of the European Airbus has decreased that share. And Toyota, with about $25 billion in the bank and possessing arguably the world's most advanced manufacturing systems, is quietly preparing to enter the commercial aircraft business. It is therefore no accident that Boeing is beginning to provide for the manufacture of aircraft components in countries that are large continuing customers. Thus Boeing, a classic international company, is leaping over the multinational stage and going straight to a transnational strategy.

Viewed from afar, multinationals superficially resemble transnationals, but the two are strikingly different in their operation, their presence in global markets, their leadership, and their ownership. Together, these differences make transnationals qualitatively distinct from multinationals and certainly from international companies.

In operation, multinationals tend to clone themselves in other countries, and, regardless of the degree of autonomy they grant to foreign subsidiaries, the center of the companies remain at their headquarters in the home market. These companies often transplant managers and invariably alter the national identities of any foreign companies they acquire. Products are generally introduced in the home market and then later rolled into foreign markets. In organization and outlook, the multinationals traditionally follow the colonial model.

Transnationals, by contrast, locate various parts of their operation anywhere in the world it makes sense to do so. Production facilities may be located in many countries to gain proximity to local markets or in just a few locations to maximize efficiencies of scale. New products are introduced simultaneously in as many markets as possible. Design functions may be carried out in areas that are rich in human talent, or marketing may find a home in several strategic locations. Research and development, one of the most important activities of transnationals, may be located in countries with superior technologies, talented researchers and engineers, or desirable markets. Texas Instruments, Procter & Gamble, Ciba-Geigy, and Carrier all maintain or plan to open research facilities in Japan. Similarly, the corporate headquarters of transnationals or their divisions may be widely separated and located to take advantage of technological or tax situations. Moreover, communications, coordination, and control are carried out through a global network, rather than radiating outward from the center, which increasingly tends to limit its activities to broad financial and strategic issues.

Part of the explanation for the difference in outlook of multinationals and transnationals lies in the distribution of their markets. According to a generally accepted definition, a company is a multinational if 25 percent of its world output is outside its home country.[28] But this definition says nothing about how that foreign output is distributed. Many transnationals, by contrast, do considerably more business outside than inside their countries of origin. IBM, for example, makes more than 50 percent of its sales (as a share of its total revenue) and 75 percent of its profits outside the United States. Dow Chemical, Gillette, Hewlett-Packard, Xerox, Reuters, and Bertelsmann all make more than half their annual sales outside their countries of origin.

Just as important, the business that transnationals do outside their countries of origin ideally generates sales and profits that are proportional to the worldwide distribution of their markets: In many cases, that means 30 percent in Europe, 30 percent in North America, 20 percent in Japan, and 20 percent in other countries. In

1990, the president of IBM, describing the American, Japanese, and European economies as three legs on a stool, said, "We want to balance this game out, so that two legs don't get bigger than the third."[29] For such companies all these markets hold equal interest, requiring an outlook that is truly global.

Perhaps the greatest strategic defect of the traditional multinational structure is the inability to grasp unusual opportunities. Again, the automobile industry provides a striking example. In August 1945, as World War II ended, Holden, the Australian subsidiary of GM, was the seventh largest automobile company in the world. Moreover, it was far and away the largest automobile company in Asia. Though GM succeeded admirably in rebuilding a strong position in Europe, its lack of a global strategic view cost it the opportunity to move Holden into the Asian markets of the Pacific Rim. The lost opportunity, of course, had enormous consequences.

The difference in outlook between transnationals and multinationals is the difference between a globe and a map. The surface of a globe has neither a beginning nor an end, neither a center nor a periphery; it is a continuous integrated whole. A map has a definite center, peripheral places, and remote corners; it is a discontinuous, hierarchical fragment. And for the traditional multinational, the home market and the headquarters stand at the center of the map and send out expeditions to progressively less important provinces. In sum, transnational corporations view the world as one vast, essentially seamless market in which all major decisions are grounded solely in the desire to gain a global competitive advantage. Multinationals make decisions to benefit the center.

Increasingly, the top leadership of transnationals is drawn from many countries, unlike the multinationals, which tend to remain firmly under the direction of board members and managers from the home country. For example, the sixteen-member board of ICI, the global chemical giant, now includes two Americans, a Canadian, a Japanese, and a German—compared to an all-British board as recently as ten years ago. And 35 percent of the company's 180 key people are non-British.[30] The top executives of Coca-Cola include two Australians, an Irishman, an Italian, and an Austrian. Asea Brown Boveri, a $27 billion transnational, born of the merger of Sweden's Asea and Switzerland's Brown Boveri in 1987, has only two Swedes on its eight-member board. The company's day-to-day operations are guided by a Swedish CEO and a twelve-member executive committee consisting of Swedes, Swiss, Germans, and Americans, who hold meetings all over the world. Business is done in English, and accounting is done in dollars. Representatives of five different nationalities sit on the board of Unilever, a British-Dutch company, and representatives of the same number of countries are on the board of SmithKline Beecham.

Transnational companies tend to have a financial structure and profile of share ownership that is also transnational, in part because of their large size and market capitalization and in part as a consequence of a truly global orientation. They sell debt and, if necessary, equity wherever the demand and the costs converge to their best advantage. Similarly, shares find their way through the global stock market to investors around the world. The profile of share ownership can change quickly, depending on investors' sentiments and corporate events, but most transnational companies seek broad share ownership around the world, believing that it helps provide a stable market for their stock. Ideally, most transnationals hope that, over time, share ownership would approximate the same geographic distribution as the company's sources of sales and profits. This pattern is already well under way. Forty to 50 percent of the shares of such transnationals as Asea Brown Boveri, Philips, Hoechst, Bayer, Siemens, and SmithKline Beecham are held outside the companies' home countries.[31]

Just as the national identities of products and transnational companies tend to become blurred, so do the normal definitions of national score keeping. A product made by a foreign-owned company in the United States and then exported, for example, to Mexico, shows up as a positive item in American trade statistics. A product made by an American company from American designs in Mexico and exported to Japan appears as a positive item in Mexican trade statistics and a negative one in Japanese trade statistics. It appears only in American calculations when a portion of the profits is remitted to the United States as a dividend; it then becomes an item in the "flow of currency" account and taxable as income to the American parent company with due credit for any Mexican income tax paid before remittance. In the case of a transnational company, however, it is more likely that the profits will never be returned to the United States, but will remain to finance growth in Mexico or be transferred as nontaxable investment capital to another country to finance corporate expansion there.

The Mexico-to-Japan trade transaction in this example that increases the wealth of the American-based transnational company by using its knowledge of design in the global market may never appear in the statistics on the flow of American trade and capital. Nevertheless, governments continue to keep score in national terms, using crude and misleading statistics like the merchandise trade deficit, although such statistics no longer capture the reality of a global marketplace and the transnational companies that operate in it. As Robert B. Reich, of Harvard's Kennedy School of Government, pointed out, "More than half of America's exports and imports, by value, are transfers of components and services within the same global company."[32] And more than half the U.S. annual trade deficit results from imports into the United States by *American* companies.[33] In fact, Reich noted, "When the foreign sales of U.S.-owned companies are calculated against the total purchases by Americans of the products of foreign-owned companies, America's trade deficit turns into a net surplus."[34] When governments adopt narrowly designed policies to increase their countries' exports or to reduce their imports, they fail to understand how transnational companies, manufacturing locally and coordinating globally through a complex pattern of plants, shipments, and sales operations, really do business.

Figures on direct foreign investments, which are often cited to support the thesis that foreigners are buying up the United States while American companies invest far less overseas, are similarly misleading. Many American companies made major investments overseas in the 1960s and 1970s, when the dollar was relatively strong. Moreover, those assets have appreciated dramatically in the ensuing years. Nevertheless, the U.S. Department of Commerce computes them in terms of their original purchase price and then compares them to direct foreign investments in the United States, most of which have been more recent. Thus a $50 million American investment made in Europe in 1965 is equated with a $50 million Japanese investment in the United States in 1990. The result is a misleading—and often unduly dire—picture of this country's net investment position.

In the transnational world the real competition is not between nations, but between global companies doing battle everywhere. Nevertheless, the ultimate winners will be the citizens of many countries, including many that were only recently thought to be in the economic doldrums, a theme to which I will return in the concluding chapter. This is not to say that the emerging transnational world is without problems. Countries like Bangladesh, Haiti, and the nations of sub-Saharan Africa remain impoverished. Desirable environmental goals—from preventing global warming to halting the stripping of the hardwood forests of Borneo—often come into conflict with economic growth, a dilemma that is likely to get worse as growth spreads. And as transnational companies appear to move beyond the power of any single government to monitor their activities, thoughtful people worry about these huge corporations riding roughshod over environmental standards, fair labor practices, regulatory control, and ethical behavior.

The dark side of globalism has been most spectacularly exposed by the corruption at the Bank of Credit and Commerce International (BCCI). Originally a Pakistani operation, the international bank operated in more than seventy countries, but it was chartered in Luxembourg and the Cayman Islands to avoid many of the regulations that govern its competitors in the United States, Europe, and Japan. Noted for attracting customers who deal in arms, drugs, and hot money, it is now being investigated for tax evasion, smuggling, money laundering, bribery, stock manipulation, and massive financial fraud, much of it allegedly carried out through a global network of dummy corporations and friendly banks. Tragically, the bank's collapse will likely mean the loss of billions of dollars in personal savings, much of it belonging to Asian immigrants in Europe and people in developing countries where bank-deposit insurance does not exist. Almost as disturbing, there was no supervisory or regulatory authority capable of keeping track of the bank's far-flung operations.

The BCCI case starkly raises the regulatory and ethical challenges posed by transnationals. Succeeding chapters will explore the nature of these large transnational companies, what they are, how they operate, and the special challenges they pose to corporate governance and ethics and the implications of their growing presence for owners, employees, customers, and the interests of the societies being served. But first it is important to understand that transnational corporations did not merely spring up for no reason.

Understanding how these companies came to be is essential to understanding where they may be taking us.

In large measure, these companies are responding to the pull of strong tides in the demands of consumers around the world whose tastes in goods and services are converging and who now universally demand high quality and good prices from whatever source. Consumers' tastes and demands are converging globally because people everywhere now enjoy easy access to common information.[35] Voice, image, and data communications are not only ubiquitous, but have become astonishingly cheap. The transatlantic telephone cable, completed in 1956 and holding forty-eight telephone lines, was laid at a cost (in current dollars) of $557,000 per line; the cable begun in 1992 will hold 80,000 lines and will be laid at a cost of $5,400 per line.[36] In satellite telecommunications, the cost of an earth station with twenty-five voice channels, capable of providing satellite access to a medium-sized phone system, dropped to about $150,000 in 1991 from $500,000 just six years ago.[37] Consequently, we witness not only the exponential growth in the wealth of information, but the rapid dissemination and easy accessibility of information on a global scale. The spread of television transmission by satellite in particular has accustomed us to the instantaneous, worldwide exchange of information. The world watches not only reruns of the same old movies and television shows, but up-to-the-minute live broadcasts of world events, from the fall of the Berlin Wall, to the release of Nelson Mandela, to the unleashing of Desert Storm. Satellite transmission to printing plants around the world makes possible the national and international distribution of newspapers like *USA Today*, the *Wall Street Journal*, the *New York Times*, and the *Financial Times*.

All these media, print and electronic alike, instantly bring advertisements and news stories about products and services to people everywhere. We can all now see what others around the world have and wish to have. And as tastes converge, global brands emerge. For example, Coca-Cola is the single best-known brand name in the world. Its consumption has spread to such an extent in the fifty years since World War II that it is now sold in 160 countries and is found in even the remotest spots on the globe. Today 80 percent of the sales and production of Coca-Cola originate outside the United States. The second best-known brand name in the world is Sony, whose astounding growth started with its farsighted application of transistor technology licensed from RCA in the early 1950s. Today more than 70 percent of Sony's sales are outside Japan, and a substantial portion of its shares are owned by non-Japanese.

The interplay of global brands and ubiquitous communications resulting in the demand for high quality from whatever source was reconfirmed by an encounter I had in a pharmacy in Beijing in 1989. The pharmacist was showing me some of the local over-the-counter products that appeared to be of uniformly low quality. These products consisted mostly of broken, powdery tablets in nondescript bottles. Just then a large man in a denim worker's suit and a Mao hat walked in and asked the pharmacist for something. The Chinese translator who was accompanying me tugged at my sleeve and said, "He's asking for Contac." Through the translator I introduced myself to the worker. He said he was from Mongolia and that he saw our advertisements there, but the product was unavailable, so he stocked up whenever he came to Beijing.

In addition to the worldwide convergence of consumer preferences, powerful business, economic, and political developments bring transnational companies into being. Some of these developments, like the opening up of formerly closed markets to foreign companies and investments, offer the opportunity for globalization. Other factors, such as the staggering costs of developing products in high value-added industries or the emergence of vast free-trade zones like the European Community, virtually demand a global response by many companies.

Opportunities for globalization have perhaps never been greater as most of the world, including a reluctant China, comes to embrace the principles of market economics and the freer flow of goods, people, and money across borders. The liberation of the countries of Eastern Europe and the collapse of Soviet communism provide only the most striking examples. But although the painful conversion from planned to market economies in those nations may take decades, numerous other countries, attracting little notice, are already moving aggressively into the global arena. Many of these countries are reversing decades of insular trade and investment policies.

Throughout much of South America, the embrace of free markets and the privatization of state enterprises are moving rapidly ahead, bringing in badly needed investments, much of them through global companies. Overall, in 1991, Latin America attracted more than $40 billion in private capital, compared to only $13.4 billion the previous year. As John Plender, writing in the *Financial Times,* put it, "The impassioned intellectuals who discussed *dependencia* are out; intellectuals who have watched the Asian dragon economies make themselves as dependent as possible on foreign multinationals are in. Three decades after the dragons dumped their import substitution programmes in favor of export-led growth, Latin America has gotten the message."[38]

Mexico, for example, has joined many developing nations that are fed up with the failure of protectionism and state planning to nourish domestic industries and provide a healthy national economy. So it has undertaken fundamental economic reforms that have propelled its industries into the global marketplace and brought the global marketplace to Mexico. To encourage export-led growth, it has devalued the peso. To encourage investment, it has eased restrictions on foreign ownership of industry. And to encourage efficiency and competitiveness, it is pursuing a policy of privatization, selling off state-owned companies, including seven of the eighteen banks it nationalized in 1982. In 1986 it joined GATT, the 108-nation organization dedicated to promoting freer trade, and lowered or eliminated tariffs on a wide variety of imported goods. The policies seem to be working. Since 1985, its exports of manufactured goods to the United States, for example, have increased by 100 percent.[39] Foreign investment, which stood at $1.8 billion in 1985, averaged $2.9 billion annually through 1991.[40] Mexico is now considering further easing restrictions on foreign ownership in banking and the oil industry, long considered sacrosanct.

Venezuela is also vigorously privatizing its state-owned industries, easing rules on foreign investments, and lowering tariffs.[41] A 60 percent stake in Viasa, the state-owned international airline, was sold in 1991 to a consortium led by the Spanish airline Iberia. Bids were also taken on the state telephone company, and a group led by BellSouth Enterprises and Racal Telecom won the right to provide cellular telephone service for the next twenty years. A natural gas-processing project involving Mitsubishi, Shell Oil, and Exxon will mark the first time since nationalization of the oil industry in 1975 that foreigners have been allowed to hold majority equities. Since 1989 import tariffs have been reduced from an average of 34 percent to 10 percent. Even an attempted military coup in February 1992 could not shake the confidence of investors in Venezuela's fast-growing economy. Within hours after the coup was foiled, contracts for hundreds of millions of dollars in new foreign investments were signed, as the country's president vowed to maintain free-market policies.[42] The net result of all these reforms is that Venezuela is once again enjoying the highest economic growth rate in the Americas.

Things are changing elsewhere, as well. India, long a bastion of anticapitalist doctrine and nationalistic economic policies, has recently undertaken sweeping reforms to attract foreign investments.[43] Foreign companies can now own as much as 51 percent of Indian companies, and foreign companies seeking more than 51 percent are guaranteed by law an accelerated approval process. As many as thirty-four major industries, including electrical equipment, food processing, and transportation, have been opened to direct foreign investment. The rupee has been devalued and governmental subsidies have been ended for sugar and fertilizers. Since the reforms, IBM, which left India in 1977 because foreign ownership of Indian companies was limited to 40 percent, announced a joint venture with the Indian conglomerate Tata Industries to turn out IBM System 2 personal computers and programs. And Ford is launching a joint venture with Maruti, an Indian carmaker, to produce aluminum radiators for automobiles. Though it is too early to tell how the reforms are working, it is worth noting that in 1990, before the changes, foreign investment totaled a dismal $70 million.

Vietnam, ostensibly a hard-line communist country, now possesses one of the most liberal foreign investment codes in all of Asia. Foreigners are allowed to own as much as a 100 percent stake in local businesses or to form joint ventures with any Vietnamese companies. British Petroleum, for example, has announced a thirty-year venture agreement with Petrolimex, the Vietnamese state-run fuel and lubricants company, to build the country's biggest and first modern lubricants plant and market its products. JVC and Sanyo have built assembly plants in Vietnam, and Honda, Mitsubishi, and Toyota all plan to follow suit. Foreign investors enjoy generous tax breaks, state-owned businesses no longer receive governmental subsidies, and price controls have been abolished.

Now China, which appeared to abandon reform following the crackdown in 1989, is inching toward a free market in some major centers. It has even devalued its currency to a point approaching free-market levels. And stock exchanges have been organized and are operating in Shanghai and Guangdong. Astonishingly, sometime in 1992, it is expected that for the first time in forty years industrial output in the private sector will outstrip that of state-run enterprises.[44]

At the other end of the spectrum, poorer European countries like Portugal, facing head-to-head competition with industrial giants like Germany when the single market arrives, have also moved aggressively to reverse decades of outdated policies. Portugal has privatized state-owned companies, reduced inflation, and induced the European Community to provide the country with nearly $5 billion for improvements in its infrastructure that have enhanced industrial productivity and attracted private investments. As a result, Portugal is now Europe's fastest-growing economy, and its per capita income has more than tripled since 1985.[45]

As more and more countries watch their reform-minded neighbors prosper, they, too, are likely to seek entry to the global marketplace. These emerging markets will mean more opportunities for globalization. Indeed, they will almost demand it. Companies expanding into these markets will naturally be afforded an even broader financial base on which to build the research and development and technology crucial to high value-added industries. And as personal incomes in these developing countries rise—thanks, in part, to globalization—the competitive advantage such companies enjoy will also grow.

In the rush to freer trade that is helping fuel the globalization of business, a strong countercurrent is, paradoxically, also fueling globalization: the threat of regional trading blocs in North America, Western Europe, and east Asia that promote free trade among their member nations but may present stiff obstacles to outsiders. The European Community plans to remove all internal barriers to the free movement of people, products, services, and money among its twelve member nations: Belgium, Britain, Denmark, France, Germany, Greece, Ireland, Italy, Luxembourg, the Netherlands, Portugal, and Spain. It will remove tariffs, harmonize regulations of products, and no longer check passports at internal borders. At a stroke, the European Community will become the largest single market in the world, numbering approximately 340 million people.

And this largest market will get larger. In October 1991 the European Community, after two years of negotiations, signed a free-trade agreement with the seven-member European Free Trade Association (EFTA), consisting of Austria, Finland, Iceland, Liechtenstein, Norway, Sweden, and Switzerland. The agreement will help pave the way for EFTA countries that want to join the European Community. Austria and Sweden have already applied for membership; Finland is expected to do so soon, and many people in Norway are rethinking their country's refusal to join. Switzerland has applied for accelerated admission, subject to the approval of its citizens in a referendum. Now some of the newly freed countries of Eastern Europe are also clamoring for admission. In any case, taking into account the EFTA countries, the European free-trade zone will number some 380 million people when the single market and the new European Economic Area go into effect.

Meanwhile, the United States has concluded negotiations in a free-trade agreement with Canada and Mexico. The agreement will create a single market of 360 million people, outstripping even the European Community proper. The United States is also contemplating bilateral free-trade agreements with Chile and other Latin American countries. If these trading blocs become a means to insulate their members from Japanese, South Korean, and other Asian competitors, then it is likely that an east Asian trading bloc will form in reaction.

The significance of these trading blocs for large companies has been clear for some time: A serious global competitor must achieve insider status in Europe, North America, and Japan to avoid being frozen out of the largest markets in the world. In short, such competitors must become transnational. Member nations of the European Community are already touting themselves to non-European Community businesses as the ideal entrée to the community. Britain, for example, places advertisements in American newspapers that proclaim "Britain's advantages for your business, as the base for tariff-free access to the European Single Market."[46]

The experience of Japanese carmakers with the European Community broadly illustrates both the challenge companies face from trading blocs and the imperative to choose the transnational response to those challenges. After gaining a significant market share in the United States in the 1980s, Japanese carmakers are now turning their attention to Europe. To protect European automakers, the European Commission decided to limit Japanese auto exports to the community until seven years after the market is unified. So until the year 2000 the community will allow no more than 1.23 million Japanese cars—about 10 percent of the current market—to be imported. But there are to be no restrictions on sales of Japanese cars produced at plants located within any of the twelve member nations of the European Community. In response the Japanese companies are rushing to build production facilities in the community. Nissan has been producing vehicles in Great Britain since 1986. Honda and Toyota will join them there in 1992. And Mazda, the only one of the big five Japanese auto companies without a European factory, is hurriedly formulating its own insider strategy.

Just what counts as insider status remains a vexed question in many locales and countries. Some members of the European Community, for example, disagree about the meaning of the automobile accord. Great Britain insists that the agreement sets no limits on sales of Japanese cars produced within the European Community. France and Italy say that the Japanese have agreed privately to such limits. In another case, ICL (80 percent of which is owned by Fujitsu) was excluded from a European computer consortium for being insufficiently European. In an even more complicated case, Brother typewriter, a Japanese company with a U.S. assembly plant in Tennessee, filed a complaint under U.S. antidumping laws against Smith Corona, a British-owned company with largely American operations. Antidumping laws are designed to protect American producers from imports sold below "fair-market value." Ultimately, the U.S. Commerce Department ruled that Smith Corona is an American producer and that Brother is a non-American producer. This ruling has also made it more difficult for foreign companies to bring antidumping actions in the United States.

All these borderline cases point to a single conclusion: The need to achieve insider status requires an unequivocal transnational response. The specter of rival trading blocs, each with huge internal free markets and external import barriers, only increases the urgency. It is just such considerations that are driving the boom in cross-border mergers and acquisitions, joint ventures, transplanted factories—and the emergence of genuinely transnational companies.

But even if rival trade blocs do not develop, the escalating costs of developing products will impel more and more companies in high value-added industries to go transnational. Two decades ago, the development of a new pharmaceutical product cost about $15 million and took about five years. Today it costs on average about $230 million and takes about twelve years. Only the global market can support such large-scale investments of capital and time. Moreover, as development times lengthen, the life spans of products have shortened — the effective twenty-year patent life of a new drug has shrunk to eight years.[47] Shortened life spans of products put additional pressure on companies to recoup their investments as rapidly as possible in as many geographic areas as possible. The same is true in many other industries.

For example, before 1950 telecommunications switching systems cost about $10 million to produce and had a useful life of about twenty-five years.[48] The digital switching systems developed in the 1980s cost $1 billion to develop and had a useful life of only eight to twelve years. The recovery of those development costs requires winning at least 8 percent of the market share, a figure that cannot be achieved by operating in, say, any single European country. So switch manufacturers must operate globally if they are to have any hope of competing in the telephone-switching business. And the greatly reduced product cycles, brought on by rapid advances in technology, require massive investments in development at ever shorter intervals. To repeat, shorter life cycles for products mean that companies must be able to roll out innovations in a hurry everywhere. The more quickly they can introduce a product around the world, the greater the benefits from market saturation and subsequent low-cost positioning.

Aircraft manufacturers, faced with staggering development and manufacturing costs, must also sell to the global market if they are to survive. The Boeing Company, a classic international company that is beginning to pursue a transnational strategy, will spend $4 billion developing its 777, a midsize, two-engine passenger jet that has greater fuel efficiency, is simpler to operate, and has a more flexible design than do comparable four-engine jets. To recover those costs, the company must corner one of the major national markets — an unlikely event in this newly competitive industry — or win significant orders all around the globe. In 1991 British Airways ordered fifteen of the planes and took options for fifteen more for a total of $3.6 billion, joining United Airlines and All Nippon Airways in committing to the 777. Thus with orders from major carriers in the United States, Europe, and Japan, Boeing achieved what must always be a central objective of a global strategy in capital-intensive, high value-added industries—significant penetration of the three major markets in the world.

Companies in high value-added industries must also stay close to the leading technology in their fields, wherever it may be found. For example, more than eighty new office copiers that Xerox introduced in the United States were engineered and produced in Japan in a joint venture with Fuji.[49] Similarly, American computer companies must also operate in Japan to get an early, firsthand look at new microcircuit technology and advances in manufacturing methods. Conversely, Asian companies must operate in Silicon Valley, which remains the foremost design center for personal computers. Hyundai Electronics recently announced that it is moving its entire personal computer operations, including design, marketing, manufacturing, and administration, to San Jose.[50] Roche and Sandoz, two Swiss-based pharmaceutical giants, have each invested many hundreds of millions of dollars in the United States to participate directly in the exploding, high-potential field of biotechnology. No other country yet rivals the United States as the location for this new technology. Consumer products companies can reap similar benefits by locating in technology-rich countries. For example, Procter & Gamble's liquid Tide uses a water-softening compound developed in Europe.

This much we know, then: The marketplace imposes a global imperative that cannot be evaded. Global economic integration requires a global response. Even resolutely local businesses must now compete with global products and services in their own backyards. Stay-at-homes cannot secede from the global marketplace because the global marketplace is not elsewhere, it's everywhere. And the playing field is not level; it's round. For many companies the transnational question is no longer *whether* but *how*. And for companies that have already made transnational moves, the question is whether the choices are correct and the pace of change is truly competitive.

What is at stake in these crucial issues of corporate strategy and competitiveness is, in the long run, survival. But although there is agreement on the need to go transnational, there is no agreement on how best to achieve it, no consensus on the optimum transnational strategy, no reliable road map to the global village. Companies may evolve logically and organically from national to international to multinational organizations, but the change to transnational status requires a total transformation that arises neither naturally nor easily—as I was to discover when many of these global forces converged with great impact on my company.

CHAPTER TWO

THE TRANSNATIONAL CROSSROADS

IN MY CASE THE GLOBAL imperative presented itself in the mid-1980s, when trends in the global marketplace and the drive for superior performance brought SmithKline to a strategic crossroads. At that time we were riding a wave of success with the revolutionary anti-ulcer drug Tagamet, but the wave was cresting and the rocks and shoals of future corporate distress were apparent. Competitors, primarily with products of Japanese and European origin, were rushing to market with so-called second-generation anti-ulcer drugs. More were coming. It was clear that the growth of Tagamet might stall. And though we were investing heavily in a reinvigorated research and development organization, the scale of our effort was less than that of our major competitors. Most important, we were painfully late in starting the revitalization of research, and promising new compounds were not moving into development fast enough, a potentially fatal problem in the new world of fast-paced, technology-driven competition. Finally, we were in the process of abandoning a previous strategic direction aimed at diversification in favor of one aimed at becoming a focused health care company.

Opportunities emerging from the exploding technology of the life sciences raised the stakes considerably. Startling new discoveries and scientific breakthroughs offered the chance to treat diseases in ways never before dreamed possible. In our case, even in the mideighties, our research scientists were pursuing promising leads in AIDS therapy; new vaccines for two scourges of humankind, malaria and influenza (regardless of strain or origin); new approaches to asthma and arthritis; and important advances in cancer therapy. These developments held out hope of relief to millions of people and, not incidentally, promised great rewards to companies that could harness them quickly, effectively, and safely.

We moved rapidly to build scientific capability in molecular biology and related disciplines of biotechnology. We constructed modern new laboratories and recruited teams of scientists, including a competitive group of molecular biologists. But with the growth of Tagamet slowing, my greatest fear was that we would be forced to reverse our expanding commitment to research and development at the very time when expanding scientific knowledge and the growing global demand for health care combined to create tremendous business prospects for our industry and our company. In short, I saw a world of opportunity for science-based health care companies such as ours, but feared we would run out of time to position ourselves to reap the rewards.

We faced a dramatic strategic choice. We could seek a safe, if unexciting, role as a relatively small niche player in our rapidly globalizing industry, or we could risk making the leap toward transnational status and global scale. Either route would lead to fateful, long-term consequences for all our stakeholders — shareowners, employees, and customers alike. Given the speed with which the world was moving and the growing pressure to maintain our growth in sales and earnings, it was not a decision we could defer for long.

Our situation was not unique then nor is it unusual now. Many companies now stand at the same transnational crossroads Smith-Kline faced in the mideighties. They have arrived there, like it or not, as a result of the many manifestations of global economic integration I previously sketched: the universal demand for global products and services; converging standards of global quality and value; the explosion of information and technology and relatively easy access to them anywhere in the world; intense competition from large companies operating on a global scale; new competitors emerging from previously remote corners of the world; and, finally, the attraction of new markets that are just rejoining the international trading system. These basic trends translate to vital strategic issues for businesses large or small.

Issues raised by technology—its pursuit, its cost, and its enormous leverage in competitive positioning—are also bringing many companies to the transnational crossroads. Since the mid-1980s, in high-technology alone, there have been more than 900 transnational alliances by American companies or investments by foreign companies in American technology start-ups.[1] And this figure does not include similar deals among non-American companies or outright acquisitions.

Because technology is an ever-increasing component of many products and services, the investment in research and development required to keep pace grows in geometric proportions. The huge scale of investment makes it imperative to commercialize technology-intensive products as quickly as possible in every available market throughout the world. And despite the strengthening of laws to protect intellectual property in most countries through international conventions, few companies have a technical monopoly. Any commercial delay will be quickly filled by a competitor's product, even at the risk of later litigation on patents, thereby strengthening the competitor and preventing the achievement of the maximum return on the high-stakes game of research and development. The strategic response, of course, is to develop in research and particularly development, on a global scale, combined with global manufacturing and marketing muscle to move products into the world's markets quickly and successfully. The failure to do so not only reduces the return on investment, it provides an opportunity to a competitor to fill any geographic void or take advantage of any time lag.

The requirements of scale in such critical functions as manufacturing and marketing are another major factor in the global imperative. Huge investments in plant and equipment and the skilled employees that work in them require the unit volume to be efficient and to gain the maximum return on the investment. As the unit volume rises, unit costs decline, thereby not only strengthening the profit-and-loss statement, but buttressing the competitive position of the enterprise. Aluminum smelters, chemicals, and telecommunications switching equipment are just a few examples of industries in which unit cost–volume relationships are decisive competitive factors. Penetrating markets all around the world to achieve the global market share and the unit volume it creates is an obvious strategy to drive unit costs down. Of course, a combination of the leading global market share and low-cost production creates an almost unassailable position of competitive strength.

Another, more subtle, factor that lends urgency to the global imperative is the need to obtain and exploit insider status not only in emerging trade blocs, but in the corridors of power in the major capitals of the world. The latter kind of insider status means gathering information that enables a company to predict events and decisions that will have a material bearing on its business. It also means gaining sufficient status to ensure treatment that is equal to that of an entrenched and well-connected local competitor. Although these objectives are easily stated, they are not easily achieved. Any foreign company that is competing in Japan, for example, will quickly testify to the difficulty and the importance of gaining some measure of insider status there. The need for insider status in Japan, and elsewhere for that matter, is one reason for the plethora of joint ventures, in which the local partner is expected to provide the necessary local coloring.

But the strongest single factor in the global imperative is the drive for superior competitive performance. As Michael Porter pointed out, "The environment in most of the developed world is one of relatively slow growth coupled with growing global competition, a dramatic change from recent decades. The emphasis has thus shifted from growth to improving competitive advantage. While largely independent business units [as in the classic multinational model] may have been an appropriate vehicle for pursuing growth, a more difficult environment has made it increasingly important to coordinate business unit strategies to exploit interrelationships."[2] Thus, competitive performance today usually translates to winning an increased market share—often, as Porter said, in low-growth markets at the expense of competitors—and continually improving productivity and efficiency to increase profits more rapidly than sales. When an industry reaches a point at which it can apply this strategy of leveraging interrelationships, the competitive forces invariably require a transnational response from the companies competing in that industry.

Thus, for many business leaders, the handwriting is on the wall, and it is easy to read. Almost every day the newspapers bring fresh stories of global events and pressures. What was once a short shelf of books touting globalism has mushroomed to a library. Professors as well as professionals offer analyses of competitive conditions that painstakingly describe the reaction of other companies to issues and opportunities that cut across many industries. Large corporations are regularly visited by battalions of consultants and merchant bankers who are only too willing to analyze the present realities and predict future developments. Concluding that basic trends in the global business environment point to a transnational corporate response is not difficult.

The hard part is deciding what to do. What is most difficult is convincing others about the validity of the decision because the transnational response is neither easy nor automatic. It does not grow naturally from previous business developments, the way many other strategic directions often do. For example, export-oriented international companies naturally tend to evolve into multinationals by reproducing themselves in major markets through gradual expansion. The transition appears organic and logical; it is measured and slow paced, and it requires no great alteration in outlook or organization.

By contrast, the transnational response requires an abrupt and often cataclysmic change in vision, mission, strategy, and organizational structure. It does not come easily and generally requires shedding many managerial and cultural habits and practices. It also requires tough decisions involving people because the emphasis on competitive performance often means fewer managers, plants, facilities, and employees. The commitment to core competencies and the people who embody these competencies on a global basis involves a stretching, mind-expanding attitude and working approach that reaches across borders and business functions. Such a radical change in attitude and approach does not come naturally to those in midcareer.

Finally, the decision to strive for transnational status is greatly complicated by the fact that the pattern of transnational strategy and structure is not clear. There is a bewildering variety of business strategies for becoming a superior global competitor:

1. internal growth over time
2. strategic alliances and collaborations
3. joint ventures
4. mergers and acquisitions.

Many firms are experimenting with several of these strategies at once, and the pace of such experiments is picking up dramatically. Thus the issue for senior executives and boards of directors is not so much whether to meet the global challenge and march down the road to transnational status, but which route to take and at what speed.

Internal growth over time as a solution to the global imperative holds great appeal because it is the most familiar and least threatening. Managing internal growth and increments of change on a day-to-day basis is, after all, what business leaders routinely do. And though internal growth to transnational status ultimately requires many of the same wrenching changes as do the other transnational strategies, it skirts the pitfalls of joining forces with other companies. There is no clash of different corporate cultures, no struggle over aims and methods, no danger of giving away competitive secrets.

Despite such attractive characteristics, however, internal growth is, in my view, simply no longer available to most companies as a response to the global imperative. When the pace of global integration was slower, some farseeing companies—most notably Honda, Nestlé, Procter & Gamble, and Sony—were able to grow to transnational status through a strategy of methodically entering key markets around the world and then leveraging business-unit interrelationships. But the breakneck pace of global integration and global competition no longer allows the luxury of relatively leisurely internal growth to transnational status. As more companies enter the race to global scale every day, the pace grows ever faster, and thus the resources required to achieve such scale grow exponentially greater. Late starters simply do not have the internal resources needed to leapfrog ahead in the race. Even those farsighted companies that initially achieved global scale through internal growth have moved beyond that strategy to maintain and enhance their transnational position. Recently, Apple and Sony forged a strategic alliance for the generation and production of a new line of Apple laptop computers and the attendant software. IBM and Apple, often bitter enemies in the past, have formed a strategic alliance to develop a new generation of computers based on a common microprocessor and common operating system. Further, IBM, crippled by a stagnant market for mainframe computers and bedeviled by more agile competitors for the personal computer and desktop business, has announced a sweeping restructuring that will emphasize joint ventures to spread risks and win new business. Meanwhile, IBM's global rival Fujitsu has taken 80 percent of the shares in ICL, thereby gaining a powerful springboard in the growing European market. Nestlé's acquisition of Perrier, the famed French mineral-water company, will make Nestlé the dominant player in every major mineral-water market, including the United States and Western Europe.

With internal growth foreclosed as an option, *strategic alliances* are the first step most companies take once they embark on the road toward transnational status. The term *strategic alliance* is usually meant to describe an agreement that commits companies to work together toward specific strategic objectives. Such alliances are often technologically based, allowing two or more companies to pool technical resources to achieve a desired result, such as a new product or a new factory. If the collaboration is successful, then the companies can move to broader areas of cooperation with better knowledge of each other and greater mutual confidence. Hitachi and Texas Instruments, for example, entered into an agreement in 1988 to exchange information on 16-megabit memory chips. Now they are embarking on a ten-year deal to develop jointly a 64-megabit chip. The partnership, motivated, in part, by similar alliances in 64-megabit technology between IBM and Siemens and between Toshiba and Motorola, allows Texas Instruments to stay at the forefront of microchip technology and gives Hitachi access to Texas Instrument's valuable Kilby patent, which covers basic technology in integrated circuits.

Strategic alliances can also pool resources to open new markets, spread risk, and combine manufacturing techniques or plant capacity. The alliances among the semiconductor manufacturers are driven, in part, by the fact that designing an advanced chip and building a factory to manufacture it requires about a half *billion* dollars. But in all cases, the allied companies retain their independence and commit to few, if any, irrevocable actions. The risk to the companies is usually relatively small, and the objectives are generally well defined and limited. The alliance of IBM and Siemens in the development of semiconductors, for example, has produced the first prototype of a 64-megabit chip, but the companies have no plans to undertake joint production.

The disadvantage of strategic alliances stems from the elements that make them attractive in the first place. Because the risk is relatively circumscribed, one or both parties can afford failure. The tentative element makes it easy to back out if conditions change. And conditions usually change. Because the initial objectives are clear and well defined, a mechanism is seldom in place for adapting the agreement to changed conditions. In addition, those who are responsible for carrying out the alliance often sense a tentative approach by one or both groups of managers and are less willing to put themselves on the line. And managerial difficulties may be compounded by cross-cultural problems that there is no long-term incentive to remedy.

The alliance between Motorola and Toshiba is a case in point. When Motorola attempted to transfer to the United States and Britain the microchip technology it developed jointly with Toshiba in Japan problems surfaced. As a Motorola executive told the *New York Times*, "In Texas, we just could not convince our managers to step aside and let people named Seki or Nishihara run their operations for a year."[3] Moreover, there was constant arguing over how to assess the trade-offs involved in the deal — Motorola's designs for the microchip in exchange for Toshiba's manufacturing technology. And both companies are reported to suspect their partner of holding back.[4]

The step beyond the strategic alliance is the *joint venture*. Joint ventures resemble strategic alliances in that the partners agree to pool certain resources or assets to reach specified strategic objectives. But there is one important difference: The resources or assets are combined and institutionalized in a legal entity that usually includes divided shareholding, a clear managerial structure, a mechanism for resolving disputes, and a board of directors to provide overall direction and governance. These institutional elements lend a sense of commitment to joint ventures, bolstering the employees' confidence. In fact, most successful joint ventures quickly develop their own organization and employees and eventually develop their own identity and culture. The structure and board often provide the ability to adapt to changed circumstances and direct the efforts of the joint venture over time.

In some countries, most notably Japan, where outright acquisitions are difficult, joint ventures may be the strategy of choice for entering a desirable market or gaining a firsthand look at emerging technologies. Joint ventures have also proved to be an affordable strategy for formerly domestic companies with limited resources to enter the global marketplace. In the United States the "Baby Bells," facing stagnant domestic markets and recent regulatory rulings that permit other companies to offer local telephone service, have found joint ventures an attractive route into the international arena. Bell-South, for example, has joined Britain's Cable and Wireless PLC and a group of Australian companies to provide telecommunications services in Australia in direct competition with government-owned companies. In 1990 Southwestern Bell joined a consortium of Mexican companies and France Telecom to buy a controlling interest in Telmex, Mexico's national phone company. As Telmex's stock has soared, Southwestern's 10 percent stake has already yielded paper profits of $1.67 billion, and the company is now looking to take part in the privatization of other national phone companies.[5]

Successful joint ventures include Fuji Xerox and Rank Xerox, which were established in Japan and Great Britain, respectively, during the early days of the breakthrough with the Xerox copying process. Although there have undoubtedly been many problems along the way, these two joint ventures have continued over time and remain the pillars of the Xerox global organization. In fact, Xerox executives credit the advanced designs and manufacturing techniques developed by Fuji Xerox with rescuing the company from almost certain defeat at the hands of aggressive competitors. Significantly, Xerox's partners in the joint ventures were not direct competitors in technology or office supplies, thereby strengthening the long-term prospects for the relationship.

The record on joint ventures in Japan is perhaps better than one may expect. Eight of the ten largest foreign chemical companies in Japan are joint ventures, as are the three largest foreign engineering companies.[6] Perhaps such successes are due, in part, to the fact that joint ventures are virtually the only way to join forces with a Japanese company and thus are entered into with the full knowledge that they must be made to work. Furthermore, many foreign companies, such as Sandoz, Bayer, and Procter & Gamble, all of which now have strong independent businesses in Japan, first entered the country through joint ventures and terminated the partnerships once their objectives were achieved. Monsanto and Ralston Purina both recently ended joint ventures with Japanese partners and now operate independently in Japan.

Corning, Inc., under the leadership of CEO Jamie Houghton,

has also successfully employed joint ventures to achieve strategic objectives. Dow Corning; Owens Corning Fiberglass; and, more recently, Corning Roche Diagnostics are among some nineteen such ventures and many more technology and marketing alliances that allow the company to bring products to market faster, free capital, and gain global clout without inflating the size of the organization. Beset in the early 1980s by falling profits in businesses in which the company had only small-to-middling market shares, the company transformed itself, largely through joint ventures. For example, a half dozen foreign joint ventures took Corning into the fiber optics business, in which it now enjoys a leading market share.

Technology sharing is at the heart of many of Corning's joint ventures. Coremtech, a joint venture with Mitsubishi Heavy Industries, manufactures pollution-control equipment for smokestacks. Mitsubishi provides the know-how to build the special smokestacks, and Corning provides the technology for producing the filters. So central is the joint-venture strategy to Corning that CEO Houghton sees his company as a global network of related businesses that share crucial technologies and personnel.

The appeal of any particular joint venture lies, of course, in an industry's competitive structure. In broadcasting, for example, the British Broadcasting Corporation (BBC) hopes to build a global news network, but in Cable News Network (CNN) it faces a competitor that is already well established in more than 125 countries. To catch up with CNN and avoid the huge financial risks involved, the BBC formed a joint venture with Star TV, a Hong Kong-based satellite network, to begin an Asian edition of the BBC's World Service TV. Star, which can reach thirty-eight countries with its satellite, sells advertising on the service and passes on a percentage of the profits to the BBC. If the plan works in Asia, the BBC will then attempt to duplicate the feat in Africa and go fully global by the end of 1993. For the BBC the joint venture makes excellent sense. Its Hong Kong partner is not a direct competitor in the news business, and the strategy allows the BBC to move quickly and cheaply, even as other European and some Japanese broadcasters are talking about forging global news networks.

One of the most ambitious joint ventures involves a complicated set of arrangements that Renault, the state-owned French automaker, and Volvo, the publicly traded Swedish car company, entered into in 1989. Together the two companies will create the world's largest partnership to produce trucks and buses. They will also try to achieve global economies of scale in their car operations. Broad agreements on components, manufacturing, marketing, and services bring each partner advantages that neither could achieve alone. Recalling Michael Porter's observation that the slow-growth business environment of the developed world shifts the emphasis from growth to competitive performance, one can readily see how this joint venture will allow the two companies' profits to grow faster than their sales. For example, their truck and car divisions have single representatives for purchasing commonly used components, which eliminates duplicated work and increases their bargaining power with suppliers. When buying from French suppliers like Michelin tire, Renault represents Volvo. On tires alone, Volvo figures to save more than $133 million annually within two to five years.[7] In manufacturing the two companies are working on commuter buses, and in Volvo's plants in Malaysia and Thailand, Renault cars are being built alongside Volvos. In marketing, they have partially merged their French sales divisions in cars and light commercial vehicles through an exchange of senior staff. In services, they have formed a joint research center and are working on a common set of accounting practices.

If their effort clearly illustrates the promise of such global partnerships, it also points up potential pitfalls. It is worth recalling that a decade ago Volvo and Renault failed to get a similar effort off the ground because they lacked clearly agreed-upon aims. And their current venture involves an apparent contradiction: On the one hand, they intend to maintain their brands' separate identities; on the other hand, they intend to "act in their partnership as if they were one company."[8] The merging of their French sales divisions, for example, excludes trucks, an area in which both partners think they compete too closely to gain any benefit from a closer relationship. And Renault is reportedly uneasy over Volvo's plan to produce cars jointly with Mitsubishi in the Netherlands.[9] What these contradictions and difficulties point up, of course, is that the two companies, no matter how closely they may work together, essentially remain competitors.

To navigate these uncertain waters, Volvo and Renault have set up three joint planning bodies that must make decisions unanimously. Though they anticipated meeting only every three months, they found it necessary to meet ten times during the first year, a circumstance that demonstrates their flexibility and commitment, as well as the difficulty of the enterprise. In any case, as in most joint ventures, they have thoroughly institutionalized their relationship, which will lead to increased understanding and cooperation and possibly to a complete merger of their car operations. On the other hand, they could come to grief either through the competitive tensions inherent in joint ventures or through their failure to win enough global advantage to match the efforts of competitors. Either way, their partnership promises to test the limits of the joint-venture strategy and therefore bears watching.

Though joint ventures sometimes succeed, they suffer from the same fundamental defect as do strategic alliances: They are not irrevocable, and having started with the best of faith on one set of assumptions, they cannot easily adapt to a new set of assumptions. Often the changes involve different people with new orientations and personal chemistry. Many joint ventures founder just on changes among top executives, a problem that frequently plagues American and Japanese joint companies. The American partners tend to change executives frequently, and the Japanese do not.

Because strategic alliances and joint ventures both generally involve the pooling or sharing of important resources and assets, they almost invariably occur between companies that are engaged in the same line of business and thus are either competitors or potential competitors. Almost inevitably, the sense of competition eventually challenges the spirit of cooperation on which the association was founded in the first place. Because joint ventures are institutionalized, they stand a better chance of success than do strategic alliances, but the record on both forms of strategic expansion is not particularly inspiring.

Chrysler's recently abandoned joint venture with Mitsubishi in Diamond Star Motors illustrates many of the weaknesses of less-than-wholehearted partnerships. And it appears that Mitsubishi reaped most of the competitive advantages. Moreover, this venture repeated the classic and disastrous pattern of the American automobile industry's relations with Japanese manufacturers — the increasing American dependence on the Japanese that allows the Japanese to make inroads in the American market without any American gain in the Japanese market or elsewhere.

The alliance of the two companies dates back to 1971, when Chrysler bought a 15 percent stake in Mitsubishi and began selling

Mitsubishi-supplied cars in the United States under the Colt name-plate. Having learned much about the American market, at little or no cost, Mitsubishi began in 1982 to sell the identical model in the United States under its own name, much to Chrysler's annoyance. Nevertheless, in 1985 the two companies entered a 50-50 joint venture, known as Diamond Star Motors, to produce three Chrysler models and two Mitsubishi models at a new plant in Bloomington, Illinois. Opened in 1989, the plant can produce 240,000 cars per year.

The relationship was further strained by Lee Iacocca's increasingly strident attacks on Japanese automakers. The venture also proved to be a drain on cash-poor Chrysler, resulting in cumulative losses of $200 million, though the plant was expected to become profitable for Chrysler in 1992. To raise much-needed cash following a failed diversification strategy, Chrysler sold its interest to Mitsubishi in 1991, walking away with less than $100 million in payment and little else.

In fact, the entire venture appears to have been a disaster for Chrysler. Mitsubishi gained an even stronger foothold in the American market, learned firsthand how its American competition works, and now wholly owns a manufacturing plant located in that market. In addition, three of the four Chrysler representatives on the venture's board of directors will remain at Diamond Star, enhancing Mitsubishi's insider status and bringing their knowledge of making and selling cars in the United States. And Diamond Star has a commercial agreement to supply cars to an American automaker through the year 2000 — that American company being none other than Chrysler. Thus Mitsubishi will continue to supply cars to Chrysler, while Chrysler's engineering and manufacturing skills continue to erode. From this distance, at least, it looks as if Mitsubishi successfully used the joint venture as a competitive weapon against its partner.

None of this would matter so much if Chrysler had been making moves elsewhere in the global chess game that is the world car market today, but it was not. The company still does 95 percent of its business in the United States and Canada and has never used its stake in Mitsubishi to make a serious attempt to crack the Japanese market. In early 1992 Chrysler sold nearly half its stake, reducing it from 11 percent to less than 6 percent, and is now considering selling the remainder. In fact, Chrysler's lack of global presence left it without effective currency hedges (discussed in Chapter Three) when the yen, which was weak against the dollar in 1985 when the joint venture agreement was signed, rose sharply against the dollar in the ensuing years. The currency fluctuation vastly increased the cost to Chrysler of Mitsubishi-supplied components, further straining the relationship.

A similarly failed joint venture by General Motors and the Korean automaker Daewoo illustrates additional pitfalls of the strategy, especially those that arise from cultural differences. In 1984 the two companies agreed to build subcompact cars together at a factory in Inchon, Korea. Seemingly a model of cross-border strategy, the 50-50 joint venture was to combine the engineering expertise of GM's German subsidiary Opel, the low-wage advantages of Korea, and the marketing know-how of the giant American automaker. The car that emerged—the Pontiac LeMans—became for many commentators a favorite example of a global product, the transnational provenance of which was dissected tellingly by, among others, Robert Reich.[10] Unfortunately, the LeMans was a lemon, the Daewoo and GM executives clashed repeatedly over basic business decisions as well as personalities, and the venture ended with the Korean automaker buying out its American partner.

Many of the car's persistent quality problems resulted from cross-cultural misunderstandings. The car's inadequate brakes, for example, were designed by German engineers accustomed to their country's wide-open autobahns, not the stop-and-go traffic of America, where the LeMans was to be sold initially. GM's American engineers reportedly had difficulty explaining the problem to their German counterparts, who, once convinced, had difficulty translating subsequent changes in design for Korean suppliers.[11] By the time the problem was corrected, the car's reputation had suffered irreparably.

Conflicting business philosophies also damaged the relationship. In an ironic reversal, the American automaker insisted on high quality, while its Asian partner was interested mainly in expansion. And, as so often happens in such ventures, the partners quickly became competitors when Daewoo negotiated a sale of several thousand cars in Eastern Europe, which was Opel's territory. Furthermore, the assumptions with which the venture began in 1985 changed quickly. The weakening of the dollar and South Korea's embrace of democracy in 1987, with a rise in union activity and a doubling of the wages of Daewoo's workers, erased the cost advantages of locating in Korea. Increasing prosperity in Korea also gave rise to a rapidly expanding domestic car market in which the low-quality LeMans was at a decided disadvantage against other Asian competitors. The venture, initially aimed primarily at exporting to the United States, was unprepared for the opportunity presented by the growing Asian market and was unable to adjust to it in time. Rounding out the list of cross-purposes, conflicts, and problems were personality clashes and bruised egos, including the Daewoo chairman's complaint that on a visit to GM in Detroit, he was relegated to the employees' cafeteria instead of entertained in the executive dining room.[12]

There is, of course, nothing unique about the tensions in the GM-Daewoo venture. Tensions arise almost inevitably anytime companies join forces. The point is that even in joint ventures a half-hearted initial commitment provides little incentive for the partners to iron out their differences over the long haul. The GM-Daewoo case, like the Diamond Star case, also drives home the larger point about choosing the wrong global strategy: The consequence of failure in the rapidly globalizing market is not merely the necessity to go back to the drawing board, but the often serious and difficult-to-reverse loss of competitive positioning. GM has not only lost a golden opportunity to gain a foothold in the Asian market at a time when the company's North American operations are hemorrhaging red ink, but it will also have great difficulty reestablishing itself in Korea because all the other candidates for joint ventures are already spoken for. In short, this heat in the global race is over, and GM has been all but eliminated.

Beyond the half-measures of such joint ventures lie cross-border *mergers and acquisitions,* in my view the strategy of choice in the emerging global marketplace. Though consultants, academics, and other strategists heavily favor strategic alliances and joint ventures, I believe a merger-and-acquisition strategy holds the best hope for large companies to remain competitive. There are two compelling reasons for this conclusion: The clock is running faster, and the irrevocable commitment of mergers or acquisitions produces faster and better results on a global basis.

As I have said, the internal-growth option is already closed for most companies, which have neither the resources nor the leisure to exercise it. Time is similarly running out on strategic alliances and joint ventures as the sole answer to the global imperative. Such collaborations are often stopgaps. They allow a company to achieve economies of scale in some area of its operations, collaborate on technological development, open markets, and spread risk. But they rarely confer true global scale or allow for the full leveraging of interrelationships among business units. Meanwhile, companies that are truly committed to transnational operations continue to bound ahead in the competition by pursuing a strategy of cross-border mergers and acquisitions.

The plight of European computer manufacturers demonstrates just how rapidly choices are narrowing. The number of European full-line computer manufacturers has been dwindling steadily during the past decade and is now down to three—Olivetti of Italy, Groupe Bull of France, and Siemens-Nixdorf of Germany. All three are losing money, and together had only 12 percent of the world market in data-processing equipment in 1991.[13] While they struggle along alone, their competitors are joining forces to create global companies that threaten to reduce the market share of the European manufacturers to perhaps as little as 7 percent by 1995.[14] In 1990, Fujitsu acquired Britain's ICL, which went on to acquire Nokia Data of Finland. Digital Equipment Corporation bought Kienzle from Germany's Mannesmann and had its eye on the minicomputer business of the Netherlands' Philips. Those acquisitions have made even the dream of a pan-European computer company evaporate, as one after another national company is soaked up by a non-European global company. Given the magnitude of the problem, it is unlikely that strategic alliances or joint ventures will allow the companies to remain full-line hardware producers, although such partnerships may enable them to survive as niche players. Groupe Bull, for example, has sold a 4.7 percent stake to NEC and a 5–10 percent stake to IBM. But if the three companies are to survive as full-line manufacturers, they must come up with a wholly transnational response—and fast.

The transnational clock is also ticking in the tire business, which has undergone rapid consolidation as a consequence of the globalization of the automobile industry. In 1980 there were six major independent American tire producers: Armstrong, Firestone, General Tire, Goodrich, Goodyear, and Uniroyal. By the end of the decade, Continental A.G., the German tire maker, had bought General Tire; Bridgestone, the Japanese tire company, had acquired Firestone; Pirelli of Italy bought Armstrong; and Uniroyal and Goodrich, which had merged, were taken over by Michelin. By 1990 Michelin enjoyed 22 percent of the world's tire market and Goodyear had 18 percent, followed closely by Bridgestone at 17 percent. Second-tier companies like Continental, Pirelli, and Sumitomo garnered, respectively, only 7.5, 7, and 6 percent of the market, dangerously small shares relative to the first-tier companies. Recognizing the danger, Pirelli attempted to take over Continental in 1991. It failed when the German company's banking allies closed ranks to help prevent the takeover, but the point is clear: Options are rapidly narrowing in global industries, and second-tier companies all face the same kinds of tough choices SmithKline faced in the mideighties.[15] Meanwhile, Continental insisted it could go it alone, though acknowledging it had also been engaged in merger talks with Toyo Tire and Rubber and with Yokohama Rubber, both of Japan.[16]

Governments, too, are recognizing the dwindling options for keeping state-owned enterprises globally competitive. In France, ailing state-owned companies are being merged in an attempt to put them on an equal footing with global competitors (and perhaps to circumvent the European Community's insistence that France stop subsidizing its electronics industry). The French government recently announced that it was combining Thomson Consumer Electronics (which includes the General Electric and RCA consumer electronics businesses that Thomson acquired from General Electric in 1987) and Thomson's semiconductor business with the nonmilitary parts of France's state-owned Atomic Energy Commission. Significantly, the French government claimed that these moves would put the new electronics giant in the same global league as Siemens and Toshiba, even going so far as to say that the new company would be modeled on the latter.[17] And there are indications that Groupe Bull and France Telecom may also be merged with this new electronics giant.[18]

Of course, it doesn't follow that because a strategy is the only one, it is necessarily a good one. Many a general, using the only strategy available to him, has gone down to inevitable defeat. With time running out in rapidly globalizing industries, cross-border mergers and acquisitions appear to be the only strategy still open to many companies. More positively, however, such a strategy is in the long run far superior to strategic alliances and joint ventures, which, though unquestionably useful, are not fully transnational responses. In a merger the commitment is wholehearted, unlike the halfhearted, even suspicious, relations that sometimes mark strategic alliances and joint ventures. Because the commitment is irrevocable, the incentive to succeed is far greater. No partner can turn back for any reason. It is the corporate equivalent of Cortez burning his boats on the beach at Veracruz as he prepared to lead his small band into the heart of Mexico to conquer the Aztec empire. Every change of business conditions does not require a laborious renegotiation of collaboration agreements or, worse, letting a project drag on past its useful life. Perhaps most important, the permanence of the relationship allows the development of a comprehensive global strategy for the new company and the creation of a new corporate culture to support it.

I don't mean to suggest that cross-border mergers are without problems. It is not easy to meld different corporate cultures, agree on the relative value of each company, or pursue truly global strategies once the merger is complete. The companies must fit strategically — wild acquisitions or mergers for their own sake belong to the bygone era of diversified conglomerates — and such fits are not easily found. And just as the incentive to succeed is greater, so are the consequences of failure. Nevertheless, as more and more business leaders come to stand at the global crossroads, they will increasingly choose the fully transnational route.

Such conclusions do not come in a blinding flash of light. They usually dawn over time, after long thought, discussions, observation, and experience with other strategies. By the time SmithKline reached its critical juncture in the mideighties, my experience with joint ventures had been disappointing. In the late 1970s, SmithKline had established reciprocal joint ventures in the United States and Japan with Fujisawa, a large and highly competent Japanese pharmaceutical company. Both joint ventures were intended to serve as the basis for the expansion of each partner's business in the other's country. Although they accomplished their basic objective and have evolved to become wholly owned operating subsidiaries of the offshore partner, I think, in retrospect, both companies would agree that they have fallen short of the deep and thorough cooperation we both believed could be constructed.

The atmosphere began to change when Fujisawa agreed to become the licensee of a competitive product to Tagamet for the

Japanese market. I did not block their taking this license, which I might have been able to do, but then I should not have had to exercise a veto to prevent long-term damage to our partnership. By the same token, SmithKline did not choose to develop some Fujisawa products for the American market because they did not meet our criteria for commercial success. Disappointed, Fujisawa questioned SmithKline's commitment in the relationship. Both these decisions, though logical from the point of view of the host partner, compounded the problem of some difficult personal relations at the operating level. The subtle climate of cooperation, which otherwise might have transformed the reciprocal joint ventures into an outstanding example of a transnational strategy, was undermined, and the chance was lost.

Though these previous experiences colored my thoughts as SmithKline faced the choice of becoming a relatively small niche player or making the leap toward a transnational status and global scale, I still did not dismiss collaborations out of hand. And in the ensuing years the company pursued a number of strategic alliances and joint ventures. It negotiated an important collaborative project on cardiovascular research and development with Boeringer-Mannheim, a German-based pharmaceutical and diagnostic company. It entered a marketing collaboration with Du Pont in the American market. It also concluded collaboration agreements with Kabi, a Swedish pharmaceutical company, and Nova, a new biotechnology company in the neurosciences. After all, I had received no sudden revelations on how the company might best make the leap to a global scale — who does? And the magnitude of the task, its enormous risk, and the practical and perhaps insurmountable difficulties of accomplishing it made easy answers elusive. But it was clear that the status quo would no longer suffice.

Even as SmithKline continued to pursue cross-border collaborations, the pace of consolidation in the pharmaceutical industry picked up dramatically. Procter & Gamble, with its acquisitions of Norwich Eaton, Richardson Vicks, and G. D. Searle's over-the-counter drugs had surged from nowhere to become number one in nonprescription drugs. It became increasingly clear that SmithKline must buy, sell, or merge. But how? I didn't see how the company could consummate an acquisition of sufficient global and strategic scale without seriously diluting our stock. Selling, on the other hand, amounted to selling out the employees and risking the first-rate research and development organization we had been painstakingly constructing. And a successful merger, on more or less equal terms, required, as one of my financial advisers put it, that "all the celestial bodies be in proper alignment for it to work." Moreover, the overheated takeover atmosphere of the late eighties complicated the problem enormously. Merely exploring the possibilities of merger ran the risk of putting our company in play and having it taken over and dismembered, a prospect I found particularly painful.

Though no great revelation descended, an answer did begin to take shape during a trip to China and Japan. Our company was one of the earliest investors in China after the overthrow of the Gang of Four following the death of Mao Zedong. As a prelude to a board meeting in Japan in October 1985, I had taken our board of directors to China to see the new factory under construction and to meet the embryonic team of managers and employees. Coincidentally, the trip took place at the very time when Richardson Vicks, a health care company of longstanding, was the target of an unfriendly takeover bid from Unilever; and Revlon, which by 1985 made two-thirds of its sales in health care products, was under a similar assault from a leveraged buyout directed by Ron Perelman. Both those events occupied my time during the Asian trip, as I talked on the telephone to the CEOs of Richardson Vicks and Revlon, both of whom were desperately searching for alternatives. Those conversations served to underscore the frenetic takeover atmosphere of the mid-1980s and the perils of inaction.

During the trip through China and Japan, there was plenty of opportunity to discuss with the board members the position the company should take in the future as I saw it. During one early morning jog through the gardens of Hangzou, I discussed the company's strategic dilemma with Bill Grant, a fifteen-year veteran of SmithKline's board and a great student of the health care industry. Together we outlined the objective of combining in some way with another major pharmaceutical–health care company to create a truly global presence. We also formulated the basic concept of spinning out to the shareholders, on a tax-free basis, the diversified companies that could stand alone and were not directly allied to our scientific base in the research and development of pharmaceuticals. And by spinning off the diversified companies and merging with another pharmaceutical company at the same time, we saw a way to increase shareholder value, protect our franchise with employees and scientists, and thwart any possible and unwelcome asset-stripping takeover.

Although we couldn't be certain, of course, we thought our preferred partner would be roughly the same size and that the combined company should have equivalent market positions in the major health care markets of the United States, Europe, and east Asia. After examining every possible combination and permutation, we concluded that we would fit best with Beecham. Like SmithKline, Beecham was in prescription drugs, animal health, and consumer health care products, businesses all linked by science and that are the core of a desirable health care strategy. SmithKline was larger in prescription drugs, but that status was precariously positioned on one product, Tagamet. Beecham was much larger in consumer products, including self-medication products sold without prescription. Its scientific competencies complemented our company's without overlapping. Beecham was strong in antibacterial chemotherapy, antiviral and antifungal research, and cardiopulmonary medicine, while SmithKline was strong in gastrointestinal and cardiovascular medicine, immunology, and molecular biology. The two companies' product-development schedules also meshed well. Beecham had four compounds in the early-launch phase, and SmithKline had a number of prospects in the intermediate and long-term phases. Perhaps most important, the geographic fit was perfect. Beecham was strong in Europe, and SmithKline was strong in the United States and Japan. In combination, the two companies would realize approximately 40 percent of their sales and profits from North America, a little less than 40 percent from Europe and Japan, and the remainder from elsewhere around the world—a distribution that would come closer than any other company in the industry to matching the proportions of the global market.

In August 1987 the desire to seek a pharmaceutical-based health care merger and spin out unrelated diversified companies became a necessity, when, to our surprise, the Food and Drug Administration (FDA) approved the manufacture of generic competitors for SmithKline's second largest pharmaceutical product, Dyazide, a treatment for hypertension. Though this approval is now known to have been obtained by two companies that submitted fraudulent documents to the FDA, the agency's surprise decision at the time led to a sharp decline in the value of our company's shares and castigation by Wall Street analysts. SmithKline became a classic "fallen angel." The tragedy was further compounded by an operating blunder in which wholesale inventories of Tagamet grew so high that sales had to be suspended for two months.

With the passage of time, I can be somewhat philosophical about all this. SmithKline was the victim of a criminal conspiracy and deception that unfairly cost its shareholders $1.2 billion in market value in just two days. The speculation in the wholesale trade on Tagamet embarrassed a management team that had already come under heavy criticism. There is no doubt that the pain of these unlikely events was decisive in pushing the company over the edge. But there is also no doubt that it was already strongly moving in that direction. The months and years of planning that began in the gardens of Hangzhou turned into serious negotiations and decisive action. The management initiated a partial spinout of Beckman shares in the fall of 1988 while conducting preliminary talks with the management of Beecham.

The merger, announced in April and consummated in July 1989, came not a moment too soon, as consolidation in the pharmaceutical industry continued unabated. Hoffmann-La Roche had made a hostile bid for Sterling Drug, best known as the maker of Bayer aspirin, that had driven Sterling into the arms of Kodak by 1988. Not more than a week after SmithKline and Beecham joined forces, Bristol-Myers and Squibb announced the largest merger in the industry's history, knocking SmithKline from its perch as number two in prescription drugs, a circumstance that only underscored the urgency of the transnational imperative. Also in 1989, Johnson & Johnson entered into a joint venture with Merck in over-the-counter drugs. Merck announced a joint venture with Du Pont to market hypertension drugs. In the same year, Dow Chemical's pharmaceutical division acquired a majority share of Marion Laboratories, which became Marion Merrell Dow. At about the same time, Rhone-Poulenc of France acquired 80 percent of Rorer's shares to create a Franco-American entrant into the transnational health care scene. In 1990 Hoffmann-La Roche of Switzerland bought 60 percent of Genentech, the world's leading biotechnology firm, a development of particular interest to SmithKline because in the United States Roche promotes Tagamet's chief competitor and ranks second to us in the clinical laboratories business.

The passage from the gardens of Hangzhou to the new Smith-

Kline Beecham nearly four years later proved to be turbulent, full of surprises, and replete with mistakes and recriminations. The hard work of creating a new company has just begun. But at the least, it positioned the merged company as a real transnational competitor. For example, at the time of the merger, the company became number two worldwide not only in prescription drugs, but in over-the-counter medicines, with many globally recognized brands, such as Tums, Contac, and Aquafresh. The new company also became number four worldwide in animal health. Before the merger, SmithKline ranked number nine and Beecham ranked number twenty-three in prescription drugs worldwide. The merger also achieved the economies of scale necessary to support a research-and-development budget in excess of $750 million annually, among the largest in the world in research on new products. And by financing the merger through a stock swap, rather than a cash purchase, SmithKline avoided the dilution of its shares, an overburdened balance sheet, and adverse tax consequences to its shareholders.

Only superior performance over time can ultimately justify the merger, of course. On the face of it, however, I think it demonstrates how the merger-and-acquisition strategy can vault aggressive companies into the transnational race and advance them in the competition far more decisively than can strategic alliances and joint ventures.

Alcatel Alsthom, a little-known French telecommunications, energy, and transportation company, dramatically illustrates the advantages of the merger-and-acquisition strategy for going global in a hurry. In 1982 it was nationalized by the Socialist government only to be privatized again in 1986. Since then, through a strategy of bold cross-border acquisitions, the company has surpassed AT&T as the number one manufacturer of telephone equipment in the world. Under a management team of many nationalities, the company acquired Rockwell International's telephone transmission equipment division, Canada Cable & Wire, and AEG Kabel A.G. of Germany. It also joined with two European and one American company to form the Space Alliance, the second largest supplier of satellite equipment in the world.

Behind Alcatel's strategy lies the familiar driver of the global imperative: the need for increased business to support costly high-technology research and development in a rapidly globalizing industry. In 1990 alone, the company spent $2.3 billion on research.

Meanwhile, AT&T has been expanding in Europe, and the threat of further consolidation among rival equipment manufacturers remains a potent spur to Alcatel's continued growth.

The strategy appears to be working. The increased research and development has already yielded telephone switches that allow phone companies to move vastly greater amounts of data, voice, and video. And Alcatel has developed a digital mobile phone that meets the new Europe-wide standard for such systems. Overall, since 1986, the company's sales have increased 77 percent and its net earnings have grown by more than 300 percent, and it is now moving strongly into the American market.

As aggressive companies expand and transform themselves into transnational competitors, the industries that serve them become just as global in the process. In effect, serving and retaining one's customers can become a global imperative.

The high-speed package-delivery industry thrives on the demand by large corporate customers for the fast delivery of documents and other paper communications. As corporate customers move to global scale, so do delivery companies, such as Federal Express, DHL Worldwide Express, and United Parcel Service. And in another little-noticed, but highly indicative transformation, the translation business, which provides translations of legal contracts, technical information, and instruction manuals, is also going global. Berlitz International, a subsidiary of Macmillan, bought six translation companies in the United States and Europe in 1991. Because global companies must tailor their products to local markets, accurate, idiomatic translation has become imperative, and Berlitz insists that its translations be done by native speakers who live in the countries where the documents are to be read.[19]

The major telecommunications carriers are rushing down the same track as are the service industries. Once content with their role as national monopolies, many of them state owned, the recently deregulated and now mostly privatized telecommunications giants are scrambling to form integrated networks to serve the already huge ($50 billion) and rapidly growing corporate demand for the electronic transmission of data, voice, and image. AT&T and BT (formerly British Telecommunications) are now running two of the three worldwide communications networks of international investment banker J. P. Morgan & Company. MCI operates Sun Microsystems's Pacific Rim network. Sprint is helping with the global communications of the Anglo-Dutch consumer products giant Unilever, which operates some 500 companies in seventy-five countries.[20] Under most of these arrangements, however, telephone lines will still have to be leased from national phone companies and many of the difficulties of trying to manage networks across countries with different technical standards and regulations will remain until a truly globally integrated telecommunications company emerges, most likely through cross-border mergers and acquisitions.

Previously, the demand for corporate global communications networks was met by cozy and highly profitable international cartel arrangements among the major carriers. The demand was so great that many companies were forced to lease their own lines between continents at exorbitant fees to be sure of access to and the timely flow of information among their major installations around the world. Competition spawned by deregulation and privatization and rapid advances in satellite transmission and digital signal technology have combined to create a mad, even unseemly, rush among the majors to form strategic alliances and joint ventures, each with the aim of integrating a truly global communications network at competitive cost. Insiders have said that were it not for the political sensitivities surrounding the recently privatized state telecommunications companies in Europe and Japan, we would soon be reading about a series of cross-border mergers aimed at the quick creation of competitors for transnational telecommunications.

Other major corporate service industries have already adapted to meet the global demands of their large corporate clients. Commercial and merchant banks serving corporate financial requirements; legal and tax-advisory services from increasingly global law partnerships; auditing services from the major accounting firms; and executive recruiting, advertising, and management-consulting services all span the globe. The old-line British merchant bank Barings recently bought a 40 percent stake in Dillon, Read & Co., the American brokerage firm, at a stroke effectively doubling the market reach of both companies. Barings got a strong foothold in the United States, which has traditionally been difficult for non-U.S. investment banks to crack, while Dillon, Read & Co. gained access to Barings's far-flung international network. It is worth noting, too, that this was a significant strategic departure for Barings, which for 300 years had expanded by means of internal growth, rather than through acquisition.

As I write, commercial air carriers are beginning to jockey for strategic positions in the global market, despite the governmental restrictions in many countries that currently inhibit them. Privatized in 1987, British Airways has enjoyed record profits on the lucrative transatlantic run at the expense of weak, debt-burdened carriers, such as Pan Am and TWA.[21] With the appearance of tough competition from the survivors of deregulation in the United States, such as American, United, and Delta airlines, the competitive environment is suddenly much tougher. Meanwhile, industry analysts are expecting a deregulated global airline industry to develop in the next decade or two. By that time an airline that has not developed a global position could be left hopelessly behind. The answer for British Airways is to find a way to expand into the huge U.S. market, which accounts for 40 percent of the passenger miles flown in the world. The stakes are huge. If British Airways fails to position itself globally, it could easily lose its lead as the number one carrier of international passengers. Worse, it could wind up as a second-tier carrier that would be forced to rely on local growth or to compete in a highly regulated regional market.

Having failed in earlier talks with United Airlines and KLM, British Airways has proposed to take a 44 percent share in USAir for $750 million. British Airways would gain access to USAir's route network in the eastern United States, the region from which two-thirds of U.S. transatlantic travelers originate their trips. USAir would gain access to markets throughout Europe, Africa, Australia, Latin America, and the Middle and Far East. USAir has accepted British Air's proposal, but the agreement still faces tough scrutiny by regulators in the United States and Great Britain and by the European Commission. In any case, it is already clear which way the tide is running. The fact that this alliance is even being attempted provides a compelling vision of the future.

Meanwhile, Europe's other small airlines are also searching for larger partners to remain competitive in the unified European market. Sabena, the Belgian national airline, has sold a 37.5 percent stake to Air France. Other airlines, such as Scandinavian Airline Systems, are likely to follow suit.

Also unfolding as I write is the mammoth deal between McDonnell Douglas Aircraft and Taiwan Aerospace, a partnership in an industry that epitomizes perhaps more clearly than any other the strategic challenges I have been discussing. The costs of developing an airliner are staggering—about *$5 billion*. Therefore, it is no surprise that there are only three major players in this high-stakes game: Boeing, McDonnell Douglas, and Airbus. Boeing enjoys more than a 56 percent share of the world market, McDonnell Douglas has about 21 percent, and Airbus has about 14 percent. (Niche companies account for the remaining 9 percent.) In 1990 Boeing delivered 379 commercial planes; McDonnell Douglas, 142; and Airbus, 95.[22] The three companies are highly competitive, and many people believe that only two can survive.

McDonnell Douglas, despite its number two ranking in commercial aircraft and its standing as the largest U.S. defense contractor, appeared to be the prime candidate for extinction. As the Cold War wound down after 1989, the company was hurt by cancellations of weapons contracts. Clearly, it needed to shift its emphasis from military to commercial aircraft, but the prospects weren't heartening. The company was burdened with debt, once as high as $3.3 billion, resulting largely from the expense of developing the MD-11 wide-body jetliner. Its commercial aircraft business had lost money for two decades and was notorious for building planes at a slow—and costly—pace. And just when it needed to make the shift, turbulence in the airline industry had greatly weakened the market.

In response, the company did what many companies do when they are faced with shrinking markets and unprofitable operations. It cut costs, slashed employment rolls, and instituted total quality management (which cut the time required to build an MD-80 from thirty weeks to nineteen weeks). All these measures made the company more competitive for the short run, but did little to solve the fundamental strategic problem: how to grow while being strapped for capital, facing a stagnant market, and being dominated from above by Boeing and threatened from below by Airbus, which enjoys millions in governmental subsidies and is well-positioned to sell planes to the national airlines of the countries that make up the Airbus consortium.

To solve all these problems at a stroke, McDonnell Douglas boldly proposed to sell 40 percent of its commercial aircraft business for $2 billion to Taiwan Aerospace, a fledgling company that is heavily backed by the government of Taiwan, which wants to encourage an indigenous aerospace industry. Together the two companies will develop the MD-12, a new jetliner to compete directly with Boeing's 747-400 long-range jumbo jet and force Airbus to play catch-up. If successful, the MD-12 would have a range 2,000 miles greater than that of the 747, making it particularly appealing to Asian airlines, which have some of the longest commercial routes in the world. And Asia is the world's fastest-growing air market, consisting of 2 billion people in sixteen countries and expected to buy $100 billion worth of airplanes annually.

In seeking a partner to take an ownership position in the new venture, McDonnell Douglas wanted one that could offer access to this potentially rich market and to a low-wage, highly productive work force. Taiwan Aerospace provides both. And McDonnell Douglas may spread an additional 9 percent stake in the venture to government-backed companies in other Asian countries, giving the entire enterprise something of the structure of an Asian equivalent to the Airbus consortium and offering the same kind of entrée to the participants' national airlines.

Though the deal is being structured as a joint venture, McDonnell Douglas is unlikely to see Taiwan Aerospace walk away from such an enormous investment to become a competitor. As the first major ownership stake acquired by a foreign company in the American aerospace industry, the deal would also offer Taiwan Aerospace a share in profits from sales of the MD-11 and MD-80, both developed long ago. Because of national security concerns, Taiwan Aerospace plays no part in McDonnell Douglas's military business.

Overall, the sheer scale of the proposed undertaking gives it the appearance of a vast new trans-Pacific merged enterprise that will bring together technological know-how, transnational manufacturing, international capital, and vast new markets. McDonnell Douglas would design the MD-12, perform the final assembly, and run the test flights. Its partners would manufacture the many individual sections of the plane in low-wage Pacific Rim countries with advanced manufacturing techniques. Thus McDonnell Douglas hopes to become the industry's low-cost producer and to undercut Boeing and Airbus.

McDonnell missed a chance in 1980 to form an alliance with British Aerospace, a move that might have slowed the rise of Airbus. Now, little more than a decade later, McDonnell Douglas has been brought to the transnational crossroads. Like SmithKline and a lot of others that were forced to confront a strategic crisis, it chose a fully transnational response.

In a world of narrowing strategic options and a clock that seems to tick faster, half-measures no longer suffice. While some companies pursue tentative strategic alliances and joint ventures, their hardier competitors will preempt them through bold cross-border mergers and acquisitions from which there is no turning back. While tentative companies collaborate with competitors to leverage a few areas of their operations, bold companies will merge with competitors to leverage business-unit interrelationships around the world. While tentative companies step gingerly onto the transnational road, bold companies will bound onto it and race ahead.

It is not an easy road to travel. There are many bumps along the way, many challenges, and much that is unfamiliar and curious. Not the least of these curiosities is one of the great paradoxes of the transnational world: Competing globally means acting locally. And that paradox points to a larger one: We now live in an interdependent world that far from effacing cultural differences seems to nourish them. It is a paradox rife with implications not only for business but for the shape of political and social life in the post–Cold War world. It is to that paradox I now turn.

CHAPTER THREE

UNDER THE MUSHROOMS

THE SLOGAN THINK GLOBALLY, Act Locally has become widely used, almost hackneyed, and is much too simple to capture the complex realities of the global economy. Realizing this, Akio Morita, chairman of Sony, coined the word *glocally* to convey the idea that businessmen, statesmen, and active citizens of all walks of life must now constantly conceptualize and act in at least two important dimensions: the global and the local.

Indeed, a greatly heightened sense of local—often ethnic or linguistic—identity is the other side of the coin of globalism. At first glance, the two forces may seem in contradiction, but they are complementary and together are the major forces shaping the culturally diverse but interdependent world that is emerging after the end of the bipolar, Cold War era.

The very act of rapid integration of the world's economies has stimulated the resurgence of local cultural identities. Examples abound: The serious consideration of independence by Quebec—long a dream of the culturally suppressed Quebecois—is becoming a reality in the presence of the Canada–U.S. Trade Pact, which effectively removes the threat of economic sanctions against an independent Quebec. The enormous magnetic attraction of the European Community not only contributed mightily to the destruction of the

Berlin Wall; it also makes it possible for Georgians, Ukrainians, Latvians, Estonians, and many other national and ethnic groups to seek political independence, hoping that somehow the umbrella of the European Community will stretch to cover them as well. In some cases, unfortunately, the resurgence of ethnic identity has also revived ancient hatreds, as in the former Yugoslavia, and it remains an open question whether the pull of global economics will be strong enough, even in the long run, to contain them.

In the United States, people wonder why recent immigrants don't seem to integrate into American society to the degree that previous waves of immigrants did. At least part of the answer lies in the fact that the flow of information around the world is so pervasive and easily tapped that people can live in a new country without losing essential cultural communication with the old. All it takes is access to a television set and a satellite antenna to pick up television broadcasts from around the world, from soccer games to school lessons to the latest news. The global trading system brings food and clothing from the home country; financial services and often hotels, movies, and, of course, telephone communication with those left behind provide a nearly complete cultural microclimate in the new country. One can now immigrate without forsaking one's culture.

Nowhere is the need greater for two-dimensional—global and local—thinking than in the large transnational corporations that are locked in fierce competition for their share of the market with other like-minded transnationals, as well as entrenched local competitors. Transnationals need to apply their resources productively throughout the world, but true success requires the additional ability to localize—to adapt to the unique requirements of cultures, markets, and governments without sacrificing the advantages of scale that are inherent in globalization.

It is not enough merely to operate globally or simply to meet global tastes and standards of value. Success comes to those companies that meet global expectations while operating and competing on a local level. Consumers want global brands and world-class technology, but they respond best when the product is presented in terms of their cultural identities and marketed in line with their purchasing patterns and preferences. The products that Coca-Cola and Sony sell are the same everywhere, but advertising, marketing, and trade practices vary considerably as the companies adapt to local customs and distribution systems. In other cases, the product itself must be adapted to satisfy local differences. In still other cases, like that of McDonnell Douglas, a local partner provides insider status. But in every case, the central paradox remains: Global competition means exquisite local sensitivity.

The lessons of localization were impressed on me years ago when, as a young manager, I was given responsibility for establishing SmithKline's business in Japan with the twelve-hour-acting cold product Contac. Thanks to one of the happy accidents of life, I had lived and worked in the Hawaiian Islands five years before I took the assignment in Japan. In the mid-1950s, Hawaii was truly the crossroads of the Pacific, where the Orient met the Occident, and provided my first introduction to Japanese people and to problems of cross-cultural understanding.

One of the earliest lessons I learned in Hawaii came from SmithKline's distributor's sales representatives, most of whom were nisei (the offspring of Japanese immigrants). I had coffee with them every morning to mine their knowledge, because they were in contact with all of our retail and hospital customers. One day the salesmen included me in a game of Guess My Age. When my turn came, their estimates of my age were off by many years—in both directions. Without a trace of irony, one of the salesmen remarked, "That's the trouble with you *haolis* [the Hawaiian word for Caucasians]. Not only can we not tell you apart, we can't tell how old you are." I can laugh about it now, but at the time it brought me up short about the kinds of parochial assumptions we all make—no matter which side of a cultural divide we find ourselves on.

Many of the doctors and pharmacists in Hawaii were first- or second-generation Japanese, so I persuaded the home office to let me hire the man who would become my lifelong best friend, Ray Kutsunai. A Japanese born in Hawaii, he was attending high school in Japan when World War II broke out and was forced to remain there for the duration. Immediately following the war, he worked for American counterintelligence, and he later attended pharmacy school at the University of Michigan. I taught him sales, and he taught me pharmacy. But the most valuable lesson he taught me was cultural sensitivity. Speaking fluent Japanese as well as English, he won over doctors and pharmacists throughout the islands. Our sales boomed. Subsequently, when I was posted to Canada, I set up a sales force of French Canadians in Quebec and Anglo-Canadians elsewhere, with similar results. If this lesson seems obvious today, I can only say that in those days of American hegemony and unchallenged assumptions about the rightness of everything the United States did, it was eye-opening.

Most important, my friendship with Ray Kutsunai introduced me to more than merely pragmatic notions of cultural sensitivity. My youthful interest in international affairs blossomed into a genuine fascination with other peoples and cultures. Among other things, I studied judo with a Japanese carpenter who spoke little English. The carpenter taught me not only judo, but something of Japanese philosophy, which is embodied in judo. Above all, he taught me to listen and observe carefully to gain understanding. "Look even under the mushrooms," he said.

My early experience in Hawaii, augmented by more traditional forms of learning, such as books and lessons, helped enormously when I traveled to Japan. I vividly recall a trip to Sendai, north of Tokyo, in 1962. I was tired and lonely, but I felt comfortable enough to stay in a *ryokan*, a traditional Japanese inn, where I was treated with great care and respect. The staff dressed me in a *yukati*—a cotton kimono—and gave me a Japanese meal and bath. The meal consisted of traditional Japanese cuisine presented with exquisite artistry in small dishes of fish and lightly cooked—often unrecognizable—vegetables. Of course, the eating utensils were *ohashi*, Japanese wooden chopsticks. The bath took place in a traditional *ofuro*, a deep, square tub of cedar filled with hot water. The washing and rinsing were performed before my immersion in the hot bath, which was as much a relaxing experience as a cleansing one.

While I was in Japan, I had perceived the country's great economic stirrings and its tremendous sense of national purpose. Yet as I watched the moon rise through an open window, I could have been in the sixteenth century. The experience was restful, pleasant, and interesting, yet alien. I was elated, but it was as if I had dropped from the moon into this timeless world. It then struck me with great force what a unique and profound identity the Japanese have: They are simultaneously modern and traditional, worldly but not of the world. And I knew, too, that I had much to learn.

I was there to figure out how to launch Contac, an American cold medicine, into the highly competitive and different Japanese over-the-counter market. First, I tried to establish a joint venture with Sumitomo Chemical, with which SmithKline had a good relationship. But Sumitomo regarded it as too risky to enter the over-the-counter market, particularly because it lacked the appropriate distribution channels. Distribution in Japan is complex, and more than one foreign company has been defeated by it. Individuals in Japan, feeling bound by the decisions of their ancestors and predecessors, find it difficult to change long-standing relationships. Sumitomo's distribution system, essentially dating back to the early part of the century, did not lend itself to an over-the-counter product, and could not have been easily changed.

Sumitomo did, however, agree to manufacture the product for SmithKline. But it insisted that I set up my own distribution network. This was a complete reversal of the usual practice. Ordinarily, a foreign pharmaceutical company would contribute technology and a unique product and the Japanese partner would provide the distribution. So I spent the fall of 1965 and all of 1966 feverishly establishing a distribution system. I studied Coca-Cola, which had succeeded in Japan with its own distribution system. I made contact with the best Japanese wholesalers and established a modern, single-tier distribution system, as opposed to the classical three-tier system. Instead of the 200-plus wholesalers that established practice required, I used just thirty-five. In working with an upstart foreign enterprise, the wholesalers wanted to show that they could perform at a high level. They also wanted to exercise some independence from the traditional Japanese business hierarchy, in which manufacturers dominate distributors. SmithKline offered them the opportunity to join the world trading system, and they gave SmithKline the means to be close to customers on a daily basis.

Through it all, my friend Kutsunai was at my side, instructing me in the culture—translating literally and figuratively. It was a great adventure, and, as it turned out, the introduction of Contac became a textbook example of a successful entry into the Japanese market. Within six years, it captured 10 percent of the cold-medicine market, even though the Japanese health authorities did not allow the company to call the product a cold medicine, as it could elsewhere in the world. Looking back, I believe two key decisions laid the foundation for success.

First, a good friend and collaborator on this project, Dr. Saburo Yamoka of Sumitomo Pharmaceutical, recommended that we consider modifying the formula of Contac to take into account the different body weight and metabolism of Japanese people. This proposal was greeted with laughter and rejected by people in the home office. "After all, people are the same everywhere," they said. "If it works on Americans, why shouldn't it work on everyone? Besides, it will cost more to run clinical trials in Japan on a different formula. This project is already too risky, and this proposal pushes it beyond reason."

But we persisted in believing that in some respects the Japanese people are different and, more important, they are convinced that they are. The primary feature of Contac that made it unique in the Japanese market was the sustained action of the "tiny time pills," not the formula itself. So we introduced a slightly lower-dosage formula, but retained the unique twelve-hour action feature of the product. As it turned out, the act of adapting the formula to recognize the characteristic body weight and metabolism of the Japanese people, rather than merely marketing the American formula in copybook fashion, became a *second* unique feature of the product.

Then I decided to concentrate my entire advertising budget on thirty-second television spots. Conscious of the fact that I knew next to nothing about the response of Japanese consumers to the message, I conducted extensive tests of various advertising approaches with live audiences. Eventually I settled on humorous scenes from everyday Japanese life that gave a distinctly Japanese character to advertisements for a new product from a foreign company. Using a Japanese agency and production company, we created ads that revolved around characters who were caught off guard by a big sneeze, which in Japan is considered more embarrassing than in the United States. The commercials were memorable and, most important, uniquely Japanese.

Today these two decisions do not appear unusual. Many successful global brands are modified slightly or adapted to the needs of the local market without losing their essential characteristics, and, of course, advertising varies considerably among markets. In fact, with the advent of global products and companies, advertising is becoming more, not less, localized. From 1976 to 1986 the percentage of companies that tailored their ads in line with regional differences jumped from 17 percent to 50 percent in Western Europe alone.[1] WPP, which owns the J. Walter Thomson advertising agency and dozens of marketing communications companies worldwide, estimated that only 10 percent of its business involves products that are marketed the same way everywhere, while fully 60 percent involves products that are marketed differently in each locale.[2]

But localization in the global marketplace today means far more than altering products or advertising. It means being willing to localize any business function, from purchasing to production to finance to anything else that seems appropriate. Which functions a company must adapt locally and in what way depend, of course, on the nature of its products or services. Consumer packaged goods, such as food, cosmetics, and pharmaceuticals, encounter the most cultural obstacles, while industrial products and consumer durables encounter fewer. Generally, however, successful localization must be

- Customer oriented

- Production oriented

- Finance oriented

- Government oriented

Whatever form adaptation takes, the aim should always be to link it to an overall strategy. Just as global scale provides a significant competitive advantage, so, too, can adaptation to local conditions.

Customer-oriented localization means operating on a daily basis as closely as possible to customers in the many markets around the globe. It often includes adapting products to local tastes, pursuing marketing strategies in line with local interests, creating advertising that speaks to particular cultures, and arranging distribution that fits local buying patterns and habits.

Customer-oriented localization requires extraordinary cultural sensitivity—the willingness to look "even under the mushrooms." Although it is perhaps the most familiar form of localization, it can also be the most difficult because it requires broad and deep knowledge of every aspect of an alien culture. From personal contacts with foreign nationals to advertising to marketing to the design of products, cultural sensitivity is key. For example, averting one's eyes during a conversation is a sign of respect in some cultures, but a sign of insincerity in others. In a culture in which prolonged eye contact is regarded as rude, the hearty backslapping style can mean the death of sales, if not the death of the salesman.

In advertising and packaging, it is crucial to understand that symbols and icons differ greatly from culture to culture. Woe to the company that uses the color white to symbolize purity and innocence in Japan, where white is the color of mourning.[3] In many parts of the Middle East it is offensive to include a person's feet in a photograph.[4] Obviously, religious differences must be respected as well. Food companies, for example, must be careful not to use animal fats in products sold in many Islamic countries.

A company that fails to understand a culture will likely fail to crack its market. In the 1970s, Kentucky Fried Chicken leaped into the fast-food market in Germany without altering its marketing technique or its products. It soon failed because it either did not know or did not care that Germans prefer chicken roasted whole, not fried in parts. Similarly, Ajax cleanser blew into Britain with the "white tornado" advertising campaign that had worked so well in the United States. It quickly expired: Britain does not have tornadoes. When the market opened up in the dissolving Soviet Union, M&M/Mars rushed in with ads for M&M candies bearing the familiar tag line "melts in your mouth, not in your hand" – in midwinter, when nothing melts there, in your hand or anywhere else. And perhaps the most famous example is the marketing of the Chevrolet Nova in Latin America, where *no va* means "doesn't go."

Mack Truck, unlike Ajax, thought long and hard about the appropriateness of its corporate symbols and advertising for other cultures. Before it entered China, it learned that the Chinese hold dogs in low esteem, a dismaying discovery for a company whose product symbol is a bulldog. Undaunted, its marketing strategy jettisoned the bulldog in favor of an old Chinese proverb: "The value of a good horse is appreciated at the end of the longest journey" – the ideograph for which also means horsepower and sounds almost like "Mack."[5]

Success comes to companies that do their homework and localize with the customer and the culture in mind. McDonald's in Japan adapts to customers' tastes literally; it offers a teriyaki burger. Meanwhile, American automakers, while complaining about the difficulty of entering the Japanese market, declined to make a right-hand-drive vehicle for Japan, where cars drive on the left-hand side of the road. Recently, however, Ford announced that it will produce a right-hand-drive vehicle at Mazda's factory in Flat Rock, Michigan, for export to Japan. The Coleman Company, the privately held U.S.-based maker of camping equipment, has seen its foreign sales grow by 30 percent annually over the past four years, primarily

because the company knows how to adapt its products to local preferences.[6] In Latin America, for example, the company sells a cooler
adapted to those countries' tall one-liter bottles. In Southeast Asia
its coolers have a strap instead of a handle. In the United Kingdom,
its camp stoves are equipped to make toast. Meanwhile, Colgate-
Palmolive, the maker of Ajax, perhaps having learned its lesson,
introduced a version of the household cleanser with insect repellent
for markets in some developing countries. It has also introduced a
sensitive-skin laundry soap for sale in markets where clothes are
washed by hand.

Perhaps one of the most successful examples of localization is to
be found with Apple Japan, which has been doubling its revenues
yearly since 1988.[7] Much of that success has been attributed to the
company's introduction of its NTX-J printer, which can deal with
kanji, the complicated pictographic Japanese system of writing.
Local Japanese software developers have rushed to produce new
software for Apple's popular Macintosh because the computer's
original design, in which the source code that drives the computer
is separated from the text messages that users see, easily allows for
adaptation to many languages.

Not every product must be altered. The trick is to know when
and what to alter. Coca-Cola is the same everywhere. Its appeal lies
in its status as a global brand. So global is its appeal, in fact, that
Coca-Cola has initiated a global marketing campaign in which a
series of identical commercials will be broadcast simultaneously all
over the world. But the Coca-Cola Company did not conclude from
the universal success of Coke that none of its soft drinks should be
altered. When it comes to fruit-flavored drinks, tastes may vary
from country to country. So when the company introduced Fanta
orange drink in Europe, it offered a tarter taste for Germany and a
sweeter taste for Italy.

Customer-oriented adaptation may sometimes involve nothing
more than a change in the size of packages.[8] It is a simple alteration,
but it can make all the difference between success and failure. In
less-developed countries with extended family traditions and high
fertility rates, Pillsbury packages food products in six-to-eight serving sizes.[9] In countries where consumers have little discretionary
income, consumer products may be sold in smaller, more affordable
packages. In Latin America, for example, Chiclets chewing gum is

sold in two-piece packs, rather than in the twelve-piece pack that is standard in the United States.[10] In Mexico small amounts of laundry detergent are sold in cheap plastic bags.

In service industries such as insurance, localization may require numerous local agents who are well versed in local conditions, are capable of assessing local risks, and are readily available to counsel customers. These agents must also offer a line of locally familiar insurance products and patterns of settling claims. Rapidly globalizing insurance companies like the Winterthur insurance group of Switzerland pursue a double strategy of preparing for cross-border contracts with large business enterprises while pursuing the business of smaller enterprises and individuals through highly localized branches, subsidiaries, and partner companies around the world.

Production-oriented localization goes hand in hand with a customer-oriented strategy, since the aim of both is to serve customers better by working close to them. Many apparel manufacturers who fled the United States for cheaper labor in Asia are now moving their operations back to the United States to be closer to their customers.[11] Because American retailers are adding "just-in-time" inventory systems, it has become increasingly difficult to order and ship from Asia. The irony here is that global competition sometimes brings a company home. A company locates its production wherever it makes the most sense to do so.

But localizing production means far more than sticking factories at strategic locations like so many colored pins on a military-campaign map. The smart global company establishes sound relations with local suppliers, uses locally available materials, locates production in areas where workers' skills are well matched to the industry, keeps abreast of superior local technology, and tailors operations for a quick response to the local market. The old multinationals of the 1950s and 1960s often supplied their overseas factories with machinery, materials, managers, and technology. Today's global companies more often depend on local means and local talent, and if it is not readily available, they help to develop it. McDonald's carefully cultivates local suppliers before it opens in a foreign country, often going to extraordinary lengths. In China, where the local potatoes make poor french fries, McDonald's food technologists spent seven years helping to develop a new strain of potato.[12]

Strengthening relationships with local suppliers allows global companies to maintain their edge in innovation, quality, and price.

And the use of locally available materials not only helps satisfy local content laws and meet customer preferences, but can hold down production costs and sometimes significantly improve the product. Matsushita Electric (UK), the Cardiff-based and Japanese-owned electronics giant, wanted to incorporate an advanced television technology into its sets for sale in Europe. Invar mask technology, as it is known, allows for much sharper television reception, but is rarely used in domestic sets because of its high cost. Standard parts for television sets can be made anywhere, of course, but with such specialized technology or with components like integrated circuits, which differ greatly in Europe and Japan, it is necessary to design and make them as close to the market as possible. So instead of turning to a Japanese supplier, Matsushita approached a major British parts supplier, Philips Components, the British subsidiary of the Dutch electronics company. Working together, the two companies improved the design of a prototype that Philips already had in development, commercialized their breakthrough quickly, and achieved a significant edge in innovation and price.

Matsushita also works to get European suppliers to adopt the Japanese view of quality: Products must be free of defects. Matsushita's representatives and their suppliers visit each other's operations frequently, share technological information, and maintain mutual loyalty. Sony, in a move that combines global thinking with local action, is instituting a worldwide system to select well-qualified local suppliers of components and materials. The company will use its quality-control manual to guide potential suppliers in Southeast Asia, Europe, and the United States and to show them how they can become preferred suppliers. The ultimate beneficiary, of course, is the customer, who gets a higher-quality product at the best price.

Local labor can make all the difference to a global-local strategy. Global companies like to locate production close to the market, but they must also make sure their labor force is well suited to their industry. For reasons of history and culture, certain geographic regions and their workers perform best in particular industries. These cultures of production may be localized within a country. For example, the labor force of the Ohio Valley in the United States seems ideal for the production of automobiles. The area that stretches from Wilmington, Delaware, to Newark, New Jersey, admirably supports the production of chemicals and pharmaceuticals. Similarly, the Rhine Valley, from Leverkusen to Basel, is the heartland of the European chemical and pharmaceutical industries.

Capturing the expertise of local workers and the local technology leads to cross-fertilization throughout a company. Stanley Works, the venerable New England toolmaker, maintains its European production facility in Besançon in the old watchmaking region of France. Though digital watches have long since decimated the watchmaking industry, the industry's former workers are well suited to making precision factory machines and using techniques of flexible manufacturing in small runs of highly differentiated products for Stanley.[13] The manufacturing knowledge that the company is accumulating there is now being disseminated throughout Stanley's operations elsewhere.

Finance-oriented localization presents some of the trickiest and riskiest problems for the global company that is attempting to operate in both the global and local dimensions at once. Few things are more local and yet more caught up in global forces than is a currency. The company must understand the vagaries of the local currencies and economies in the countries where it does business, and it must simultaneously defend itself against ruinous currency fluctuations in the $700 billion-a-day foreign-exchange market. Adverse currency movements can wipe out profits, devalue capital investments, and place the company at a disadvantage with competitors. Thus, companies must develop appropriate reinvestment strategies, establish effective hedges, and formulate company-wide treasury procedures that are simultaneously global and local. Most important, the policy on currency must move beyond the treasurer's office and be integrated with all aspects of the company's strategy.

Take, for example, the hypothetical case of a French subsidiary of a U.S.-based machine-tool company. Suppose the company sold ten machine tools in January for 100,000 francs each for a total of 1 million francs, payable upon delivery of the merchandise in June. In January, the dollar buys only five francs, but by June it is bringing ten francs. When the company converts its 1 million francs in June, it will receive only $100,000 instead of the $200,000 it expected to recover when the dollar was weaker in January.

The machine-tool company could avert such a disaster through several familiar hedging strategies. One local strategy is the natural hedge. Instead of converting the francs to dollars, the company simply uses those francs to purchase materials and supplies locally, thus avoiding the problem of foreign exchange altogether. Although the natural hedge appears to be an elegant and simple solution, it points up the need for a company to integrate its policy on currency with its overall strategy. Should the machine-tool company choose a local supplier because of quality and price or simply because it is a convenient way to protect exposed cash flows? And how prominently should considerations of currency figure in strategic decisions like the location of factories and the choice of markets?

Alternatively, the company could buy a currency-forward contract in the foreign-exchange market in January, guaranteeing the delivery of a currency at a set price in the future to lock in the value of a big sale. Armed with such a contract, the company would receive $200,000 for its 1 million francs in June, despite the strong run-up in the dollar.

Another possibility for hedging lies in currency options. Currency options cost more than do currency-forward contracts, but they ensure against big exchange losses and allow the company to take advantage of a currency movement in its favor. The machine-tool company would purchase in January an option to buy dollars in June at the January rate. If the dollar was bringing ten francs instead of five by June, the company would exercise its option and buy dollars for five francs each, thus avoiding a big loss. But if the dollar has grown weaker against the franc, bringing only, say, 2.5 francs, then the company would forgo its option and exchange the francs for dollars at the June rate. The value of the sale, after the exchange, would then be $400,000 instead of the expected $200,000. The company would not only avoid an adverse currency movement, but would profit handsomely from an advantageous one. Currency futures offer something of the same safe haven, but they are traded in fixed amounts on formal exchanges, unlike options, which are negotiated in private. Companies may also use various combinations of currency trading instruments, but all are essentially insurance against an adverse move in the currency in which the company is operating.

All these hedges can work well in clearly defined contractual situations. But in markets and industries where volumes are high and unpredictable and currency risks are enormous, larger strategic considerations must come into play. In such circumstances perhaps the best financial strategy is the transnational solution itself. Global companies reduce their huge exchange risks in high-volume markets by diversifying into many different markets and currencies. In contrast, companies that are closely tied to a few currencies may be badly hurt. Porsche, Volvo, and Saab all concentrated heavily on expanding into the U.S. market while their production remained tied to their home currencies. When the dollar declined, all three companies suffered big exchange losses, and they consequently shifted some of their focus back to the European market.

Global companies must also take into account the currency structure of competitors. For example, currency fluctuations may raise one company's costs while a competitor with a different currency structure remains unaffected or enjoys lower costs. A company with production costs that are tied to a falling currency and sales revenues earned in a rising currency benefits all around. A competitor whose production costs are tied to the rising currency will suffer. As the dollar falls, domestic U.S. automakers have a competitive opening against manufacturers whose production is tied to the yen. Of course, transnational companies like Honda protect themselves by locating production in the large markets they serve. In general, many companies have been content to match the currency structures of their competitors. But some global companies are developing the capacity to shift production and resources with great rapidity and flexibility, thereby not only reducing their currency risks but gaining a real competitive advantage.

Government-oriented localization is rarely a matter of choice. Companies must conform to the governmental and regulatory rules of each locality in which they operate. Consumer products companies must satisfy regulations governing the purity, labeling, and licensing of products. Manufacturers must observe environmental and labor laws and often must meet local-content requirements. Service providers, like banks and insurance companies, must operate within highly complex rules governing their industries. And all companies must, of course, comply with trade regulations and tax laws. Moreover, within a particular country, laws and regulations may vary from region to region or city to city. Automakers, for example, must meet far more stringent auto-emission standards in California than in most other parts of the United States.

Companies must also become as familiar with the informal rules, customs, and expectations that govern their industry as they are with the more formal arrangements. Meeting these challenges often requires enlisting a local partner to lead the way through the regulatory maze and to help navigate the political back channels. Thus mergers, acquisitions, joint ventures, and strategic alliances, though often driven by imperatives of global scale, are also indispensable for successful localization.

Though SmithKline's long-standing ally in Japan, Sumitomo Chemical, was unable to help with the distribution of Contac there, it was indispensable in helping the company overcome Japan's regulatory hurdles. As the importer of Contac and, soon after the product's introduction, its manufacturer as well, Sumitomo Chemical was responsible for clearing it through regulatory channels. It conducted the appropriate clinical trials with carefully chosen academics and ran the necessary stability and pharmaceutical tests. In most countries, but particularly in Japan, the complicated dealings with regulatory agencies require great experience and knowledge. Most companies find it advisable to work with local companies until they and their local staff have acquired the requisite experience and know-how.

Insider status is more a matter of local behavior than of corporate strategy, although the extent of local investment in plant, technology, and the corresponding employees is a vital prerequisite. Investment and employees do not count for much, however, if the organization's behavior is characterized by insensitive or high-handed actions or a consistent disregard for local sensitivities. The measures of insider status vary by country and by society, but usually bring substantial benefits to the corporations that earn a high level of public esteem. In Japan, a consistent measure of insider status is the ability to recruit the highest-quality university graduates from the best campuses. This measure is considered sufficiently important that companies closely follow the graduates' relative ranking as determined by annual nationwide polls of the graduating classes. The rankings are considered so newsworthy that they appear on the front pages of most national newspapers. IBM, Nestlé, and the joint-venture company Fuji-Xerox are among the relatively few foreign companies that consistently appear in the most-attractive-employer category. In the case of Japan, insider status is measured primarily at the national level.

In the United States, insider status is measured primarily at the local level. Without public support from the communities in which plants and offices are located, even the most expensive Washington lobbyists will not make much difference. With strong community support, expensive lobbyists are seldom necessary or even desirable. Strong support at the local level inspires members of the House from that area and the senators of the state to go to bat for a company that is known to be a good employer and conscientious citizen of the community. Such support, in turn, is a prerequisite for legislators from other districts and states to take up the company's cause. When the Japanese family that owns Nintendo and lives in Seattle offered to buy the Seattle Mariners baseball team to keep the franchise from leaving the city, many Americans saw it as Japan "buying up the national pastime." Not the people of Washington state, however; they hailed the Japanese investors as heroes, and the state's top officials vigorously supported them. In fact, Nintendo president Hiroshi Yamauchi pointed out that the governor of Washington and one of its U.S. senators first approached him. When Major League officials expressed their reluctance to allow Japanese ownership, there was an outpouring of local support for the Japanese investors, especially in light of the fact that Yamauchi's son-in-law, who would be chairman of the buyer group, had lived in Seattle for fifteen years, which was fifteen years longer than any previous owner of the Mariners.

Astute international companies are beginning to understand the virtues of good community relations in the United States, and more are joining the ranks of good corporate citizens. In 1987, Japanese subsidiaries in the United States gave about $30 million to nonprofit organizations; by 1990 that figure increased tenfold to $300 million. Toyota, for example, runs a corporate-contributions program that donates some $10 million annually to local institutions.[14] Fujitsu America, based in San Jose, is a pacesetter in Silicon Valley, where 800 of its more than 5,000 American employees are located. The company sponsors the annual Cable Car Classic; a college basketball tournament; and the Fujitsu America Essay Contest, in which two flights of schoolchildren, grades six to eight and nine to twelve, write about whom they most admire or aspire to be like. More than 2,000 entries were submitted in 1991, many heartwarming and inspiring, competing for the cash prizes awarded to first-, second-, and third-place winners in each flight. In addition to prizes for the students, Fujitsu provides awards to their teachers and the schools that the top six students attend. About the program, Arthur J. Gemmell, senior vice president for strategic planning, said, "Everything we've done . . . has reflected well on our company. It's impossible to measure the impact in dollars, but it's worked out well for us."[15]

In the case of SmithKline Beecham, with half the shares denominated in dollars and half denominated in pounds sterling and with significant employment and facilities in the United States and Britain, the company has tried hard to maintain the strong, positive insider status that both originating companies enjoyed before the merger. It has refocused and increased the overall amount of corporate philanthropy with increased emphasis on scientific education for elementary school children, an area of great need in both countries. SmithKline Beecham is the sole sponsor of a new, pioneering program, Science in Summer, that teaches young children the fascination of science in otherwise empty U.S. schoolrooms during the summer months. In Britain, the company is using a similar theme with exclusive corporate sponsorship of a permanent exhibit at the National Science Museum on health and health care that is aimed at schoolchildren. We believe these are good ideas that will blossom over the years. In a similar fashion, many other large global companies are playing a stronger and more visible role in the societies they serve, believing that good works are the foundation of good business.

All these forms of localization offer real opportunities for competitive advantage. But they are not a simple checklist that can be completed in a linear fashion. Achieving the right mix and the right emphasis is a matter of overall strategy, of asking tough questions, and of weighing often mutually antagonistic considerations. Should production sites be chosen for their proximity to a market or to reduce costs? Should a market be avoided or abandoned because currency risks are high? At what point does localization work against transnational economies of scale?

In addition, localization is not a purely chameleonlike adaptation to the local culture, nor does it leave that culture unaffected. The global company does, after all, introduce real changes—a new product, involvement in global trade, the training of local staff and employees, and perhaps new business arrangements and practices—even while it strives for localization. When SmithKline enlisted independent Japanese distributors for Contac, it was going against the grain of traditional distribution methods in Japan. The Japanese distributors were engaging in an act of independence and were being drawn into the global trading system, which is no small thing. Localization should not mean always accepting the status quo. When Toys 'Я' Us entered Germany, it encountered widespread resistance from toy manufacturers, which were accustomed to selling their products through small specialty shops, not warehouse-size self-service stores.[16] Local officials refused the company permits for suburban store sites on the grounds that toy stores belong in city centers. To force the officials' hands, the company, led by its German managing director, then requested large sites in the city centers. Eventually, the company prevailed. A toy manufacturers' boycott of the stores evaporated, and booming toy sales bolstered the entire German toy industry.

Percy Barnevik, the president and CEO of Asea Brown Boveri, aptly described the push and pull of cultural innovation versus adaptation: "Global managers have exceptionally open minds. They respect how different countries do things, and they have the imagination to appreciate why they do them that way. But they are also incisive, they push the limits of the culture. Global managers don't passively accept it when someone says, 'You can't do that in Italy or Spain because of the unions,' or 'You can't do that in Japan because of the Ministry of Finance.' They sort through the debris of cultural excuses and find opportunities to innovate."[17]

The key is to work in both dimensions at once—the global and the local. That is a business imperative, but it is based on a fundamental human condition: People the world over are simultaneously different and the same. An amusing early experience I had in Japan makes the point. The chairman of a Japanese pharmaceutical company invited me to dinner at one of Tokyo's oldest and finest geisha houses. I arrived around 6:30 P.M.—evenings begin early in Japan—and joined the chairman and four or five of his Japanese colleagues. The easy conviviality was augmented by much sake, and still more sake, circulating among us as we sat on the floor around the table. Around 10 P.M., to my astonishment, the chairman simply fell over backwards; he had passed out cold. (In Japan it is no disgrace to be drunk after 6 P.M.) Two brawny men appeared and carried him out. No one seemed to take it amiss, so I continued to socialize with the remaining guests. One by one they, too, began to pass out. And in due course each of them was carted away, until I was the sole remaining guest. Still I stayed, finishing the last of the sake and perhaps taking a bit of macho pride in having outlasted them.

When the place closed, I walked back to the Imperial Hotel feeling shipshape and soon went to sleep. The next morning I stepped out of bed and fell flat on my face. I felt as if a brick had been dropped on my head. And then it struck me: The Japanese metabolize quickly and Anglo-Saxons metabolize slowly, but we all end up on our hands and knees. (In a literal sense, that was the key to the reformulation of Contac—a different dosage, same ingredients). The point is that one has to be sensitive to differences, but alive to similarities. And it is in the area of the similarities—the widespread desire for quality and price, for example—that a company can push the culture a little, doing things differently to gain a competitive edge and to realize the benefits of globality.

To work purely locally is to return in many ways to the era of the multinational, customizing everything at the sacrifice of the economies of scale that can be realized in many aspects of the operation. The most striking examples—which illustrate the differences between modern transnational business strategies, which integrate the global and the local, and those of the older international and multinational-national companies—are found in the automobile industry.

The strategy toward Japan that the American automobile companies adopted in the 1960s and 1970s was to associate with Japanese companies through joint ventures and purchases of minority equity positions, thereby enabling the American companies to obtain parts manufactured in Japan on favorable terms. Ford owns 25 percent of Mazda, Chrysler has a joint venture in Japan with Mitres Motors, and GM owns about 33 percent of Isuzu and 5 percent of Suzuki.[18] Until recently, none of the Big Three automakers attempted to use these arrangements to market its products in Japan.

Incidentally, this was a major departure from the strategy employed by Ford and GM in Europe. In Europe the two large American companies have, for decades, operated wholly owned subsidiaries that are managed with considerable local autonomy. Both Ford and GM, through Opel in Germany and Vauxhall in Britain, have produced models that are thoroughly European and highly competitive. In fact, the European strategy succeeded so well that for both companies profits from the European subsidiaries covered the deep domestic losses experienced in the 1980s under the onslaught of competition from Japan. The only rational explanation for the dichotomy between a successful European strategy and the failure to grasp the strategic importance of Japan, and indeed the entire Pacific Rim, is the absence of a true global vision.

The aim of the American automakers was to keep U.S. costs down by importing Japanese components. That part of the strategy worked, but there were other, unintended consequences. The American purchases increased the volume of the Japanese companies, reducing their costs even further and strengthening their financial base. With this newfound financial muscle, the Japanese companies have been able to compete in world markets. And, of course, the American imports of parts and even finished automobiles have greatly added to the notorious trade deficit between the two countries. For several years Chrysler was the largest single importer of manufactured products from Japan—larger than Toyota or Nissan or any other Japanese company with subsidiaries in the United States.

The Japanese strategy, in contrast, has been to strengthen their ability to compete on a global basis. The key, once again, was localization. In approaching the huge American market, they quickly moved to design products that are especially suited to American tastes. They moved far ahead of their American competitors to capitalize on the demand for highly reliable cars and low operating costs. But their understanding of American tastes and desires has been much more subtle and sophisticated. This is a crucial point. Successful localization does not mean merely copying domestic products in foreign markets; it means exceeding the domestic competition in sensitivity to local tastes. Most automobiles that are sold in the American market by Japanese companies have been styled and designed by Americans working in design studios in California. These designs are then tested with American consumers, in much the same way that SmithKline tested its Contac commercials in Japan twenty-five years ago. It is no accident that the largest-selling model of automobile in the United States today is the Honda Accord, made in Ohio and now exported to other countries.

Following their market successes, the Japanese automobile companies have moved manufacturing from Japan to locations that are best suited to supply the global markets. In doing so, they are no different from other transnational companies. In the American markets, more and more Japanese cars are made in American plants by American workers, and as suppliers are developed and trained, more and more components and parts will be made in the United States, Canada, and Mexico as well. The same process is occurring in Europe, where the major Japanese companies have located plants in Great Britain as the launching pad for gaining entry to the European Community.

The point is that the success of the Japanese automobile companies does not stand only on their cars' engineering and quality, as important as these ingredients are. The additional dimension has been the companies' great sensitivity to the special needs and tastes of their customers and their ability to adapt their business practices to meet these needs better than can the local competitors without sacrificing their global strategic advantages.

As the competitive battles rage and ratings of market shares ebb and flow, the major benefactors are consumers around the world. I like to think that SmithKline brought relief from cold symptoms throughout the day or night to millions of Japanese and in the process brought Japan one step closer to the world market for health care products. Few doubt the consumer benefits gained from the Japanese assault on the world's automobile markets. Consumers certainly are driving better automobiles from all manufacturers as a result. I also believe that the global competition for the American automobile market, although immensely difficult for American manufacturers, has strengthened the American manufacturers' ability to compete at home and abroad. The voices crying for protectionism have to answer not only how consumers will be better served, but how the manufacturing companies being protected will become better competitors in the global marketplace.

Other global companies, besides Japanese automakers, have learned the lessons of global scale and local adaptation. Electrolux is now the largest manufacturer in the world of household appliances and durable consumer goods. Originally a Swedish-based company, its sales have increased fivefold during the 1980s to achieve the position of world leadership in a highly competitive industry.[19] The primary strategy has been growth by acquisition, including such well-known brand names as Zanussi in Italy, Tricity and Bendix in Britain, Corbero and Domar in Spain, Zanker in Germany, and White in the United States. But Electrolux has not pursued an asset-stripping strategy similar to that of financial acquirers like Carl Icahn or Sir James Goldsmith. Rather, it has combined transnational production and financial strategies with the delegation of design and marketing to the local level. This approach allowed the management team to turn Electrolux around in the first place, followed by similar success with Zanussi and approximately

100 other acquired companies around the world. Now headquartered in Switzerland, with an international team of managers, Electrolux has evolved into a true transnational company with a global vision and strategy to match, complemented by the excellent adaptation of the design, advertising, and promotion of products and sales and distribution tactics to local needs and preferences.

Motorola, once the beleaguered victim of the Japanese attack on televisions and consumer appliances, has reshaped its strategy and become a global competitor in innovative and high value-added electronic products and components. Few companies are as competitive and successful in the global battle for the market share of the electronics industry as is Motorola. Applying global production and marketing strategies, Motorola has taken the battle to Japan and was awarded the hotly contested cellular telephone contract in Tokyo. Possession of the best technology and best product is not enough to win a battle of this kind. Bob Galvin and the management team from Motorola mustered the local knowledge and savvy, including the right friends in the right, highly placed positions, to beat NEC, Toshiba, and Hitachi to the finish line.

The interplay of global imperatives and local prerogatives is not confined to the automobile, durable-goods, and electronics industries. Nor does it always operate in the same way in every business. But it does operate, the larger point being that the global and the local, two apparently antagonistic, if not contradictory, dimensions are the forces that now define the world. The wine business is a striking case in point.

Wine conjures up images of candlelight, conviviality, and romance. And rightly so! And the wine business evokes pictures of generations of family winegrowers sharing the treasures of their personal cellars with discerning patrons. After all, few businesses that are based on agricultural production can be owned and managed on a family basis all the way from cultivation of a crop to the appearance of a premium-priced product on a restaurant table or a shelf in an exclusive shop. Add to that heady mix the deep cultural history of wine as a symbol of civilization, friendship, and even religious spirituality, and the image is romantic, indeed.

In 1980 my wife and I purchased a vineyard in northern California, in part as a refuge—a place to rest, reflect, and gather strength for further forays into international business. We found all that and more. Within a few years we were drawn into making wine from our estate-grown grapes and then naturally, of course, into offering the results in the market, adopting the name Quivira (pronounced *kee-veer-a*) after the legendary kingdom sought by Coronado and other Spanish explorers, lured by reports of a fabulous city where the people habitually ate from gold plates and caught fish as big as horses. The legend of Quivira endured for more than two centuries, with the kingdom appearing on European maps of North America as late as 1752 and located in the area where our vineyards are today.

Though we entered the market on a relatively small scale, we soon found that even the wine business is bound by many of the fundamental trends we recognize easily in manufactured products like automobiles or computers. Visit your local wine shop, and you will find wine from all corners of the globe. Australia and New Zealand are certain to be represented, alongside the well-known wines from France, Italy, and Germany, as well as those from Chile and Argentina, Bulgaria and Spain, Israel and Hungary. Of course, California wines will be well represented (there are nearly 750 bonded wineries in California), but you're sure to find Pinot noir from Oregon and perhaps a Chardonnay from Texas, along with sparkling wine from New York. There are, in fact, few shops or retail outlets of any kind where so many parts of the world are represented by the origin of the packages on the shelves. Yet your local wine shop is no different from those in London, Amsterdam, Chicago, or Tokyo. Few other products are so ubiquitously global and yet so intensely local in character.

In part, the story of global and local forces in the wine business, as in many other industries, begins with technology. During the past thirty years or so, the technology of wine has undergone something of a revolution. That revolution began at the University of California at Davis in the 1960s. Researchers there applied the processing technology developed in the biochemical industry to wine production. In so doing, they brought the scientific method to an ancient process that is usually governed by folklore and tradition. The use of stainless steel and other hygienic methods brought some of the more random and wilder strains of microbes under control, and rigorous experimentation created reproducible methods of making wine of consistently high quality. During the same period, the researchers at Davis perfected the use of secondary fermentation—malolactic fermentation—for red wines and some white wines. Secondary fermentation added a softer finish to the wines and reduced the astringency common to many red wines, thereby making long periods of aging in bottles unnecessary. The wines can be enjoyed sooner and are generally more accessible.

The technical revolution at Davis reinvigorated the California wine industry, bringing it out of the aftermath of prohibition with such force and impact that it sent shock waves through the traditional wine regions of Europe, as well as the newer wine regions around the globe. The world took notice and, after a decade or so of skepticism, began to apply the same techniques and use the same equipment. As in most other fields of endeavor, scientific information is shared freely through publications, symposia, and personal visits. The results are apparent. Wine lovers have seen a tremendous improvement in quality and consistency, particularly in the wines from the traditional regions of Europe. All winemakers are now making wine in essentially the same manner everywhere in the world.

As the California wine business, boosted by the work at Davis, reemerged from the devastation of prohibition, the labels expropriated many well-known European regional names. Label designations, such as "Hearty Mountain Burgundy," "Chablis," and "Champagne," introduced a whole generation of Americans to California wine in the 1950s and 1960s, but greatly angered European producers, who threatened retaliation. The Bureau of Alcohol Tobacco and Firearms (BATF), which regulates the American wine industry, sided with the European producers and initiated regulations that led the American industry into varietal labeling. The idea was to provide greater information to consumers by labeling wines according to the variety of grapes such as sauvignon blanc or zinfandel, of which a wine is comprised. It was certainly a step beyond the use of ersatz European names, but it was based on the foolish idea that a grape from one region is equivalent to grapes of the same variety from other regions. This approach has led to the generic varietal labeling of American wine and has certainly condemned American wine to a lower price class than wines from the best regions of Europe.

Recently, the BATF established a system of local appellations, known as American Viticultural Areas (AVAs), to designate the specific locale in which the grapes are grown and the wine is made. There are now 112 AVAs in the United States, 63 of them in California. The industry is still stuck with generic varietal labeling, but can now describe in an orderly fashion the locality of its products. Locality has always been important in wine, and the great wines of Europe are known by their location and certainly not by their grape variety. For example, Châteauneuf-du-Pape is a specific place. The wine known by that name typically contains about seventeen different varieties of grapes. Within the appellation, over time, some growers and some wine estates achieve recognition for the superior quality of their wines. Allowing plenty of scope for artistic genius, it is generally conceded that certain local characteristics of soil, drainage, and climate combine to produce distinct differences in the nature and taste of wines.

Vineyards that are best known for producing consistently high-quality wines in California are beginning label their wines vineyard-designated wines. Some of the better known examples are Three Palms Merlot from Duckhorn, Les Pierres Chardonnay from Sonoma-Cutrer, and Monte Rosso Sonoma Valley Cabernet Sauvignon from Louis Martini. These designations refer to specific locations, usually the exact vineyards from which the grapes are taken. It is useful because the names of the vineyards and names of the relatively few estates that grow their own grapes and make wine exclusively in their estate wineries are the ultimate designation of locality, which, until recently, was the missing element on American wine labels but the dominant description on European labels for centuries.

With the spread of virtually identical wine-making techniques around the world, the technical emphasis has shifted from the wineries to the vineyards. And even in the vineyards there is a great similarity among grapes—most wine-growing regions work with the same clonal varieties. The European varieties, known as *vinefera*, are grown in most parts of the world and are often grafted to American rootstock of the *labrusca* variety because of *labrusca*'s resistance to phloxyera, the pest that decimated the vineyards of Europe a century ago. So the current effort is focused on such viticultural practices as trellising techniques, canopy management, pruning, grafting, soil cultivation, and the precise control of irrigation. Once again the experiments and the results are being shared around the world. In our vineyard, for example, we are experimenting with trellising and canopy-management techniques based on work done in New Zealand. There is no doubt that the application of the scientific method to the ancient practices in the vineyard will also contribute to the improved quality and consistency of wine in all the wine-growing regions of the world.

The international trading system is bringing these wines from all over the world to local wine shops and restaurants. The consumer now has an immense selection of wines from which to choose. But as wine production and vineyard practices converge around the world, what will distinguish one wine from another? The answer, of course, is the specific location in which the grapes were grown and the wine was made.

In the modern global environment in which the ancient art of wine making now finds itself, local identity has become much more important than ever. The informed consumer of American wine is already searching out Chardonnay from Carneros, zinfandel from Dry Creek Valley, and Pinot noir from the Willamette Valley, just as the consumer of European wine looks for Brunello di Montalcino from Tuscany and Montrachet from Burgundy. But competition for the attention of the informed consumer is so intense that it is incumbent on the various appellations, particularly in California, where the concept is new and not yet well defined, to provide a clear and consistent identity for their chosen localities. The failure to do so will eventually cause their products to disappear from the global market.

As it turns out, the wine business, although a source of immense pleasure and personal satisfaction, is certainly no refuge from the pressures of the global economy. Quite the contrary! On the other hand, a strong and well-defined sense of locality, which has always been a factor in wine grapes, is clearly the road to competitive success.

There is yet one further dimension to localization—personal adaptation. Managers who would work in a different culture or even do business with one from a distance must enter into the spirit of that culture in more than a superficial way. It is less a matter of action than of personal reorientation that must precede action—a willingness to learn, to listen, and to look "even under the mushrooms." Judo requires an analogous mental discipline. To understand judo, it is first necessary to understand certain principles of Zen and only then to apply them to the sport itself. My judo instructor in Honolulu was adamant about making certain that my mental posture was as correct as my physical posture before he would teach me a throw.

Even for people of manifest goodwill, personal reorientation often means struggling against the dismaying tendency to substitute racial, national, and ethnic stereotypes for real understanding. Even more fundamentally, openness to other cultures means overcoming deeply ingrained beliefs and habits, most of them acquired so early in life that they seem like immutable natural facts or just plain common sense. (The eminent anthropologist Clifford Geertz brilliantly showed that all cultures have beliefs that they hold to be "common sense" — the things that anyone with his or her head screwed on straight can be counted on to believe — and that these supposed self-evident truths vary dramatically from culture to culture.[20]) For many Westerners cross-cultural understanding comes particularly hard because of the Western insistence on universal and absolute truths.

From my experience, I would have to say that the highest value in Japan is not truth, which is regarded as relative, but harmony. Harmony means coexisting serenely with other people; achieving smooth and seamless change in all endeavors; and reaching mutual understanding about feelings, attitudes, and perspectives. Above all, harmony finds its highest expression in sincere behavior. Sincerity doesn't require verbal expression. It appears unobtrusively in one's way of receiving others, of listening, and of comporting oneself. It may consist of speaking only with the eyes. But however expressed, the individual's sincere behavior, in the service of harmony, wins the confidence of others.

As with other forms of localization discussed here, personal adaptation does not require a chameleonlike metamorphosis, à la Woody Allen's *Zelig*. Nor does it even entail trying to achieve something like the participant-observer ideal of anthropology. And, in any case, it would be facile and arrogant to believe that we can so easily enter other cultures, even those that are not so far removed from our own. Moreover, if a global enterprise is to work, the company must also have an overarching corporate culture that holds it together and to which the manager also adapts. But at the least, personal adaptation requires a willingness to take seriously the customs, expectations, and social rituals of the host culture.

This lesson was vividly brought home to me during my early

days in Japan, when two of the wholesale distributors of Contac fell into an acrimonious boundary dispute in Osaka. One wholesaler appeared to be using Contac to enter the other's territory. The accused wholesaler denied it, and there were charges of bad faith all around. The dispute grew so rancorous that it finally fell to me to resolve. Ordinarily, I would have traveled to Osaka, met the two wholesalers at a hotel, and settled the dispute. But I was assured by my Japanese friends that it would have been considered presumptuous and arrogant to summon the wholesalers to a Western hotel. Nothing short of settling it in the time-honored fashion of the daimyos (the former landholders who commanded Japan's castle towns), second in Japanese tradition only to the shoguns (the former military governors of Japan), would do.

In ancient Japanese practice, the daimyo sat on a huge tatami, flanked by samurai warriors and facing rows of supplicants, whose fate he decided. I was advised that I must conduct a similar ceremony with the warring wholesalers. So I chose a distinguished ryokan, which had once been visited by the emperor, for the meeting. The ryokan was situated on the boundary between the two wholesalers, so we could all come to the meeting without losing face. I found myself on my knees in a gray flannel suit in the ryokan's huge tatami room, facing a roomful of wholesalers. My role was to speak sternly, extract promises, delineate boundaries, and get them to agree, which I did. It was a dramatic confrontation, but in the old Japanese style, and it was followed by a banquet on the tatami as in the days of the Black Ships and Admiral Perry.

I make no special claim to having mastered Japanese cultural practices. I was distinctly uncomfortable kneeling on the tatami, feeling out of my depth and perhaps a bit foolish, on the one hand, and eager to do the right thing, on the other hand. But what I learned is how very far we *can* go in attempting to adapt to other cultures and how far we have to go. It is the most personal of the transnational challenges facing the global manager and, in a rapidly integrating world, each one of us.

PART TWO

FROM STRATEGY
TO STRUCTURE

CHAPTER FOUR

THE WORLD UPSIDE DOWN

IF GLOBALIZATION REQUIRES the personal transformation of managers, it also requires the complete transformation of the company. That is the real issue posed by global markets—nothing less than a new kind of corporation. A truly global orientation makes new demands on strategy, organizational behavior, and organizational structure.

It is easy to assess competitive conditions and to decide to make the leap to transnational status. And I think it is becoming clear that, in many cases, a decisive move, as in a cross-border merger or acquisition, is the best way to attain global status. And a responsiveness to local conditions and consumers is certainly the best way to keep it. But these steps are only the beginning. The more profound challenge, which I address in this and the following two chapters, is just how strategy, behavior, and structure work after the transnational leap has been taken. What features describe and distinguish transnational corporations? How do companies move beyond traditional international and multinational models to adopt genuinely transnational strategies in which global efficiencies and responsiveness to local conditions complement, rather than contradict, each other? In turning the world upside down in search of competitive advantage, globalization turns the familiar world of the company upside down as well.

The outline of the new corporation may appear dim initially, but it can be brought into sharper focus by looking first at the nature of the strategy dictated by globalization. In the past decade, global strategy has moved to the forefront of managerial consciousness. Globalization, many managers will now concede, is an imperative; localization is its corollary. But to many managers, globalization is merely a slogan. Even when it is well understood, it is a broad concept. On the one hand, it includes *international* strategies in which competitive advantages gained in the home market are systematically exploited abroad through exports, an approach pursued most successfully by Japanese automakers and American commercial aircraft manufacturers. On the other hand, globalization may also include *multinational* strategies, in which companies expand globally by reproducing their high value-added functions in each of the world's major markets, a game plan that has been executed adroitly by companies, such as Unilever, ITT Corporation, and Nestlé.

Companies that pursue an international strategy primarily focus on efficiency and competitive cost advantage through economies of scale. For decades Boeing has rigorously implemented a classic international strategy, successfully exporting jetliners from its two factories near Seattle to the rest of the world. More than half the jetliners that have ever been built were built by Boeing. Specifications for jetliners are universal. They require virtually no tailoring to local markets. And because the costs of entering the industry are so high, foreign countries, lacking their own aerospace companies, have never erected special barriers to the import of commercial aircraft. Building on the security of its enormous American market and enjoying the huge economies of scale that went with dominating the world market for jetliners, Boeing had little incentive, until recently, to do other than it did: build more airliners faster and at a lower cost than its chief rival, McDonnell Douglas, and export them to the world.

Multinational companies, in contrast, are primarily interested in attracting customers to their high value-added products by developing a competitive response to local market conditions. Global food companies, such as Nestlé, have traditionally pursued multinational strategies, primarily because food preferences are decidedly local. Historically, such companies have been willing to sacrifice the advantages of global scale by locating as many elements of

the value-added chain as are necessary in foreign countries to satisfy local tastes and to market their products. Nestlé, for example,
operates nearly 400 factories on five continents and does 98 percent
of its business outside its home country of Switzerland. Unilever,
another company that is highly responsive to local tastes, makes
more than 200 different formulations of margarine in highly segmented markets around the world. What such companies lack in
efficiencies of global scale in manufacturing, they make up in their
well-honed responsiveness in thousands of local markets.

Each of these two familiar strategies embraces half the global-local
equation—the international emphasizing global scale, and the multinational emphasizing local response. But neither strategy brings them
together and fuses them into a seamless and multidimensional competitive approach. *Transnational* strategies seek to blend into a syn-
chronous whole the concept of global-scale efficiencies and market
responsiveness. It is not a simple matter of allocating some resources
globally and others locally, but of leveraging the interrelationships
across the two axes of transnational operation while focusing managerial attention on those distinctive skills—or "core competencies," as
they are labeled in business journals—that are needed to gain and sustain a competitive advantage. Thus the three essential elements of
such a strategy are (1) lines of business, (2) customer-
oriented business-unit relationships, and (3) the corporate-driven
coordination and exploitation of the core competencies.

Lines of business define the market segment being served—
whether it's instant coffee, airliners, mainframe computers, consumer electronics, or pharmaceuticals—which, in turn, defines
competitors, market-share dynamics, and cost positions. A global
analysis of the competition, market shares, and relative costs
defines the requirements of scale. In most cases, a global scale,
strong market shares, and low relative costs reinforce and complement each other to create powerful corporate strategies.

Customer-oriented business-unit relationships are usually coordinated on a local scale. These relationships include coordinated sales
activities for common customers; coordinated advertising purchases; the use of a common corporate identity to relate one line of
business to another in the customer's mind; and the coordinated
use of common logistics, such as distribution centers, transportation
suppliers, joint billing, and receivables management.

The corporate driven coordination and exploitation of core competen-

cies is carried out on a global scale. Core competencies are the business functions and technologies that are essential to the competitive survival of the enterprise. They are often embodied in research and development and manufacturing organizations, but can also include financial functions, personnel, information technology, and other functions. Invariably, core competencies are represented in the primary products and services that are delivered to customers. Often they describe essential strategic elements that differentiate the corporation from its competitors.

Leveraging these global and local interrelationships means thinking not just in two strategic dimensions, but in three: lines of business (scale), core competencies (skills), and global presence (scope). Thus, the three dimensions of a transnational corporate strategy can be conceptualized as a cube:

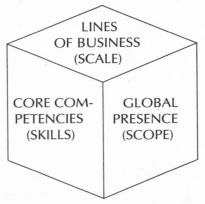

The purpose of this "transnational strategy cube" is to illustrate the strategic integrity required to articulate a business strategy in three dimensions. Each dimension is important in its own right and supports the integrity of the entire structure. Remove or ignore one dimension, and the entire structure collapses.

The management of corporate interrelationships on both the *local* and *global* dimensions holds great potential for vastly improving corporate performance. The additional complexities of constantly thinking and working in three essential strategic dimensions are substantial, but they are increasingly viewed as the keys to long-term competitive success.[1]

Michael Porter pointed out that economies of scale are not all equivalent.[2] The *relevant* measure of scale differs among industries, firms, and business functions. For some high value-added activities, such as research and development, global scale is relevant; for others, such as advertising, the local scale may be the cost driver. Porter noted that the appropriate measure of scale is often a matter of choosing a policy. Products can be standardized worldwide, thereby achieving global economies of scale, as is occurring with pharmaceuticals and semiconductors. Alternatively, products can be designed to accommodate local or regional tastes, thereby considerably reducing the volume produced and efficiencies of scale in return for products that are better tailored to customers' preferences. In other words, the challenge is to mix skills, scale, and scope in appropriate and advantageous proportions. Transnational competitors often have a wide range of strategic choices in this regard, depending on their customers and their competitors, as well as the economics of each choice.

Many American chemical companies, for example, have found the formula for global success that has eluded not only numerous other American companies in other industries, but Japanese chemical companies as well.[3] The U.S. chemical industry derives significant economies of scale from huge, world-class petrochemical plants built near cheap sources of energy around the Gulf of Mexico, and the companies export enough chemicals to achieve record export surpluses. So great are the efficiencies that these American plants have achieved that many foreign users have found it cheaper to import chemicals from the United States than to build their own plants. In addition, with a long history of direct investment in foreign countries, the American companies ship about 40 percent of their exports to overseas affiliates, which, in turn, produce higher-cost specialty chemicals tailored to their specific markets. In contrast, the Japanese industry made a few foreign acquisitions in the 1980s but pulled back from them when an overcapacity in world production depressed the prices of chemicals. Now, lacking the strategic mix of scale and market penetration achieved by the American companies, the Japanese companies simply are not as competitive in world markets.

In many important respects, the pharmaceutical business, the industry with which I am most familiar, illustrates the primary components of a transnational strategy. As the industry separates into large global competitors and smaller niche players, it is clear that the global imperative has taken hold. The demand for modern, scientifically based drugs derived from advanced research has become universal, as is vividly illustrated by China, for decades one of the last great holdouts from the world trading system. Following the death of Mao Zedong, China became the last major market to accept modern medicine. If SmithKline Beecham's success there is any indication, and I believe it is, China is rapidly moving from traditional herbal medicines to world-class scientific pharmaceuticals of proven safety and efficacy. And China has also acknowledged the importance of intellectual property rights, having agreed in January 1992 to enact laws to protect American pharmaceuticals (as well as books, computer software, and recordings) from illegal copying. According to American trade associations, China's past violation of pharmaceutical patents alone resulted in losses of approximately $400 million annually to the industry.[4] China has also agreed to extend patent protection to twenty years from fifteen years, which is crucial for pharmaceuticals because they must be patented as soon as they are formulated, but may require as many as ten years of safety testing and regulatory approval before they reach the market. By honoring international standards and extending patent protection, China, a nation of more than 1 billion people, is opening the door to global products and the companies that produce them. In its own way, China has recognized the global imperative, at least with respect to medicines.

Universal demand, expanding the protection of intellectual property rights, rapidly evolving technology, and the fast and widespread dissemination of scientific information are all elements of the global imperative for the pharmaceutical industry. And with the convergence of regulatory policies around the world, the global imperative for individual companies grows even more urgent. Recently, the regulatory agencies for the world's three largest markets—the United States, the European Community, and Japan—adopted a joint view that recognizes the global nature of the industry and its products. In November 1991, at an extraordinary press conference in Brussels, Belgium, representatives of the U.S. Food and Drug Administration (FDA), the European Commission, and the Japanese Koseisho (Ministry of Health) announced the results of a two-year effort by more than 1,200 people to harmonize and streamline approval procedures for new drugs. This initiative promises to eliminate the duplication of procedures from country to country and to prune many unnecessary testing procedures.

For pharmaceutical companies, the result of this historic international agreement will be even greater globalization of an already rapidly globalizing industry:

• National differences in regulatory review and approval procedures will disappear. Such differences have always acted as invisible trade barriers that provided some measure of protection for local companies and tended to disadvantage global companies. As the regulatory differences vanish, so will the local companies's insulation from the full rigor of global competition.

• National differences in labeling (the official statement of indications, warnings, and contraindications that guides physicians in the use of pharmaceutical products) will also vanish. The labeling of pharmaceutical products will become nearly identical everywhere and so will the marketing and use of pharmaceuticals.

• National differences in medical and pharmaceutical practices will gradually disappear, particularly for medicines that are intended for the treatment of serious diseases. Today, for example, at least several dozen pharmaceutical products that are widely prescribed in Japan for cancer will never be approved elsewhere. Such products and similar examples in other countries will gradually disappear, further diminishing local companies and providing an additional advantage to global companies that offer products that measure up to international standards.

As the larger pharmaceutical companies become even more committed to a global view of their destiny, they must make markets, scale, and skills work together to create a truly transnational strategy. Universal demand and regulatory convergence mean that rules and regulations are virtually identical in all markets. Vast, uniform markets mean opportunities for achieving significant economies of scale in research and development, manufacturing, information technology, and the support and marketing of products. Economies of scale in such crucial business functions impart power and scope to the application of skills, which, in turn, translates into more competitiveness and a growing penetration of the global market.

More concretely, one can see how issues converge in key parts of an organization, especially those parts that house a company's core competencies. In the pharmaceutical business the quintessential core competence resides in research and development. (In other industries the core competence may lie elsewhere. In the automobile industry the convergence of strategic factors appears most clearly in design, engineering, and manufacturing. In a service industry, such as high-speed package delivery or the clinical laboratories, they are seen in the fusing of the logistics of distribution and customer satisfaction. In the packaged-foods industry they come together most clearly in marketing.) In the past, all that was required for successful pharmaceutical research was a high degree of scientific skills. But great advances in the life sciences and in the use of new technologies have produced elaborate and important new therapies in recent years that have increased the costs of research and development far beyond the resources of small companies, no matter how skilled their researchers. Today, scale, as well as skills, is a necessary component of competitive success.

The financial stakes alone argue for a high degree of scale. Annual research and development budgets in excess of $500 million are commonplace. And annual sales of recently introduced products in excess of $1 billion may not yet be commonplace, but they are no longer rare. Vasotec, a blood-pressure medication, and Mevacor, a cholesterol-lowering drug, both produced by Merck, reached sales of $1.75 billion and $1.09 billion, respectively, in 1991.[5] Pravachol, a similar cholesterol-lowering agent developed by Bristol-Myers Squibb, rang up $35 million in sales during its first quarter on the market and $70 million in its second quarter and was expected to exceed $400 million in its first year.[6]

The nature of modern research also requires large-scale operations. As research advances, it becomes more complicated and far more difficult to carry out. Today, medical research increasingly focuses on the highly complex and still incompletely understood physical and chemical systems that control many of the processes of the human body. Further, the distinctions between scientific and technological disciplines have become blurred as ever more sophisticated technology has become indispensable in research and as escalating costs compel a closer union of basic research and applied development. For all these reasons, most research, even in the early discovery phase, is carried out by multidisciplinary teams. For example, teams conducting early research on new approaches to the treatment of ischemia would certainly include cellular biologists, pharmacologists, medicinal chemists, animal pathologists, and perhaps molecular biologists, along with such clinical specialists as cardiologists and neurologists. The various scientific disciplines must be located close enough to each other to allow for their integration and yet be flexible enough to work on more than one project at a time. Such a requirement argues for a high level of scale in any given location. The nostalgic image of the lone scientist working to earn a Nobel prize no longer fits the realities of modern science. Likewise, many of the essential support services, including mandatory testing for toxicity, are usually done most efficiently in large-scale centers that then disseminate the results throughout the world.

Once a promising new compound has been identified and characterized, skill and scale converge even more dramatically in the development of a new product, which usually consumes about 70 percent of the total budget for research and development. Much of that money is spent on extensive tests on animals and on human trials that are designed to prove the therapeutic value of the concept emerging from the research and to satisfy regulatory authorities of the safety of the new agent. For commercial and regulatory reasons, these tests must be conducted simultaneously on a global scale. Despite the harmonization of international regulations, many national regulatory agencies require local tests, and physicians like to see published studies by local clinicians of tests on local patients. And because of global competition in the industry, it is essential to introduce important new therapies in markets around the world in the shortest possible time. Typically, development projects culminate in large-scale trials involving thousands of people and often more than 100 individual clinical investigators. The demands of data analysis and storage are enormous: Most new drug submissions require hundreds of volumes of supporting data and are delivered to the FDA and other regulatory agencies by truck.

From development emerges the competitive profile of a new product and a full understanding of its potential. The information amassed during the development of the product and presented to the regulatory agencies determines the product's officially approved description, known in the trade as "labeling." This approved labeling, which defines *exactly* what can be said about the new product, indelibly imprints the product's usefulness in physicians' minds. Articles about the product in medical and scientific journals strengthen these initial impressions.

In most cases, the competitive battles of the pharmaceutical industry are won and lost in development of products—not in the market. The competition between Tagamet, SmithKline's pioneer ulcer medication, and Zantac, Glaxo's competitive response, stands as a vivid example. It has become a famous case, but, as someone who was deeply involved in the struggle, I think its real character has been missed. The popular business press described the contest between these two highly effective products as a marketing battle between SmithKline and Glaxo. Though I know SmithKline could have improved many aspects of the marketing program for Tagamet, it really lost the advantage to Glaxo in development. Glaxo won regulatory approval for a twice-daily dose of Zantac, in contrast to Tagamet's four-times-a-day dose and at a lower overall total daily dose in milligrams. Physicians drew the obvious inference: Zantac appeared to be a more potent and longer-acting agent. Moreover, when Zantac was introduced, its official labeling listed fewer side effects than did the labeling for Tagamet, which by then had been widely used and extensively reported on for more than six years. All Zantac's initial comparative advantages, except the total daily dosage in milligrams, have largely disappeared as a result of the continuing clinical development of both products. Both can now be administered once a day, and the side effects noted in Zantac's labeling have increased extensively. Nevertheless, the initial impression of Zantac as a more potent and longer-acting compound with some safety advantages remains firmly fixed in the minds of many prescribing physicians, and Zantac outsells Tagamet by better than two to one worldwide. Glaxo won the battle in development, long before its product appeared on the market.

The development of a new product is not only a battle for the product's positioning and relative claims of safety and efficacy, it is also a race against time and money. Costs rise exponentially with time because data continue to accumulate. All the data, no matter how trivial, must be processed and analyzed and eventually are incorporated into applications for the approval of the new drug by drug authorities. Unnecessary time expended in development often creates needless work, costs money, and can actually depreciate the drug's value. There is always a great temptation to add one or two more clinical trials to the development plan to examine relatively minor issues. Prestigious clinicians also exert tremendous pressure on a company to conduct extra trials. Finally, once a trial is con-

cluded, many physicians naturally want to continue giving the
investigational medicine to their patients. In all cases, data accumulate beyond what is needed to register the new drug. Yet the regulatory agencies insist on examining *all* data, relevant or not, before
they will license the production and marketing of the new drug.
The accumulation of such superfluous data adds exponentially to
the time and cost of production and ultimately leads to the loss of a
competitive advantage. Time in development means time not on the
market. Sales are lost, and the door stands wide open to competitors
who are developing a similar product.

How can a pharmaceutical company win this development race?
Once again, the answer is a global scale, and perhaps what may be
surprising, local responsiveness. Competitive success depends on
timely, efficient, large-scale development conducted simultaneously
in major markets throughout the world. The company must conduct
sizable clinical trials on a *global* scale while involving leading clinical
experts in important *local* markets. Such strategically effective clinical
trials require extensive global planning, intensive input from local
markets, and a rigorous determination to follow the plan without
adding extraneous activities. Execution makes great demands on
the company's global communications network and data-manage-
ment system. Ultimate success depends on skillful planning, disciplined follow-through, and the ability to manage data quickly and
accurately.

The necessity to conduct development simultaneously in many
places leads to the third dimension of the transnational-strategy
cube: markets. No less than skills and scale, the scope of engagement in key global markets impinges on research and development
and converges with them. Global players no longer conduct
research only in their home market. It has become common practice
to establish drug-discovery units in the triad of the United States,
Japan, and Europe. U.S.-based Merck, the world's largest pharmaceutical company, has three laboratories in the United States and
seven outside the country (in Kirkland, Quebec; Riom, France; Ter-
lings Park, England; Madrid, Spain; Pomezia, Italy; Meguro, Japan;
and Okazaki, Japan) that are engaged in the research and early
development of new drugs. The company also conducts clinical trials on tens of thousands of patients in dozens of countries. Six other
American pharmaceutical companies do basic research in their own
laboratories in Japan, the world's second largest prescription drug

market after the United States. Four Japanese drug companies — Eisai, Kirin, Tanabe, and Yamanouchi — have set up research facilities in the United States. SmithKline maintains research and development facilities in the United States, Britain, Belgium, France, and Italy and has ambitions to add discovery work to its development unit in Japan.

It's important to note what the globalization of research and development really means for markets. Formerly, the location of research and development in foreign countries was aimed primarily at helping tailor products to the local market. For many health care products, particularly those sold over the counter, such local tailoring, as with Contac in Japan, remains a primary function of these local units. But as pharmaceutical companies move toward producing universal products, the globalization of research and development has become a much more tightly integrated mechanism for gaining new markets around the world. These far-flung units are highly prized by the host countries and contribute in important ways to gaining insider status in desirable markets. Furthermore, they allow a company to employ local academic consultants as an important component of the intellectual mix. The employment of these consultants helps companies to participate early in emerging technologies and quickly relate those technologies to research efforts throughout the global organization. For example, both SmithKline Beecham and Bristol Myers–Squibb have established research units at Oxford University that focus primarily on neuroscience and the search for new drugs for Alzheimer's disease and other conditions of the central nervous system. Finally, the discovery units located in various markets are linked by information technology in a global network in which tasks are allocated to various units according to their proficiency and capacity, thus intertwining markets, skills, and scale.

Though these three elements — skills, scale, and scope — remain conceptually distinct, operationally they become indistinguishable, each fortifying the other in a three-dimensional transnational strategy that is simultaneously global and local. In short, they achieve that elusive quality of synergy — to use a word much abused by business journals — in which the three elements together produce a competitive advantage that none could produce individually. For example, scale that is unrelated to core competencies yields poor results, as many companies that wildly diversified into unrelated businesses have painfully discovered. In a sense, such companies viewed management, especially financial management, as a core competence, which it rarely is — being largely abstract and not a distinctive feature of any product or service. Core competencies show up in products, not just in financial statements.

SmithKline Beecham is currently engaged with Glaxo in a new competitive battle that is being fought in the new terms of a transnational strategy. The contest involves a new class of compounds, known as 5-HT$_3$ antagonists. This important class of new products blocks even the most severe nausea and vomiting induced by powerful anticancer agents. As many as 80 percent of the patients who received chemotherapy for cancer failed to complete the course of treatment because of the terrible, wracking side effects of severe nausea and vomiting. Traditional antiemetics, though useful at extremely high dosages, also have undesirable side effects because of their inherent toxicities. The new 5-HT$_3$ antagonists stop the nausea and vomiting in up to 80 percent of the patients who would otherwise drop out of treatment and appear to be far safer than traditional antiemetics. The new compounds are doubly important because of the far greater number of people who now initially survive cancer as a result of advances in its treatment. And the effectiveness of the compounds promises to make possible even stronger regimens of chemotherapy and radiation treatment, leading to even higher survival rates. Both SmithKline Beecham and Glaxo are now developing new 5-HT$_3$ antagonists and are racing to reach the market first with the best "approved" profile.

Although SmithKline Beecham made many of the pivotal discoveries in the use of 5-HT$_3$ antagonists, the real contest is taking place in development, just as it did in the case of Tagamet versus Zantac. In the race to be first on the market, Glaxo is clearly ahead in the United States and marginally ahead in Europe, but Smith-Kline Beecham is at least one to two years ahead in Japan, a market for anticancer drugs that is nearly as large as that of the United States. In this instance, a well-managed and disciplined development effort in Japan put SmithKline Beecham ahead in that crucial country. Likewise, Glaxo stole the march on SmithKline Beecham in the United States with a fast start and well-managed clinical development program. The stakes are large for both companies, and every day counts.

Speed isn't everything, of course. Again, just as with Tagamet and Zantac, the success of the development effort also depends crucially on *what* is developed and how it is initially perceived. In this case, Kytril, SmithKline Beecham's product, appears to be more potent and longer acting than is Glaxo's Zofran. And just as Zantac's simpler dosage gave it an initial advantage over Tagamet, Kytril initially enjoys a simpler dosage than does Zofran. On the other hand, Zofran is currently available in tablet form in several European markets, as well as by injection, while Kytril is not yet available in oral form, which may give Glaxo a temporary marketing advantage. In any case, clinical trials comparing the two drugs are now going on, and the results will have important consequences for their ultimate reception in the market.

No single consideration, by itself, may be decisive for the ultimate success of one product over the other, but taken together, they illustrate how little margin for error exists when two global companies, after enormous investments of time and money, go head to head around the world. Merely to have a fighting chance, the competing companies must have all the elements of a global strategy in place and working together: global scale and the huge resources that scale brings to the battle; an established presence in the triad markets of the United States, Europe, and Japan, where the resources can be applied with local sensitivity and effect; and sharply honed core competencies in both the discovery and development of drugs that are applied with great care and discipline globally and locally.

Although research and development is usually a good place to begin examining the strategy at work in the pharmaceutical industry, in many other industries the best place to start such an analysis is in the manufacturing systems involved in making the company's primary product or in the company's means of producing its chief service. And there one finds that traditional notions of scale—understood in terms of volume-cost relationships—have been turned upside down by global companies that have the elements of a transnational strategy working together in novel ways.

For generations of managers, volume-cost relationships have been well understood and accepted as gospel: The higher the volume of units, the lower the cost to produce each unit. Certainly, in the automobile industry the assembly-line techniques developed by Henry Ford strikingly embodied the principle and became an accepted manufacturing doctrine. However, new production techniques pioneered by Japanese manufacturers have dramatically altered the equation. These new techniques stem directly from the work of two Americans: W. Edwards Deming and Joseph Juran. Experts on building quality into the production process, these men were part of the Allied effort to help revive the Japanese economy following World War II. They lectured extensively throughout Japan in the 1950s and 1960s to larger and more receptive audiences than they were able to attract in the United States. Building on the insights of these two prophets, leading Japanese companies have developed quality-oriented manufacturing systems and techniques, including total quality management, just-in-time manufacturing, and flexible manufacturing systems that incorporate fast setup times and short production runs. All these approaches to manufacturing are founded on a common philosophy of giving absolute priority to building in quality throughout the production process, striving for the utmost customer satisfaction, and pursuing continual improvement in the productivity of all work.

Total quality management illustrates how radically these new techniques differ from the older philosophies of production. Previously, quality assurance programs simply inspected finished products and eliminated defective ones. Inspections were usually carried out by a quality-control department that was separate from manufacturing. Gradually, there developed the practice of inspecting the product at every stage of manufacturing. The aim was to build in quality from the first and to improve the manufacturing process itself. Now the concept of quality has been expanded to the design stage at the front end and to customer use at the other end. As Toshiro Fujiwara, the director and general manager of Nippon Steel explained, "In response to changing needs, the concept of production of goods has shifted from *'product-out,'* which places emphasis on production, to *'market-in,'* which responds to market needs, and more recently, to *'customer-in,'* which pays more attention to individual customer needs."[7]

At Beckman Instruments, the California-based manufacturer of diagnostic and analytical instruments that SmithKline spun off to its shareholders at the time of its merger with Beecham, total quality management, just-in-time manufacturing, and flexible production have been applied with dramatic results. Since 1986, when the program went into effect, manufacturing space has been reduced by better than 25 percent, and sales have increased 40 percent. Perhaps what is most impressive, whereas the manufacturing process formerly required six to eight weeks, depending on the complexity of the instrument, today the process requires only four to eight *days*. Costs are down, quality and reliability have improved, and customer satisfaction is up. The consequent reduction in the plant's overhead and inventories has improved the return on investment and permitted increased investment in research and development. The company has grown more profitable and competitive, selling more products worldwide and growing steadily—even in Japan—with products made in the United States.

The effect of total quality management at Beckman has proved to be much more important than even a significant reduction in cost or reduced working capital. It has altered the competitive landscape in other ways as well. The time now required to develop new products has been shortened considerably, making Beckman a much more potent competitor that is able to outpace many companies that serve the same customers. But the most important result is the significant increase in customer satisfaction and the reduced requirements for after-sale service and adjustment.

Beckman Instruments performs a sophisticated analysis and provides the user with information about microscopic quantities of biological materials. In other words, it sells instruments, but the customer is also buying a reliable source of precise information. The reliability and consistency of information, as well as the ease of use, have improved measurably through total quality management, thereby further strengthening Beckman's bond with its customers. That is a far cry from the days when volume-unit cost relationships were the chief measure of manufacturing prowess. The manufacturing of high-quality products has become a sales and marketing advantage.

High-quality production techniques produce equally dramatic results in most industries, but the competitive impact is greatest in low-growth markets in which the technology is old and therefore breakthrough innovation is unlikely to change competitive relationships. The automobile industry fits this description, so it should be no surprise that advanced production techniques are substantially altering the industry's competitive terrain. Because the Japanese automakers have been developing and refining quality-oriented production techniques for more than two decades, the advantages such systems provide are strikingly apparent when compared with those of American automakers.

Differences in the quality and production costs of U.S. and Japanese automakers have been devastating for the American auto industry. In December 1991, GM announced its intention to close twenty-one plants and eliminate 74,000 jobs. This was not the first such announcement from GM, nor is it likely to be the last. GM's North American operations lost $15 million *per day* throughout 1991. The magnitude of the problem appears most starkly in the contrast in productivity between GM and its Japanese competitors. Each GM worker produces, in effect, thirteen cars in one year, whereas each worker at Toyota Motors Corporation produces forty-five. And that simple statistic does not measure differences in quality, reliability, and customer satisfaction.[8]

Of course, the impact of these statistics on productivity is magnified because Toyota, in common with many large Japanese manufacturing companies, uses an extensive system of subcontractors to obtain parts and components. In fact, it manufactures less than half the cars it sells. Furthermore, it is well known that Japanese workers, as a matter of practice, donate "free" work time to their companies. In effect, this unbilled overtime, which can range as high as 10–20 percent of the total work time annually, skews comparisons of productivity. Nevertheless, in England and the United States, the Japanese transplant factories consistently reproduce the high rates of productivity achieved in Japan. Thus, it is clear that the differences in the productivity of Japanese and American companies are not a matter of national or ethnic character, but of a different corporate concept of the production process and a radically different level of respect and esteem for customers. It is American workers, after all, who efficiently build those Accords in Ohio and Nissans in Tennessee. In the final analysis, the differences can be traced to corporate strategies — to skills, scale, and scope.

For forty years Chrysler enjoyed a well-earned reputation for excellent engineering, a reputation that endured well into the 1960s. Its styling and dealer organization may not have equaled those of its competitors, but customers kept returning because of the quality and reliability of the cars. Engineering was the company's core competence, a precious competitive advantage passed from Walter Chrysler, the founder of the company, to successive generations of managers and employees. But gradually Chrysler began to lose its way and eventually turned its back on its engineering heritage. The decline began in the 1970s, when the company began buying engines, of all things, from suppliers in Asia and then assembled them in Detroit. Other components followed. Now Chrysler is critically dependent on suppliers in Japan, Korea, and Taiwan for highly engineered components. By failing to invest in engineering technology, training, and the best plants and equipment, Chrysler lost its lead in engineering excellence, the one undeniable advantage that had always distinguished it from its competitors.

The bitter experience of the American automakers can teach us a lot about skills, scale, and scope. The Big Three always enjoyed the advantages of scale. They still do. GM remains the largest industrial corporation in the world, and Ford is still the second largest automaker in the world. Even Chrysler, for all its troubles, doubled its output of cars and trucks during the past decade and now makes some 2.3 million per year and has become the industry's low-cost producer. Furthermore, all three U.S. automakers are situated at the heart of the world's largest automobile market, another significant advantage of scale. Their real strategic problem lies in the realm of skills. The production techniques pioneered by the Japanese followers of Deming and Juran changed the skills required to make cars to such an extreme degree that the competitive tables were turned. *Skills* transformed the competitive definition of *scale*.

The Toyota worker's higher productivity, which obviously lowers unit costs, flows from the company's advanced manufacturing skills, not simply from its global scale. Just-in-time manufacturing, in which components arrive on the assembly line from suppliers at precisely the time they are needed, shrinks the inventories of parts, saves working capital, requires less factory floor space, and greatly increases the efficiency and productivity of each worker. Fast setup times and rapid factory changeover permit smaller production runs and thus greater responsiveness to customers' preferences. Total quality management produces reliable products that keep customers coming back and saves ruinous warranty costs later. These advantages result not directly from scale, but from skills applied intelligently to scale.

When the problem of scope is factored in alongside scale and skills, the depth of the American automakers' strategic failures, as they converge in manufacturing, becomes apparent. Just as skills can alter scale, scope can alter skills. The U.S. automakers have behaved as if markets mattered only as a basis for large scale. Though Chrysler doubled its output in the past decade, it continues to do 95 percent of its business in the United States and Canada. Ford and GM are well represented in Europe, but neither pursued a genuinely global strategy in the Asian market. Since they failed to build factories or locate design and development facilities in Asia, they did not gain early access to the innovative manufacturing systems and technology, despite the fact that advances in automotive technology, from fuel efficiency and low emissions to advanced automotive electronics, have been coming from Japan for two decades. The American companies' early purchases of minority stakes in Japanese and Korean car companies served yesterday's strategy of obtaining low-cost components, but are not yet part of an aggressive assault on Asian markets.

In today's global marketplace, skills, scale, and scope work together, each altering and redefining the other. Scale cannot be uncoupled from skills or markets from either. Markets not only provide scale, but contribute importantly to maintaining skills. For example, it was Beckman's decision to become competitive in Japan that led to its wholehearted adoption of total quality management. The result was greatly improved competitiveness everywhere. These interrelationships and their power to generate superior corporate performance are now being recognized even by companies that have historically pursued only international or multinational strategies.

Boeing, under pressure from Airbus and from McDonnell Douglas's bold proposal for a trans-Pacific partnership with Taiwan Aerospace, is beginning to adopt some of the elements of a transnational strategy for the production of its new 777 widebody plane. In Airbus and McDonnell-Taiwan Aerospace, Boeing faces what are in effect transnational companies that are partially underwritten by governments whose national airlines are likely to be customers. So Boeing has contracted out the manufacturing of about 20 percent of the 777's structure to a Japanese consortium, made up of Fuji Heavy Industries, Kawasaki Heavy Industries, and Mitsubishi Heavy Industries. Enjoying a strong backlog of orders and little indebtedness, Boeing could easily manufacture the entire plane at home, but its management believes that the alliance with the Japanese consortium is crucial to the company's prospects for selling the plane in east Asia. The decision to perform some of the manufacturing in the world's fastest growing market for commercial aircraft lends the company at least a patina of the insider status enjoyed by true transnationals and is, in effect, a gesture of local responsiveness. The arrangement also taps the technological superiority that the Japanese possess in the lightweight composite materials that will replace heavier aluminum alloy in some parts of the plane. Thus the imperatives of global markets, borderless technology, and transnational competitors are now moving Boeing beyond its purely international strategy.

Boeing has not, however, adopted a fully transnational strategy, because as with many such strategic alliances, it must try not to give away its core competence for the sake of markets. Boeing's core competence is the design and integration of the many complicated technological systems that make up a modern jetliner. Its managers believe that they can farm out the manufacture of structural elements of the plane without giving away anything in systems integration.

The stakes are enormous. Both Airbus and McDonnell Douglas already produce similar wide-body planes, and Airbus plans more. In the 1970s when Lockheed, Boeing, and McDonnell Douglas competed directly with the first wide-body planes, Lockheed was forced out of the commercial aircraft business. Boeing is unlikely to be the loser, but since it now faces transnational competitors, the company has recognized the limits of its international strategy.

Starting from the other end of the spectrum, multinational companies, such as Unilever, have historically moved toward fuller transnational strategies. With more than $35 billion in worldwide sales and more than 500 operating companies in seventy-five countries, Unilever is the world's largest consumer products company, selling packaged foods, personal products, detergents, and hundreds of other everyday items. Because consumer preferences in such products vary greatly from country to country and market to market, Unilever has pursued the classic multinational strategy of reproducing its value-added operations in many local markets to satisfy its customers. Two decades ago, operating from separate units based in each market, Unilever made most of its sales in Europe. Today, however, it makes 60 percent of its sales in Europe, 20 percent in North America, and 20 percent in the rest of the world.[9] In line with its broader global scope and as a result of converging global tastes and Europe's move toward a single market, the company has been consolidating factories, reducing product configurations, and restructuring its operations. All these moves are designed to realize greater efficiency and economies of scale without losing sight of the company's responsiveness to customers. In Europe, for example, the number of soap factories has been reduced from twenty-two to three. Now instead of twenty-five different sizes of Unilever toothpaste, there are only two. Perhaps, what is most important, the company's three-dimensional matrix structure — products, areas, and functions — has been redrawn to give greater emphasis to product lines across areas and functions.

As more and more global companies — international and multinational alike — move toward transnational status, they will inevitably find themselves remaking more than strategy and structure. They will also find themselves on that often-shifting middle ground between the two: the realm of organizational behavior and culture. Though these issues enjoyed a great vogue several years ago, many people soon wearied of their sometimes ill-defined concepts and their difficult-to-quantify origins in human behavior. Nevertheless, such issues are real, and in a world where the notion of culture and cultures is not merely metaphorical — a transnational world — they have reared their heads again with a vengeance.

CHAPTER FIVE

THE SOFTWARE OF BUSINESS

THE WORLD CHANGES RAPIDLY, but organizations often do not. Despite the changed conditions that obtained in modern warfare by the time of World War I, for example, the British army continued to use outdated and often suicidal tactics. Its attacks on the Germans proceeded like clockwork—and in thoroughly predictable fashion. In the early morning hours the troops shelled the German positions, hoping to soften them up. Promptly at dawn, the artillery ceased and the assault began: Waves of British troops marched in close formation across no-man's-land. The Germans, having waited out the artillery barrage in their well-fortified bunkers, then emerged with machine guns and systematically mowed the British down. As Paul Fussell pointed out in *The Great War and Modern Memory,* other tactics were available.[1] The British could have feinted by suspending the shelling and then resuming it when the enemy machine gunners appeared. They could have advanced their troops behind a creeping barrage of artillery, or they could have had them run from cover to cover. Instead, for complicated cultural and organizational reasons, millions of men were marched sportingly to slaughter.

The intransigence of the British command starkly raises the question of why some organizations persist in behaving foolishly even in the face of certain and repeated disaster. Why do they refuse to change, even when all the conditions in which they must operate have changed so obviously and completely? Conversely, why do some organizations accept change and adapt to it smoothly and with the agility of a broken-field runner sidestepping a tackler? Why do others ossify even when faced with the certainty of cataclysmic disaster? What causes great names in the commercial world and great positions of international leadership, such as Pan American World Airways, to dry up and disappear?

The answers to these and similar questions are to be found in the cloudy realm of organizational behavior at least as much as in corporate strategy. Strategy is the sum of the decisions, objectives, and allocation of resources to which the firm is committed: the lines of business it pursues, the markets it enters, the competitive positioning it adopts. In effect, strategy is the "hardware" of corporate business. Organizational behavior is the collective pattern of action that grows out of the values, norms, and human preferences that add up to the corporate culture. In any enterprise, culture is, in effect, the "software," and organizational behavior—the way in which work gets done—is its result. A particular kind of software makes some kinds of work possible and some kinds impossible, no matter what the capacity of the hardware. To run properly, all organizations, regardless of their size, ownership, or purpose, need organizational software that is compatible with their hardware. Corporate culture must encourage organizational behavior that is compatible with corporate strategy. Large, complex, global organizations need sophisticated and robust organizational software—a single, well-understood corporate culture capable of functioning across many national cultures and in an environment of constantly changing conditions.

During the early 1980s, the essentially anthropological idea that companies, like cultures, function through formal and informal systems of rules, norms, and attitudes was all the rage. Bemused executives attempted to order up new corporate cultures overnight. But corporate culture begins in shared values and a common understanding of the organization's purpose, not in exhortation. When values are widely shared throughout an organization and everyone understands and accepts the fundamental purpose of the corporation, remarkable accomplishments can become commonplace. In the absence of shared values and an understanding of the organization's purpose, organizational torpor and sloth and inability to rise to the occasion often rule.

In a crisis, when people must act quickly under stress and the white-hot glare of publicity, the strength and character of the corporate culture become readily apparent. Instructive contrasts in corporate cultures are offered by two widely chronicled cases of corporate crisis — the poisonous tampering with Johnson & Johnson's popular pain remedy Tylenol and the discovery of benzene contamination in Perrier water.

In 1982, a murderous lunatic laced several bottles of Extra Strength Tylenol capsules with cyanide and placed them on the shelves of stores in the Chicago area. Seven people died as a result of ingesting the capsules. Something approaching a nationwide panic set in. Led by its chairman, James Burke, Johnson & Johnson didn't hesitate. Even though the company was in no way responsible for the tainted capsules, Johnson & Johnson did everything it could to inform and protect the public, at whatever cost to the company, even after the FDA, early in the crisis, gave the company a clean bill of health. The company opened its doors to the press. Instead of putting public relations executives out front to fend off reporters, Burke himself stood in the glare of the cameras almost daily and forthrightly answered whatever questions were put to him. The company immediately offered to exchange all Tylenol tablets for capsules. For the long term, it abandoned capsules for tamper-proof caplets. But by far the boldest action was Burke's decision to recall all 31 million bottles of Tylenol capsules from store shelves across the country, no matter how much it cost. The FDA opposed the decision on the grounds that it would increase the growing panic. The FBI objected that the recall would only teach terrorists how to bring down giant corporations. Nevertheless, Burke went ahead with the recall, at an after-tax cost to the company of some $50 million.[2]

Burke was not the only one to respond at Johnson & Johnson. The staff, at all levels, acted quickly and often without direction from the management. The company's speed and openness won praise from all directions. Following the incident, the reputations of the company and the product were actually enhanced, and Tylenol's share of the over-the-counter pain-reliever market, which had plunged from 35 percent to 7 percent in a matter of days after the incident, had climbed back up to 24 percent in fewer than three months and to 30 percent within a year, despite widespread predictions that the product would never recover.[3] Ultimately, a strong corporate culture that valued public trust as an end in itself saw the company through the wholly unforeseeable crisis.

By contrast, Source Perrier of France, long known for its secrecy, reacted with disdain for public opinion when in February 1990 some of its bottled sparkling mineral water, in several countries, was found to be contaminated with minute traces of benzene, a toxic solvent suspected as a cause of cancer. The drama began when the president of Perrier Group of America ordered a halt to distribution in North America because a North Carolina laboratory discovered the contamination. Officials of the company strongly contended that the contamination had affected only a few bottles shipped from France to the United States. Subsequently, however, distributors in Japan, Denmark, and the Netherlands began recalling the product. The company concluded that the contamination had occurred as a result of its failure to clean water filters at its plant. Belatedly realizing its mistake, Perrier finally undertook a worldwide recall. Though the company ultimately did the right thing—and at an after-tax cost of some $30 million—much of the damage had already been done by its initial defensiveness and slowness to react. Analysts predicted at the time that the fiasco could likely force the sale of the company, and, indeed, little over a year later, Perrier was acquired by Nestlé.[4]

What accounts for the difference in the behavior of Johnson & Johnson and Perrier? Why did the Johnson & Johnson employees, at every level of the company, instinctively do what was right without having to be told? Burke credited Johnson & Johnson's well-known Credo with creating the organization's ability to respond quickly and automatically to an unexpected event. The Johnson & Johnson Credo, which has been in existence for many years, states the basic values and the social as well as business purposes of the company. Created after several years of discussions with employees, the Credo is the first thing a visitor to Johnson & Johnson's headquarters in New Brunswick, New Jersey, sees. It is displayed on large tablets in the main reception area. Widely known and respected by the company's employees, the Credo begins: "We believe our *first responsibility* [italics added] is to the doctors, nurses and patients, to mothers and fathers and all others who use our products and services." Nothing could form a clearer basis for the quick and responsible actions that members of the company took, and nothing could offer clearer proof than those actions that the Credo is a living document at the company.

Although often greeted with polite disdain, especially in Europe, such statements of corporate values and mission as Johnson & Johnson's Credo, often called vision statements, are becoming more common. For transnational corporations, they are indispensable, provided that the senior management understands that a corporate culture cannot be created by fiat. A few weeks after the announcement of the intent to merge SmithKline and Beecham in April 1989, months before the merger was to be completed by a vote of the shareholders, I set to work drafting a statement of what we intended the new company to become. Entitled "The Promise of SmithKline Beecham," it included a statement of vision, a statement of purpose, the charter of our business, and an elaboration of the values and long-term corporate objectives in one document. The senior executives of the yet-to-be-merged companies carefully reviewed the initial draft, and work continued on it until they were satisfied. Their suggestions and changes not only improved this important document, but ensured that the key managers had a sense of ownership of its contents. "The Promise," as it came to be known, was reviewed and approved by the board of directors at the first board meeting following the shareholders' approval of the merger on July 27, 1989. The document was promptly distributed widely throughout the company. It was not all things to all people, nor did it answer all the questions and concerns the employees had about the reasons for the merger. It did, however, address those questions, and, above all, it provided a sense of higher purpose to the merger that went far beyond cost cutting and achieving the obvious efficiencies that the combination of two large companies brings about.

Looking back over the more than three years since the merger was announced, I believe the quick dissemination of "The Promise" was instrumental in bringing the two originating companies together quickly and relatively harmoniously. It provided a sense of mission and a clear statement of values. Most important, the fact that a number of senior managers participated in its framing assured that those values were widely shared before the final document even appeared. In the long run, of course, "The Promise" must be lived; only the senior managers' actual behavior will bring it to life for the organization as a whole.

A statement of vision and values is obviously more important for a large new company created by the merger of two old well-established companies than it is for many other companies. Yet today most global companies are as large or larger than SmithKline Beecham, and in many cases they, too, are composed of people brought to the company by merger or recruitment from other companies. Most important, such statements help to guide managers' behavior across many societies and ethnic cultures and across many functions and business units. It is difficult to imagine transnational companies operating successfully without the cultural direction and social binding that such statements help to create.

Ultimately, however, a corporate culture is created much more by the way people — particularly those in leadership positions — behave than by what they say or write. Employees are guided in their behavior by example more than by words, as Johnson & Johnson's employees were guided by the exemplary actions of their chairman. And it is collective behavior that defines what is now termed "corporate culture." If corporate leaders behave in a trusting manner to each other and to their fellow employees, then the groundwork is laid for a corporate culture that is characterized by mutual trust. A culture in which internal trust predominates, in turn, generates external trust with shareholders, customers, suppliers, and others who are asked to place their faith in the corporation. And in times of trouble, such a corporate culture can be a source of great strength. When a plant has to be closed, for example, corporate values take on real meaning. Then words like *integrity* and *human dignity* come to life in the way people behave and respond to each other's needs. But whether such ideals are enunciated in a document or widely shared through tradition and example, common values and a sense of purpose are the foundations upon which a positive corporate culture must be built.

On the other hand, strong, well-defined corporate cultures can just as easily become self-defeating obstacles to change. Change more than ever seems to be the order of the day, particularly for large transnational corporations. Consequently, the corporate landscape is strewn with examples of serious clashes between the established culture and the urgent need to change a corporate strategy.

Throughout 1991, the business press relentlessly recorded the difficulties at IBM as the global manufacturer, long considered the flagship of American industry, struggled to adapt to slowing market growth and increased competition.[5] In the wake of a huge write-down of assets and the announcement that 20,000 employees would be laid off, IBM's management was clearly charting a new course for the company. The very fact that IBM, long considered a haven for lifetime employment, had decided to lay off employees signaled a dramatic change in its approach. The idea was not only to become leaner but to become more responsive to market opportunities and to place greater responsibility—and accountability—on individual employees. Yet, judging from Chairman John Akers's public remarks, the work force at IBM was not responding. Akers's statements, both prepared and spontaneous, displayed uncharacteristic frustration, not with market conditions or competitors, but with his own employees. Remarks such as, "From now on, we're going to spend less time gassing around the water cooler and more time selling computers" were widely reprinted in the business press.

Ironically, people at IBM cannot remember seeing any water coolers in the company's facilities. Obviously, there is a mismatch between IBM's corporate strategy and the deeply rooted IBM culture. Perhaps Akers believes he doesn't have the time to work to change the organizational attitudes and patterns of behavior among his more than 250,000 employees. If not, his only alternative is to manage by exhortation. It won't work. Any significant change in corporate strategy requires a corresponding change in the way managers and employees see their duties and the patterns of work among them. It inevitably requires going back to basics with co-workers and addressing the shared vision of the future and commonly held values in the context of the new corporate goals.

The way people work together and think about themselves at IBM received another shock in October 1990 when executives of IBM and Apple announced a major strategic collaboration. The announcement astonished the computer industry not because the business logic wasn't sound, but because the cultures of the two companies differ so dramatically. In fact, Apple launched its successful Macintosh line of computers in the mid-1980s with a famous commercial that was a direct slap at the culture of Big Blue, as the IBM organization is known. The ad depicted men in blue suits marching like lemmings off a cliff. Apple unveiled another celebrated ad during the broadcast of the Super Bowl. Directed by Ridley Scott of *Blade Runner* fame, the futuristic ad evokes all the oppressive horror of George Orwell's *1984*. A giant talking head, projected on an enormous screen, harangues a vast meeting of gray functionaries. But help is on the way in the form of a brave young athlete who breaks into the meeting and hurls a sledge hammer through the screen, overthrowing the sclerotic bureaucracy. The implication was clear: Big Blue equals Big Brother. Apple equals individualism and vigor.

Now these same two companies have announced the boldest and most sweeping collaboration in the computer industry. Initially, they will concentrate on enabling communication between computers that use different programming languages and operating systems. For the longer term, they hope to develop superfast microprocessors. Most important, they will cooperate to create entirely new, revolutionary software to link computers and ordinary household appliances, thereby bridging the gap between computers and consumer electronics products. John Sculley, president of Apple, stated, "This relationship touches potentially every area of importance in the 1990s in terms of foundation technologies."[6]

Many observers see the collaboration as a response to the dictates of global competition. They suggest that by combining through these joint projects, Apple and IBM are coming to grips with the challenge from Japan. Certainly, the respective strengths of the two companies are complementary. Apple's dedication to software, particularly to the "end-user interface," (that part of the program the user actually experiences) and IBM's tremendous installed base in businesses, the design of advanced microprocessors, and systems capability make for a potentially powerful combination.

But the collaboration also raises grave doubts. There is a great disparity in the size of the two collaborators—$69 billion in revenues for IBM versus $6.3 billion for Apple. More important, the two companies' nearly opposite organizational traditions and patterns of behavior are likely to clash. IBM has always been known for its stolid, "buttoned-down," and regimented approach (so acidly satirized by Apple in its commercials), whereas Apple, since its founding in a garage, has been known for its loose, somewhat rebellious and iconoclastic corporate culture. In California, the shock caused by the announced collaboration has been profound—Apple is "sleeping with the enemy." Among IBM employees, the Apple collaboration is only one among many disturbing changes that have descended on them from the corporate suite. One measure of the difficulty of bringing these two cultures together lies in the fact that fully five months were required to decide on a chief executive for the venture. Ultimately, the success or failure of the collaboration will not be decided by the quality of technology or the logic underpinning the various joint ventures. It will be decided by the thousands of engineers, programmers, and project managers who must work together on a daily basis but come from different organizational cultures and patterns of behavior.

The current difficulties facing the automobile industry offer another example of the clash between culture and change on a global scale. The advanced manufacturing techniques emanating from Japan that give Japanese competitors such tremendous advantages in productivity and costs over their American and European counterparts are well known in the United States and Great Britain. United Motors in California, Honda in Ohio, and Nissan in Tennessee have all successfully applied these techniques with their American work forces. Nissan and Honda are performing in Britain in similar fashion with British workers. Honda works closely in Britain with Rover, a division of British Aerospace, to apply advanced manufacturing techniques to the Rover and Range Rover series of vehicles. Nissan owns and operates a large plant in Sunderland that is currently producing about 240,000 vehicles annually for sale in Britain and the common market.

For more than a decade, Toyota and GM have operated United Motors, a joint company in Fremont, California, with the express purpose of providing a training ground for GM managers in the application of total quality management, just-in-time manufacturing, and flexible manufacturing systems. And for decades GM, Ford, and Chrysler have been purchasing important components, indeed in some cases entire cars, from Japan. Chrysler's recently abandoned joint venture in Illinois with Mitsubishi Motors in Diamond Star Motors dates back to 1985. Ford owns 25 percent of Mazda, and GM owns 37.5 percent of Isuzu. These companies are not strangers to each other, nor are they unfamiliar with how the others go about their business.

But if there are no secrets in the automobile industry, one wonders why advanced manufacturing techniques are not being applied by all car companies. The question is more germane, given that these techniques have been used with great success by many non-Japanese companies operating in the United States and Europe—Milliken in the textile business, Hewlett-Packard in computers and sophisticated instruments, Xerox in office copiers, and Beckman Instruments in advanced analytical and diagnostic instruments. If these non-Japanese companies can do it, why can't GM? The answer lies in deeply ingrained patterns of organizational behavior, in cast-iron cultural values, and in leadership practices that provide the strongest barriers to change.

Ironically, it is often the most successful companies that find it most difficult to change their managerial attitudes and organizational habits. Few companies enjoyed more success in the three decades following World War II than did GM. In 1947 Peter Drucker, in his ground-breaking book *Concept of the Corporation,* extolled GM as the best example of the modern American corporation and pioneer of many of the most advanced managerial techniques. In 1991, he said that GM has become "a victim of its own success."[7] He was referring, of course, to the hallowed managerial practices that once worked well for GM, but now present the most impenetrable obstacles to the acceptance of change. That is the core of the problem for the company. The people who run GM do not lack desire, nor are they ignorant of what must be done to compete with the Japanese in manufacturing. But the enormous institutionalized organizational patterns of behavior that continue to focus on ways of doing work that are out of step with advanced production techniques and current market realities apparently render the company powerless to do other than it has always done.

Anecdotes abound about GM's often overbearing, rigid management style. One supplier is described as rolling his eyes when speaking of an effort to trim costs; an effort that was brought to failure inside GM's giant bureaucracy. A Chevrolet dealer is reported to have complained that his telephone calls to divisional headquarters were not answered.[8] Managers complain about mountains of paperwork, endless and often inconclusive meetings, and vicious office politics. Petty rules, such as the requirement that managers leave a clean desk at quitting time, focus on appearance, rather than substance.

GM's hierarchical management style and its rigid system of controls clash directly with the organizational element that is essential for advanced manufacturing: the involvement of every manager and every worker in continual improvement. That is the key to advanced manufacturing—not automation, not robotics, and certainly not Taylorite applications of them. To use the current jargon, the "empowerment" of each individual to take the initiative in systematic ways to improve the productivity of the manufacturing process is fundamental to any program of continual improvement. Empowerment pushes responsibility downward and outward. It requires mutual trust among managers and workers, respect for the intelligence of all employees, and a willingness to experiment.

Many companies are moving to empower their employees. Du Pont is giving greater responsibility to middle managers in the interest of getting products to market more quickly, while PepsiCo is attempting to push decision making to ever lower levels.[9] Johnson & Johnson has been doing it for decades, believing that small, self-governing units are more responsive to markets and more accountable. Even some companies that have earned fearsome reputations for their summary treatment of employees have begun to see the virtue of such empowerment. In an extraordinary turnabout, General Electric's chairman John F. Welch, long noted for his autocratic (and highly successful) management style, called for—in the company's 1991 annual report—his managers to have "the self-confidence to empower others and behave in a boundaryless fashion."[10] Welch and vice chairman Edward E. Hood, Jr., wrote: "In an environment where we must have every good idea from every man and woman in the organization, we cannot afford management styles that suppress and intimidate." They further stated that the ability to help dictatorial managers to change "will be the ultimate test of our commitment to the transformation of this company and will determine the future of the mutual trust and respect we are building."

General Electric has already seen concrete evidence of the improvement that the empowerment of employees can bring. At its plant in Schenectady, New York, teams of hourly workers operate $20 million worth of new milling machines that they specified, tested, and approved for purchase. As a result, they have reduced the time required to fabricate some critical components of steam turbines by 80 percent. As Welch wrote to his stockholders, "It is embarrassing to reflect that for probably 80 or 90 years, we've been dictating equipment needs and managing people who knew how to do things much faster and better than we did."[11]

GM's command-and-control mentality, on the military model, withholds responsibility from workers and managers alike and, in the long run, encourages a hierarchical separation from them not unlike that of the British officer corps from the enlisted men in World War I. Just how deep that separation runs in GM was unwittingly revealed in an advertisement the company unveiled during Super Bowl XXVI in January 1992 as part of its "Putting Quality on the Road" campaign. In the ad, a well-dressed female GM executive is speaking to a group of casually dressed workers, telling them about a "profound change" taking place: American workers are once again doing high-quality work. She exhorts them to greater effort, reminding them how angry it made them as children when someone told them they couldn't accomplish something. No doubt the ad is meant to show a dynamic company moving forward, determined to produce high-quality cars. But it unintentionally suggests that the decline in quality was the fault of the workers in the first place. Moreover, it suggests, also unwittingly, that the workers must be appealed to as children.

The GM executives, who, after all, approved the ads, apparently refuse to take responsibility for their company's problems. Their disdain for their workers is so deeply ingrained that it inadvertently finds its way even into their advertisements. A Toyota Camry advertisement aired on the same Super Bowl broadcast offers an instructive contrast. Toyota proudly presents its American workers at its Georgetown, Kentucky, plant. Toyota takes pride in its work force, whereas GM lectures its workers.

A visit to Honda's Marysville, Ohio, plant even more concretely reveals the contrast in the organizational behavior of GM and its Japanese competitors.[12] Honda's top manufacturing executive, for example, dresses in grease-stained overalls, has a desk in a room shared with forty other people, and is a constant presence on the manufacturing line. At GM, the plant manager wears a business suit, spends much of his time at meetings with other executives, and occupies the corner office on the top floor. And though in most GM plants workers are urged to become more involved in quality control, designing parts, and dealing directly with suppliers, many supervisors and managers still wear white shirts and neckties and insist on exercising the authority they have always enjoyed.

With the December 1991 announcement of the closure of

twenty-one unidentified plants and the elimination of 74,000 unidentified jobs, no one at GM knows whether he or she will be in or out of GM's future. And the survivors of the cuts are likely to remember the anguish and uncertainty the company put them through. In such circumstances, it's hard to expect a positive attitude toward any kind of change. Downsizing may be necessary to adjust capacity to the realities of demand, but managed in this fashion, it cannot contribute positively to a change in an organization's culture.

Even after the plants to be closed and jobs to be eliminated are identified, it will be difficult to imagine productivity improving substantially in traditional American automotive factories until the top managers' behavior demonstrates on a daily basis to all employees that organizational habits must change to fit the dictates of the new corporate strategy. Such a change by senior managers requires their absolute commitment to the long-term future of the corporation and their willingness to place the interests of the corporation, including those of the employees and customers, above those of the short-term interests of the executives and shareholders. Perhaps, instead of complaining about "uneven playing fields" in foreign trade, senior executives would do well to look at their own practices and the general environment for assessing corporate and managerial performance.

The difficulties adapting organizational behavior to changing circumstances are not peculiar to large American corporations. Despite its problems at home, GM was recently called upon by Isuzu Motors to supply a key executive for its Tokyo headquarters. GM owns a substantial portion of Isuzu shares, 37.5 percent, much larger than any other shareholder, and operates eight joint ventures with Isuzu around the world, including jointly owned companies in Australia and the Middle East. In addition, Isuzu manufactures the Geo Storm model that GM imports and distributes in the American market. GM buys Isuzu diesel engines for the United States and assembles and sells Isuzu light commercial trucks in Africa and Asia. In a surprise press release in December 1991, Isuzu named an American executive from GM to its second highest management post following a series of mounting operating losses in the company and a major reorganization of its head office in Tokyo.[13]

The ties between Isuzu and GM are obviously strong and have been built over several decades. Still, I can't think of another example of a major Japanese company seeking managerial help from a foreign company, even one that holds a substantial number of its shares. Indeed, there are few, if any, examples of non-Japanese managers reaching senior executive levels in Japanese companies. The conventional wisdom has been that foreign executives, even those with fluency in the language and long service with the company, would not be able to function in Japanese organizations, with their distinctively Japanese and deeply entrenched cultural patterns of behavior and value systems. The need for *nemawashi* (consensus building) and unfailing loyalty to the company, rather than to the individual, are two of the many cultural barriers that are often invoked.

But times are changing in Japan, just as they are elsewhere. The effects of global interdependence are apparent in the choice of the American executive appointed to the new position in Isuzu. Before taking on the job at Isuzu, the executive served GM on three continents, gaining direct experience in the markets of the triad regions. Previously, he had been group director of GM's Chevrolet-Pontiac-Canada Division; did strategic planning for GM in Europe; and, in his last position with the Chevrolet division, worked with Isuzu on Geo Storm sales.

The unique attributes of the Japanese organizational culture that make it difficult for foreign executives to rise to positions of corporate responsibility often make it equally difficult for otherwise well-managed and competitive Japanese companies to become global players. Kao Soap, Procter & Gamble's great Japanese rival, is an example. Kao is a well-established, extremely successful manufacturer of detergent, soap, and consumer products. It has applied advanced manufacturing techniques with great success to its diverse line of consumer products and is a formidable competitor in the Japanese market. Kao's sensitivity and ability to identify completely with its customers in Japan are legendary. A story is told of a consumer complaint coming to Kao headquarters from a certain neighborhood in Tokyo regarding Kao's laundry soap. The customer claimed that the soap just didn't seem to work as well as the company claimed. After detailed investigation, Kao managers determined that the neighborhood in question, along with a few other sections of Tokyo, had especially hard water. The company promptly reformulated a special brand of laundry detergent for high pH water and marketed its new formulation only in the pinpointed districts. Its market share shot up, and competitors wishing to penetrate those neighborhoods now face an impossible task.

Despite its excellent products and exquisite sensitivity to local conditions in Japan, Kao has yet to develop any significant international business. Of course, competition from established global players, such as Unilever and Procter & Gamble, is strong everywhere, but Kao's Japanese managers don't seem to be able to adapt their well-honed Japanese cultural sensitivities to foreign environments. Likewise, by their own admission, Kao's managers have been unable to accept foreigners of stature into management positions in their company. Consequently, to the delight of Unilever and Procter & Gamble, Kao remains a giant in Japan, but a runt on the global market.

How do you change a corporate culture? Widely shared and agreed-upon vision statements help, as I have said, but in the long run it's not what people say but what they do that adds up to culture. Another answer — so simple to say and so difficult to do — is to remake the company and culture will follow. But, of course, it's a chicken-and-egg proposition. A willingness to remake the company suggests that the company's culture has already changed. To an extent, that's the case. A company that acts decisively and intelligently in the face of the global imperative already has a robust culture, one that, at the least, is open to change. Nevertheless, for companies that are still groping their way toward a viable culture, it is possible to come at the problem from the other direction. In fact, it may be their only realistic chance of survival. First, they must adopt a multidimensional transnational strategy. But they can't stop with that strategy. They must analyze the kind of organizational behavior such a strategy requires and then plan and work relentlessly to encourage it. Companies with a new strategy and structure will, with proper leadership, elaborate and develop the kind of culture required not only to make the leap but to land on their feet. Above all, it is important for the senior managers to understand and articulate the essential complementarity of the strategy and the organizational culture. Focusing on one while ignoring the other inevitably leads to frustration and failure. Usually, it is best to begin with a careful examination of the organizational behavior necessary to implement the chosen strategy fully. A conceptual approach runs along these lines:

• Begin by recalling that a transnational strategy may be conceptualized as a three-dimensional cube, to keep in view the structural integrity and interrelationships of its three chief elements: scale, skills, and scope:

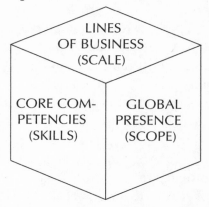

LINES
OF BUSINESS
(SCALE)

CORE COM-
PETENCIES
(SKILLS)

GLOBAL
PRESENCE
(SCOPE)

• Now ask what particular kinds of organizational behavior are essential to the key strategic elements of skills, scale, and scope in the company. What must be done on a daily basis to enhance core competencies? How do we make sure we are effectively leveraging our global-scale advantages and local-scale requirements under constantly changing conditions? What habits and attitudes are necessary for competing in the world's markets, taken together and individually? Obviously, many kinds of organizational behavior are desirable in any enterprise, but the task is to focus on those practices that are at the heart of a successful transnational strategy for a given corporation.

In examining core competencies, one would find that total quality management, applied with such success by high-performing Japanese companies, would be high on the list of desirable organizational behavior. As I showed earlier, the results are often dramatic. Greatly improved quality lowers costs while improving customer satisfaction. Soon it spreads to other functions throughout the company, often with similarly dramatic results. At NEC, for example, total quality management is a comprehensive management approach that is found throughout the company: in research, product development, manufacturing, new product planning, and sales and marketing.

The basic organizational requirement of total quality management is a high level of mutual trust—sometimes called a risk-free environment—at all levels of the company, which facilitates the employees' involvement in planning and improving the way work is done. The practice requires a highly disciplined systematic analysis and understanding of work processes. The people doing the work, wherever it is performed—on the production floor, in the laboratory, or on the loading dock—participate directly in the analysis and then take direct responsibility for suggesting ways to improve the way work is done.

In addition to a high level of mutual trust, the organizational prerequisites for a successful program of continual improvement are excellent training in the techniques of analysis and work processes; the true delegation of authority to the lowest levels; a system of control that is oriented toward process as much as to results; and, finally, a system of reward that is directed to positive reinforcement rather than to punishment. In sum, these prerequisites are the essentials of a successful organizational culture. Continual improvement is the result of such a culture.

When fully implemented in an organization, continual improvement in all essential work becomes the norm of the organization. Productivity often improves by orders of magnitude. Thus the core competencies—the vital skills that differentiate the company and provide the ongoing sources of competitive strength—are honed, polished, and enhanced by the very people who are most directly involved in doing the work.

Building a culture oriented toward continual improvement takes many years, but, as I have said, it is best to begin with the work that is considered vital to the implementation of the company's strategy. In the pharmaceutical business that work would certainly include the development of new products, an area in which the competitive battles are won and lost. In the consumer-products business it may include advertising and promotion. In advanced instruments it would certainly include design and engineering and production.

Eventually, a culture that is dedicated to continual improvement will permeate the entire organization. All functions, in all lines of business, in markets all around the world, become engines of continual improvement. A few leading Japanese companies, including Canon, NEC, and Fuji Xerox, are moving toward such an organizational culture. In the West, companies, such as Millekin,

Beckman Instruments, and Hewlett-Packard, although perhaps not as far along as the Japanese companies, have made great strides in recent years. And, of course, many Japanese "transplant" factories successfully apply continual improvement techniques in a Western setting.

Boeing, with its core competence in the integration and design of systems, offers a splendid example of improved productivity linked to skills. It is pushing for radical improvement in its core competence by designing the 777 entirely on computers, creating the world's first "paperless" airplane.[14] Computer design will allow Boeing not only to design the plane faster, but to do it right the first time, giving the plane a chance to become the first two-engine jet to win immediate certification from the Federal Aviation Administration for over-the-ocean flights.

The pattern of organizational behavior that is usually applied for the strategic pursuit of advantages in scale, globally and locally, is constant *learning and communication.* It is often said that information is now chief among what economists used to call factors of production (which also include capital, facilities and equipment, and labor). Acquiring information and disseminating it throughout a company are certainly the keys to the transnational application of scale. Scale requires learning and communication because it is not just a simple matter of establishing economies of scale, but the constant and supple allocation of resources worldwide. In the pharmaceutical business, for example, both the discovery and development of new products, conducted on a global basis, are areas of advantage in scale for the large transnational pharmaceutical companies. But scale yields a competitive advantage only when it is used effectively. And effective use requires that people have full knowledge of the company's technologies and strategies and have the flexibility to apply them across national borders, as well as functional lines. A company's ability to use all the modern techniques of communication, including routine global videoconferencing, for example, is as or more important than is sheer size.

Dow Chemical's worldwide sourcing system stands as an example of learning and communication tied to scale.[15] With more than 100 production facilities in twenty-nine countries, the company certainly operates on a global scale. But it leverages that scale most effectively by requiring the separate sales and marketing functions in each geographic area to supply their territories with Dow products at the lowest possible cost. That is, they are not required to take products from any particular manufacturing facility, even in their own territories. Moreover, decisions about sources can be challenged by any internal customer or any alternate source of supply in the company. Challenges trigger a global study to see if the lowest-cost source is being used. The system encourages manufacturing plants to keep costs down and sales departments to seek meaningful differences in the cost of supplies. The key to the system is the rapid worldwide exchange of data among the managers who really need the information. Managers throughout the global system can gain immediate access to detailed information on costs, revenues, and profits for any Dow product in any geographic territory. Thus the company maximizes its scale advantages through widely shared information among managers who are empowered to press those advantages across borders.

With respect to scope, the desirable pattern of organizational behavior stresses *responsiveness to customers*. In each of the many local markets that make up the global market, a focus on customers means honoring different cultural values, striving to meet local tastes, and working to fulfill expectations. It means fitting the company's products, services, and ways of doing business into particular ways of life. Obviously, responsiveness to customers is an aspect of localization, but it has a global component as well. It means constantly striving for customer satisfaction with agreed corporate standards and operating at uniformly high ethical standards the world over, especially with regard to the safety and efficacy of products.

Responsiveness to customers has been applied with great success in businesses as disparate as SmithKline Beecham Clinical Laboratories and Appleton Papers, which produces paper products. In both cases, a total orientation to customer satisfaction has transformed the organizational culture throughout the company, bringing the business strategy to life for every employee. The business results are impressive in all respects, but what is even more important, both companies have created an almost unassailable position of competitive advantage with their customers.

These, then, are the three distinct patterns of desirable organizational behavior: (1) the enhancement of productivity through continual improvement, (2) learning and communicating on a global scale, and (3) a total focus on customer responsiveness. Once it is successfully implemented in an organization, each pattern of behavior takes on a life of its own, gaining momentum and spreading to different lines of business and across borders and functions. Before long, the patterns interweave. A focus on customers becomes an integral part of total quality management, as does a bias toward communication and learning, which, in turn, reinforces the training and development of personnel. As the patterns fuse, a distinct company culture is formed that reinforces the company's competitive strategy. The company develops, in effect, an integrated personality with distinct and recognizable features that distinguish it from its competitors and make it readily identifiable.

The three dimensions of corporate culture can be visualized as a cube. Just as with the dimensions of strategy, they are interdependent, each relying on the other to create an organizational culture of strength and structural integrity.

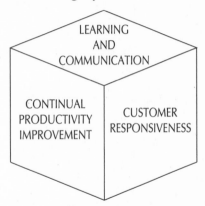

The three dimensions of organizational behavior, fused to form a definite company culture, in turn, interrelate intimately with the three dimensions of a transnational corporate strategy. For example, responding to customers in various local markets means determining which aspects of the product or business can be standardized globally and which aspects must be tailored to local tastes. The exchange of information ultimately speaks to the requirements of scale. Similarly, improving productivity also means organization-wide exchanges of information and learning. Or, to come at it from the direction of strategy, the interrelationship of the strategic elements—skill is scale is scope—should mean that the behavior essential to one strategic dimension will penetrate the other dimensions, as the two cubes, which now embody organizational behavior as well as strategy, are meant to suggest.

But at this point, the conception represents an incomplete model. There must be a mechanism for linking behavior with transnational strategy in such a way that the synergies implicit in a multidimensional strategy are achieved. Returning to the metaphor used in the beginning of this chapter, if corporate strategy is the hardware and organizational patterns of behavior are the software, the operating system that is the essential link between the two is the organizational structure.

CHAPTER SIX

MELODIOUS ARCHITECTURE

TWENTY YEARS AGO I worked as a management consultant with Louis A. Allen, a great student of management and author of numerous books on management as a profession. Allen described organizational structure as the way work is identified and grouped and, through the process of delegation, assigned to people.[1] The organization's structure, which defines its decision-making authority, is the connecting fiber between corporate strategy and organizational behavior. When things are working properly, the organization's structure channels organizational behavior in directions prescribed by its strategy.

Just as in other aspects of corporate management, structure can be strong or weak, old or new, conservative or progressive. The compatibility of structure with corporate strategic objectives and the realities of organizational behavior can greatly affect the way a company goes about its business and its competitive performance. As all the management textbooks say, structure should be the servant of strategy, but frequently strategy serves structure. An old structure can scuttle a new strategy. Equally, in real life, structure often disconnects strategy from organizational behavior.

In practical terms, organizational structure defines hierarchies; job titles; and, most important, rank and personal income. In other words, it is the organization's structure that brings home most of the awards and rewards that are meaningful to people. It is no wonder then that organizational structure is the aspect of corporate life that is most resistant to change and, even under heavy pressure, is amazingly resilient. Strategy may change, organizational culture may change with it, but unless the structure also adapts to the needed change, all efforts may fail.

Historically, multinational corporations have tended to structure their organizations by geographic location with strong, semiautonomous local operating companies. International corporations have emphasized strong worldwide product structures. As a result, the full set of business functions soon tends to become global in international companies and highly local in multinational companies. But neither form of organizational structure simultaneously captures the kinds of global-local synergies of skills, scale, and scope now considered necessary by aggressive transnational companies.

Behind both multinational and international organizational structures stands the traditional notion of hierarchy, often embodied in the divisional organizational structure that was pioneered by Du Pont and brought to its zenith by GM. In *Concept of the Corporation*, a seminal book first published in 1947 and reprinted many times thereafter, Peter Drucker carefully analyzed GM's divisional structure and advocated its virtues to a wide audience.[2] At the time Drucker examined GM, the company had clear strategies for each of its five automobile divisions—Chevrolet, Pontiac, Oldsmobile, Buick, and Cadillac—based on the different economic strata of their customers. The five divisions allowed GM to implement its corporate strategy of reaching the full spectrum of possible customers with appropriate models and marketing appeal. Each division offered its market relatively few models and each division's products differed distinctively from the products of the other divisions. The offering of relatively few models enabled long manufacturing runs and kept costs low. Profits were high and the employees' productivity led the automotive world. The divisional structure served the reality of the market perfectly. It was employed by GM in many countries and is still emulated, with various degrees of success, by numerous companies around the world.

Forty years later almost everything about the automobile market, the competition, and the techniques of production have changed. The GM structure has not. In fact, some observers believe that the deeply imbedded strength of GM's traditional divisional structure impedes the strategic and organizational changes the company so badly needs to make. Yet when the latest round of plant closures and layoffs was announced in December 1991, Chairman Robert Stempel went out of his way to state that the traditional GM structure, consisting of five divisions, each with its own management, support staff, factories, dealerships, and marketing organizations, would not be changed. He reaffirmed this structure even though self-image and life-style are now much greater determinants of consumers' purchasing decisions than are economic strata.

The five GM divisions now spread their models so they overlap target groups of customers. The number of models has increased manyfold as producers design for and target ever smaller market segments, thereby reducing production runs and ceding cost and marketing advantages to competitors that use flexible production methods. At GM, costs are up, profits are down, and productivity is lagging far behind that of its key competitors. The structure no longer serves the reality of GM's market or its apparent strategy and the needed changes in organizational behavior.

During the heyday of the industrial conglomerates, the divisional structure described by Drucker was carried to extremes. The conglomerates claimed they could manage any kind of business by applying the techniques developed by Du Pont and GM during the 1930s and 1940s. The common thread was thought to be financial management based on the false assumption that all businesses yield a common result—money. Today, however, former conglomerates, including British American Tobacco, Gulf & Western, and ITT, among many others, have been forced by competitive pressures or irate shareholders to shed many of their unrelated businesses. Managerial speeches and annual letters to the shareholders now use terms, such as *focused; core businesses;* and *shared resources, shared technology* in describing an "integrated" business strategy.

Nevertheless, the divisional structure remains the most common form of corporate organization, perhaps because it has the cardinal virtues of simplicity and a clear chain of command. But life is increasingly complex, and the special strategic and organizational demands on transnational companies make the classic divisional form of organization correspondingly less appropriate. The very simplicity of the divisional structure handicaps transnational corporations that are pursuing the twin goals of local responsiveness and global scale. Transnationals require some form of matrix structure so that crucial functions, such as information technology, manufacturing, and the development of new products, can be managed to gain a global advantage while the design, marketing, and sales of products are directed with exquisite local sensitivity.

Yet the full-blown matrix organization, which was used extensively in the defense industry during the military buildup of the 1960s and 1970s, suffers from serious disadvantages. This structure, in which functional departments, such as new-product development, product design, marketing, and so on, interlock at every level with product-line divisions, is far too cumbersome and confusing to operate on a global scale for long periods. Matrix organizations seem to work best with specific time-limited projects. But over more extended periods, they can become muscle bound and paralyzed by paperwork and the bureaucratic process.

The structural solution for transnational companies seems to be emerging in the form of modified, matrix-based, multifunctional teams. The objectives of transnational business place great importance on obtaining the advantages of both scale and skills and on pressing these advantages home within and across markets around the world. By definition, the attainment of these objectives requires cutting aggressively across organizational boundaries just as much as across national borders. That is, organizational structures must be created in which common business functions can be managed to achieve the advantages of scale and critical core competencies are kept clearly in view so they can be continually enhanced and sharpened in all business and geographic sectors. Managers must break down the boundaries of the divisional structure. As the interior walls fall — and they are already coming down in a number of advanced transnational companies — organizations apply a form of pragmatic matrix management in which flexible teams of managers, representing different functions, disciplines, and cultures, are deployed to deal with opportunities or issues that are strategically important. Until a better label appears, one may call it *flexible matrix management*.

The transnational flexible matrix is being applied within *well-focused businesses* operating *globally* in which the matrix consists of both local and functional command and decision structures. The essential load-bearing elements of the organizational structure are strong local management teams with the prime responsibility for customer-focused functions, including sales; marketing; and, where appropriate, the design of products and management. Meanwhile, global efficiencies are pursued at the corporate level by functional groups, such as manufacturing, information technologies, and research and development of new products, with worldwide responsibility.

The transnational flexible matrix must be kept simple; it must eliminate layers of management, not generate new ones. An ill-designed matrix can be even more hierarchical, bureaucratic, and unwieldy than can a divisional structure. Such a poorly conceived matrix can become not only tall, like the hierarchical divisional model, but broad, rising high above the disenfranchised employee in the manner of the old pyramidal structures, but without ever appearing to come to a point. Ideally, the transnational flexible matrix broadens spans of control to flatten hierarchies and empower employees. It must also work along the global and local dimensions simultaneously without subjugating employees further by making them serve two masters. On the other hand, the matrix must not divide loyalties between the local and the global, leading to turf wars and poisonous organizational politics. In allocating responsibility along two dimensions at once—the global and the local—the transnational matrix broadly serves the transnational strategy by keeping the company moving simultaneously on both tracks.

A further word of caution about structure in general is in order. It was Friedrich von Schelling, the nineteenth-century German philosopher, who once described architecture as frozen music. Schelling's observation is memorable not only because it makes us see architecture in a new way, but because it makes us meditate on the concept of structure itself. In organizational design, the notion of *structure* is essentially an architectural metaphor. I have used it here in writing about "load-bearing" elements. But an organization is dynamic and temporal like music, not static and spatial like archi-tecture. Structure must channel organizational behavior into strat-egy, not simply provide a static reflection of strategy. It is possible to establish a transnational matrix that abstractly mimics the two dimensions of global strategy, but fails to provide the required dynamism. Structure then becomes a frozen strategy.

Thus the matrix alone is not enough to evoke and channel the organizational behavior that is essential to a transnational strategy. The matrix identifies, groups, and allocates the work, to be sure. But the success of the enterprise depends on the day-to-day activities of thousands of employees who respond to customers, work to improve productivity, and share knowledge and information. As I noted in Chapter Five, each of those essential organizational activities must be integrative, qualitative, and timely. In the world of transnational competition, integrated, high-quality information must be brought to bear fast. In the organizational structure toward which transnational companies are evolving, the primary structural element for evoking such behavior is the multidisciplinary team that is invested with powerful decision-making authority.

Managers are increasingly using multidisciplinary project teams to identify problems and to plan and recommend solutions. Vested with the authority to make decisions, teams that are multilevel and multicultural, as well as multidisciplinary, enable a faster response and more sensitive understanding of important local and global nuances. Their widespread use contributes to reductions in levels of management. Teams can be created and redeployed quickly. Most of all, they are splendid environments for organizational learning and for redirecting patterns of behavior. In technology-intensive organizations, especially in research and development, team-oriented management structures have become the norm.

But the complexities of rapid technological change and rapidly shifting planning assumptions don't stop with research and development. Similarly, yet coincidentally, the advanced production techniques now being applied in many businesses use teams of people to establish the need for strategic and organizational change and to develop specific plans for improving methods and processes. Inevitably, teams bring together people who are responsible for getting the work done and require a considerable delegation of authority in an atmosphere of trust. As total quality management, just-in-time manufacturing, and flexible production techniques take hold in companies, the effects soon spread beyond the production floor to encompass all the important business functions. When they do, multidisciplinary teams become the primary mode of organizational structure throughout the organization.

The movement toward widespread use of teams representing different disciplines, different functions, and different geographic perspectives is breaking through traditional organizational barriers.

Such teams become agents of change, but of change for a clear and well-defined purpose. And as internal walls come tumbling down, a new, more flexible organizational form arises in which teamwork becomes the organizational function and teams themselves, the form.

NEC, the Japanese computer company, illustrates how the use of multidisciplinary teams typically spreads through a company to meet global strategic imperatives. With 118,000 employees, forty-nine factories in Japan and twenty-nine in other countries, and worldwide sales of $26 billion, NEC is becoming a truly global company, well focused on its core businesses of telecommunications, computers, and semiconductors and intent on pursuing its clearly stated strategy of linking computer and communications technologies. Taking the view that a company's manufacturing excellence is reflected in the least amount of work-in-progress inventory, NEC began a program in 1989 to halve its total lead time from receiving an order to shipping the product to the customer.[3] Previous attempts to reduce the inventory had been left to the line, with staff, in the manner of staffs since time immemorial, merely advising and criticizing. The company had failed to heed W. Edwards Deming's admonition that the entire organization, from the formulation of strategy to its daily implementation, must be designed with quality in mind; it cannot be relegated to only one or two functional areas.[4] This time around, however, NEC first set out to involve the entire company in the effort, in effect, remaking the culture of the corporation through a variety of participative learning and informational activities. Then three model plants, one in each of NEC's core businesses, were selected to attempt breakthrough innovations in reducing the lead time, with a view to disseminating the results throughout the company's manufacturing operations.

The key to the program's success was a thirteen-member multidisciplinary team made up of specialists from corporate staff divisions, such as manufacturing, systems analysis, and accounting, working with members of the manufacturing subsidiaries and the operating divisions. In a remarkably short time, the team achieved impressive results at the three model plants. In two years, NEC's microwave communications plant cut the lead time from ninety-eight to thirty-nine days. After only one year, the lead time at the office automation equipment plant dropped from twenty-seven days to five days, and the plant that makes electron devices slashed its lead time from twenty-two days to nine days.

From manufacturing, the team concept then spread to the development of new products. Previously, the development of new products had proceeded sequentially. First a new product was conceived and designed. After the design was reviewed, a prototype was manufactured and evaluated. Finally, mass-production design and retooling began. Functions were kept rigidly separated. Research and development threw the concept over the wall to design. Design then dropped it in the mail to manufacturing, which eventually passed it on to marketing and sales. Sometimes one of the functional areas threw it back, resulting in costly and time-consuming changes in the product. The entire process, from specification of the product to the start of production, usually required from six to eight months. But to develop its first notebook personal computer (PC), the company broke down the barriers between the functional areas, bringing them together in a team from the very inception of the product.

The effort was more than an experiment. NEC had always commanded more than 50 percent of the PC market in Japan, until Toshiba introduced the first notebook PC there. Within a matter of weeks, NEC's market share plummeted from 52 percent to approximately 25 percent, while Toshiba's skyrocketed from a 2 percent share to more than 30 percent.

NEC's new-product team went to work. Its task was to consider from the outset all aspects of the product's life cycle — the requirements of users, quality, cost, and product support — and to design them in from the first. Called "concurrent engineering," the process eliminates the endless tinkering with specifications by functional areas at each stage of the development process. Specifications can be frozen at an early stage of development; retooling can begin quickly; the writing of documentation can proceed without fear of last-minute changes; and the whole process can be managed with a clear strategic goal in mind, part of which is based on the product's timely introduction.

NEC's team was able to eliminate the prototype stage and to pass technical evaluations early. The time required for specifying the product, formerly one to three months, was cut to two weeks. Far from compromising the design, this accelerated, integrated approach yielded a design that required *no* engineering changes after production began and that produced a product that passes the key electromagnetic-interference test on the first attempt. As a result, the product was developed in 3.5 months, less than half the time previously required.

Had NEC developed the product in the old way, it estimates that its market share would have dropped even further, perhaps as low as 10 percent. However, through the timely introduction of its new notebook PC, it quickly regained its former market share and even greatly exceeded it, achieving a 75 percent share. Fresh from its success in the development of new products, NEC is now spreading the program throughout the company.

Teams can improve the performance of many kinds of companies, but when a company is a transnational, their use becomes doubly important in encouraging supple organizational behavior across borders, as well as across boundaries. For example, in almost any organization that uses teams, communication and learning will occur at a faster pace, with information flowing across all functional boundaries at once, instead of inching along through sequential steps of a process. In a transnational company, however, the information must flow across borders if the company is to realize such advantages of a global operation as the ability to roll out high value-added products in many world markets simultaneously. Teams also consider customers' concerns in the earliest stages of development—and they sometimes include the customers themselves as members. Responsiveness to customers is no longer merely a matter of honoring warranties or of grudgingly customizing a product for a favored customer long after the product is in production; it is a matter of having a customer-driven product-specification process from the beginning. (Apple Computer, for example, sends employees to participate in Apple user groups, the hobbyists who often determine the uses to which products are actually put.) Furthermore, the timely delivery of new products that teams achieve is itself a feature of responsiveness to customers, for many of whom time is paramount. Such responsiveness is important to almost any company, but for transnationals that operate in scores of markets with often vastly different characteristics, the need to be responsive to customers is both more acute and more difficult to achieve. Faced with such a problem, transnationals are finding that multicultural, cross-border teams are often the best means for quickly integrating and globally coordinating the requirements of their many different kinds of customers—and doing it in such a way as to avoid creating an unwieldy bureaucracy that is the antithesis of responsiveness. In sum, transnational flexible-matrix teams represent the best hope for meeting the apparently contradictory demands of global size and local responsiveness, demands that are peculiar to transnationals.

But it must be understood that if such teams are to live up to their potential, they must function in the right organizational culture. The senior management must have sufficient confidence in the people and the process to invest the team with full authority to make decisions. Similarly, colleagues throughout the company must also have enough confidence in the team to follow its orders. In short, multidisciplinary teams can operate only in a climate of high mutual trust and organizational alignment.

Rover, the smallest of Britain's three remaining car makers and the most vulnerable to intensified competition, offers an interesting study in matching strategy to structure through the use of teams. As the Common Market becomes a reality, the leading Japanese automakers have established "greenfield" plants in Britain from which to launch themselves into the European market. The new Japanese factories are especially competitive because in addition to the established strength of the companies, they are operating facilities without having to cope with trade unions or single-union agreements.

From Honda, which holds a 20 percent stake in Rover, the small British company has learned much about advanced manufacturing practices and the use of teams as a primary organizational form. But Rover's management was acutely conscious of the vast cultural differences between their British workers and Honda's employees in Japan. So in 1990, Rover dispatched a team to the United States to study the behavior and organizational structures at the Honda plant in Ohio, reasoning that British workers, in terms of culture, differed less from American than from Japanese workers. What they found intrigued them. As Rob Meakin, now personnel director of British Aerospace, Rover's parent company, explained, "The workers at the sharp end had authority for a whole range of activities, from training to control of materials supply, which in this country are done by somebody else. As a result, there was an enormous sense of involvement and participation in the operation."[5]

Rover plans to move quickly to the new organizational form, eliminating the industrial-class distinctions that are still characteristic of British companies. Workers will be paid monthly, just like white-collar employees. The time clock will be eliminated. Pay and conditions will no longer be negotiated by individual trade unions, and all workers will be organized in teams of about fifteen members each. Each worker will be trained in a variety of skills, allowing them the flexibility to perform multiple jobs. "We want a different relationship between the organization and the people within it," Meakin said.[6]

Clearly fighting for survival in the highly competitive and slow-growth European auto market, Rover is matching its structure to its strategy to change its organizational behavior — indeed its entire culture — constructively. Rover is by no means a transnational company, although its parent company, British Aerospace, is a large, technology-intensive company with a broad global reach. Nevertheless, Rover shows every outward sign of recognizing not only the need to change in order to survive, but the need to link its strategy and patterns of organizational behavior by means of a revised organizational structure that is based on teams and built from the bottom up.

In the future, more and more companies, especially transnationals, will adopt multidisciplinary, and increasingly multicultural, teams as the primary instrument of their organizational structures. A borderless world requires such borderless teams in which the elements of desirable organizational behavior converge and from which such behavior radiates outward, implementing a tightly integrated transnational strategy. Multidisciplinary teams see that behavior is not narrowly focused on one function or one element of strategy, but encompasses all of them at once, so that the strategic interrelationships are realized. The global strategy, desirable behavior, and organizational structure all work together, each fortifying the other. Structure not only serves strategy, but concentrates it and keeps it circulating throughout the company. And as the walls between functions break down, blurring their lines of demarcation, one may think of the edges of the strategy cube (presented in Chapter Four) softening accordingly, forming something akin to a globe, at the center of which sit multidisciplinary teams. If the new corporation has a real center, it is there — "at the still point of the turning world," to borrow a phrase from T. S. Eliot — not at some headquarters at the center of a map, but conceptually at a point equidistant from all other points on the globe, no matter where a particular team is actually located.

SmithKline Beecham is only beginning the journey toward a

transnational flexible structure. It cannot do so quickly because strategy, structure, and organizational culture must shift and adapt to change in concert. When any of the three elements is out of step, things grind to a halt.

The company did use multidisciplinary teams to great effect in the nine months following the merger. More than 300 teams were deployed throughout the entire corporation and around the world, developing objectives and plans for the new company. Now we are implementing functional management with global responsibility, beginning with the development of pharmaceuticals, purchasing, and information resources. Other multidisciplinary teams are planning manufacturing and logistics.

But it is not easy. People tire of incessant change; they become anxious to return to a stable and predictable organization. Most of all, everyone is already extremely busy and has little capacity to undertake new tasks. Yet the need for continued change in our company, as elsewhere, is real. Finally, before we can move fully to the use of transnational flexible-matrix teams, we must be sure that all internal contradictions are removed and that our strategy and organizational behavior are consistent with the new structure.

One company that has, in my view, brought together all the strands of the transnational concept is Asea Brown Boveri, the giant transnational forged in 1987 from the merger of Sweden's century-old company Asea and Switzerland's equally venerable Brown Boveri. Though few people may have heard of it, the company is the world leader in the development, manufacturing, and delivery of the latest in all phases of electrotechnology and power generation, including everything from fuse boxes to full-fledged power and industrial plants. Its electronic-transmission systems send electricity coursing through electrical grids throughout the world. Thirty percent of Los Angeles's electricity is transmitted by high-voltage DC systems built on a turnkey basis by Asea Brown Boveri. The company's pollution-control equipment cleans energy plant emissions in Stockholm, Sweden; Oklahoma; and many points in between. Its robotics systems help Ford manufacture cars in Cologne. Its transportation equipment delivers power to commuter trains in Brisbane, Australia, and its locomotives pull superfast tilting trains over existing tracks in Europe. More than any company I know, Asea Brown Boveri comes closest to being a true transnational, combining strategy, organizational behavior, and structure to gain an enormous competitive advantage in markets around the world.

Like many companies, including SmithKline Beecham, Asea and Brown Boveri were brought to the transnational crossroads in the mid- to late 1980s. From the late 1970s through the mid-1980s, the electrotechnology industry had been undergoing major international restructuring, largely because the growth of the world's consumption of electricity slowed down. By 1987 the rate of growth had dropped to less than half that of a decade before. The overall industry was mature and was even shrinking in such sectors as the generation of power. Increasingly, global giants, such as Siemens, Hitachi, General Electric, Westinghouse, and Compagnie Generale d'Electricite, were dominating the industry. Small and medium-sized companies were disappearing. Asea, by pursuing a niche strategy in areas like the transmission of power, had managed to achieve profitability that was higher than the industry average, but the global imperative had taken hold. A shakeout was taking place, and companies were faced with the stark strategic choices of dropping to the status of niche player or taking the leap to global scale.

Asea had begun to internationalize in the 1960s and had stepped up the pace in the 1980s. But it had no significant presence in North America and had not succeeded in entering the European market outside the Nordic countries. In fact, it had pursued what it called a "Nordic strategy," progressively strengthening its position in its national and regional markets, where it led the industry in Sweden and Finland and rose to number three in Denmark and number four in Norway. But the strategy was only half complete, slowed, in part, by stiff competition from Brown Boveri. Asea's aim was to be number one in all the Nordic countries, but given the speed with which the industry was restructuring, time was running out.

The obvious was staring Asea in the face: In mature, global industries with slow-growing markets, the competitive advantage often lies not in new products but in efficiencies of scale, improvement in manufacturing, and the rationalization of business functions, all of which minimize tied-up capital and help increase profits faster than sales. Asea clearly needed such efficiencies if it was to keep up with similar advantages enjoyed by other global companies in the industry. A transnational merger promised the fastest route to a competitive scale. But sheer size is not enough, and as

Asea approached the merger, it clearly recognized the limitations of seeking merely to achieve a large scale.

"Being the largest is not always the best thing," Percy Barnevik, then president and CEO of Asea, said. "Contemporary industrial history is full of illusions of grandeur and poorly supported company acquisitions, where company managements in their eagerness to become large destroyed what they were intended to administer. The era of conglomerates in the 1960s and the 1970s constitutes one example of how there are always good reasons to examine critically giant company mergers."[7]

The key to a sensible merger is the strategic fit of the two companies. The merger must not only produce advantages of scale, but must maximize the additional strategic elements of skills and scope. Such fits are easier to imagine than to find.

For Asea and Brown Boveri, the fit looked good. By 1986, one year before the merger, the companies were of roughly equal size, though historically Brown Boveri, a more advanced multinational player, had always been larger than Asea. (Interestingly, the idea of combining the two century-old companies dates back to the 1940s, and for six years, from 1968 to 1974, the companies discussed merging in the nuclear power field and cooperating in large turbines and in other areas, but the talks produced meager results.) The rough equality of the two companies was an important consideration for both partners, just as it was for SmithKline and Beecham. It would allow a merger of equals from which there was no turning back and in which the distinctive talents of both companies could combine and thrive.

The scale advantages of the merger were obvious. In the electrical business, the merger immediately vaulted the new company far ahead of its nearest competitors—Siemens, Hitachi, and General Electric. More important, the two companies' production and development capacities were complementary, which allowed the creation of a company that would be much larger, but relatively much leaner than the two original companies. For example, Brown Boveri was the second largest in the world in the field of gas turbines and was twice as large as Asea in industrial equipment and electronics, bringing greatly added muscle to the new company. However, in many fields, including the transmission and distribution of power and the manufacture of transportation equipment, the two companies were of equal size, offering them the opportunity to shrink their excess production capacity greatly. And, of course, they would benefit from large-volume purchases from suppliers and long production runs.

As the only two large companies in the electrical field that concentrated primarily on the electrotechnical market, Asea and Brown Boveri brought the same, highly focused core competencies to the partnership. In research and development, where much of that core competence is housed, the companies were complementary: Brown Boveri tended to do more theoretical research, while Asea emphasized the development and commercialization of products. Together they would make a powerful combination, while allowing for the elimination of some redundancies in their research and development units.

The merger also promised to broaden dramatically Asea's market scope. It would complete the company's Nordic strategy, making it the industry leader in all the Nordic countries and nearly doubling the number of employees in Scandinavia (from 35,000 to 65,000). The new company would also gain a firm foothold in the European Community, where Brown Boveri had always been strong. Though the new company would initially be weak in North America, with only 6,000 employees, it was well positioned in many of the markets of Asia, Africa, and Latin America, where rapidly increasing populations and migration to cities would create an enormous demand for the supply and transportation of electricity. In fact, with some 30,000 employees in Third World countries, Asea Brown Boveri would be the leading local presence in the electrical industry there.

A look at electrical transformers, one of the company's power-transmission products, demonstrates the potential of the transnational merger, despite a mature industry and slow growth. At the time of the merger, the demand in the field of power transmission was low; there was excess manufacturing capacity for power-transmission products throughout the electrical industry, and mergers by competitors were stiffening the competition. Following the merger, Asea Brown Boveri would have forty-four transformer factories in twenty-eight countries and fully 25 percent of the world market, more than three times as much as its nearest competitor. Research and development costs would be spread over a larger volume at the same time that the company's local presence in many countries would present opportunities to manufacture specialized

products. The company would move on three fronts simultaneously—concentrating on special transformers, conducting large
power-transmission projects, and gaining an insider status in protected markets. As Percy Barnevik told Asea's shareholders six days
before the merger, "If we cannot earn money against this background, then I don't know how it will be possible."[8]

Nevertheless, a fully transnational vision had still not emerged.
As I have said, the fully transnational solution often dawns slowly
and usually develops in evolutionary fashion, though sometimes
with dizzying rapidity. The new company possessed distinctive
skills and a global scale, but it still lacked a global presence and
sales in proportion to the world's markets. Two-thirds of its business was still done in Europe. The company's literature at the time
of the merger still talked of creating a truly "Nordic industry" that
would seek to dominate selected markets and to export products
from its now-consolidated home markets to North America and
Asia.[9] As the example of the transformers suggests, the new company made great strategic strides, but the overall strategy was still
Asea's previous international strategy on a larger scale.

Following the merger, Asea Brown Boveri moved quickly to
make aggressive acquisitions, especially in North America, where
the company was strategically weak. In 1989 it acquired Combustion Engineering, a manufacturer of power-generation and process-
automation equipment, for $1.6 billion. Also in 1989, it acquired
Westinghouse's transmission and distribution operation, the latter
composed of twenty-five factories and businesses, with revenues of
$1 billion. Now its North American operations employ some 40,000
people, as opposed to 6,000 immediately following the merger, and
generate $7 billion in annual revenues. The company has 10,000
employees in India and 10,000 in South America, and it is investing
aggressively in Eastern Europe.[10]

Overall, Asea Brown Boveri acquired or has taken minority
positions in more than sixty companies and now employs 240,000
people worldwide—as opposed to 180,000 immediately after the
merger—and earns revenues of more than $25 billion.[11] Operating
more than 1,300 local companies around the world, it now has markets that are well distributed globally: Europe accounts for 60 percent of the company's revenues (split about equally between the
countries in the European Community and the Scandinavian, Austrian, and Swiss trading bloc), North America accounts for about 25

percent, and Asia accounts for 15 percent.[12] Though it is still heavily dependent on Europe, it has moved closer to the 40-40-20 distribution of the true transnational.

Perhaps, what is most significant, there is no longer talk of being a Nordic company. By 1991, Barnevik was telling the *Harvard Business Review:* "ABB is a company with no geographic center, no national ax to grind. . . . Are we a Swiss company? . . . Are we a Swedish company? . . . Perhaps we are an American company."[13]

Today the company's approach is a paradigm of the transnational strategy, leveraging the interrelationships of skills, scale, and markets. Barnevik summed up the three principles this way: "First, we know what core technologies we have to master, and we draw on research from labs across Europe and the world. . . . Second, we structure our operations to push cross-border economies of scale. . . . Third, we recognize the limits of specialization [across borders]. We can't ignore borders altogether."[14]

To illustrate, Barnevik offered the example of the European locomotive industry, running at only 75 percent of capacity and fragmented into twenty-four competing companies, some of which produce as few as ten locomotives a year. Asea Brown Boveri has factories that produce ten times that volume and that specialize in components for locomotives all across Europe, giving them huge cost advantages. But the scale and scope of these factories also give them an advantage in skills. Locomotive manufacturing requires the mastery of several demanding disciplines: power electronics, mechanical design, and communications software. Unlike most of its competitors, Asea Brown Boveri can draw on the latest advances in those fields from its research laboratories around the world because the company's presence in many markets provides not only the broad customer base necessary to support such a scale, but the best new technology, wherever it may be emerging. And, of course, the cost of research is spread over a greater volume. Most important, not only do production costs go down, but quality goes up.

The elements of the transnational strategy can be made to work in other equally powerful and often highly creative ways. In India, where Asea Brown Boveri employs 10,000 people, there is a strong demand for locomotives, but the government insists that they be built locally. The company is glad to oblige, but it still has to import many components. To pay for these imports, the Indian government needs soft credit. Because Asea Brown Boveri manufactures many components in Germany and Italy, two prime sources of soft credit, the company can persuade Bonn and Rome to help India with financing. Thus the company's insider status in the local markets of Germany and Italy gives it additional leverage in a third market. Not many of its competitors can match such advantages.

In power-transformer operations the company's strategy is now turning relationships of skills and scale upside down, just as the Japanese did in the auto industry. The forty-four transformer factories have been shrunk to twenty-five, and most of the remaining ones are much smaller than the industry standard, with annual sales ranging from $10 million to $150 million.[15] Yet these factories are not only profitable, but their profits continue to grow, though traditionally the industry has always competed by lowering prices in soft markets. Although Asea Brown Boveri reaps a cost-volume advantage through its global strategic purchase of materials — insisting on good prices, zero defects, and just-in-time deliveries, it is on the factory floor that the company really outperforms its rivals. Using just-in-time manufacturing and flexible production techniques, the company has greatly reduced the manufacturing time. Just as important, flexibility and speed allow each factory to meet the special needs of local customers. Thus the transformer operation is simultaneously broadly global and intensely local, with each factory profitable on small volumes that, taken together, add up to $1 billion in annual revenues worldwide.

As all these strategic triumphs demonstrate, Asea Brown Boveri exemplifies the requisite organizational behavior for transnational competition — communication and learning, increased productivity, and responsiveness to customers. At the time of the merger, Barnevik made it clear that the new company needed a culture of mutual trust globally, entrepreneurship in the local companies, and flexibility. Communication is vital to global coordination, so the company, like many others, places great value on a sophisticated management-information system. But equally vital human communication — the cross-border exchange of ideas — is accomplished through rotating people to various countries and through the extensive use of multinational teams. Business-area leaders, located all over the world, are assisted by five-member management teams. Thus for the fifty business areas, some 250 people of many nationalities meet regularly to share perspectives and solve problems.

Through such coordination and communication have come the kinds of improved productivity that occurred in the transformer operation and, in one of those apparent paradoxes in the transnational world, a simultaneous improvement in the quality of products and in the company's responsiveness to customers.

Fostering a culture of trust that encourages learning, communication, and improved productivity means pushing responsibility downward and outward. At the time of the merger, Barnevik insisted that the most important job was to nurture flexibility and initiative in the local companies. "It is better," he said, "to lose something of the co-ordination and large-scale operations than to lose enthusiasm and the driving force in the many different profit centers."[16]

The structure that Asea Brown Boveri relies upon to channel such desirable behavior into its transnational strategy is a global matrix.[17] In the company's matrix the fifty worldwide business groups intersect with national companies serving their local markets. Leaders of worldwide business groups coordinate globally, overseeing factories in far-flung locations, allocating export markets, realizing economies of scale, and ensuring that quality and performance meet global standards. On the other hand, national companies in each market are responsible for their own profits and are organized in local divisions and subsidiaries that are also responsible for their profits. The presidents of these local companies—which number approximately 1,300—report to both the leader of the global business group and to the president of the national company of which the local company is a part. Thus each local company remains sensitive to customers while holding to global standards of performance, quality, and efficiency. The overall direction of the company is coordinated from the lean corporate headquarters in Zurich, with a staff numbering only about a hundred. The fifty business areas are grouped into eight segments, each of which is the responsibility of a different member of the executive committee, to whom leaders of each business group report.

The global matrix is flexible enough to accommodate the varying proportions of the global and the local in the company's lines of business. Some of the businesses, like service and electrical installation, are highly local. Others, like steam and gas turbines and power transmission systems, are highly global—only three or four high-voltage DC power stations are sold annually around the world. Still others, like transformers, motors, and drives have significant product development and production operations in several countries. The relative freedom enjoyed by the national companies ensures that units in Asea Brown Boveri's most global lines of business will remain attentive to local markets, while global coordination gives even the smallest and most local companies in the group opportunities to increase international sales.

The results achieved by Asea Brown Boveri's American acquisitions demonstrate the advantages of operating in a global matrix. Exports at Westinghouse's power-transmission business and at Combustion Engineering had been negligible before their acquisition by Asea Brown Boveri in 1989. Within one year, the export business shot up to $1 billion and is expected to double in the next few years.[18] So successful is this global matrix and the strategy it serves that IBM, after a series of executive-level meetings with the company, based its sweeping reorganization, announced in November 1991, on that model.[19]

The cross-border merger of Asea and Brown Boveri offers an additional lesson. Although both were strong companies before the merger, their home markets were small compared to those of the global companies that had originated in the United States, Japan, or Germany. And both Sweden and Switzerland are outside the European Community. But by accomplishing a transnational merger of equals, the two middle-sized regional companies instantly became one giant global company to which the distinction of domestic and foreign markets is meaningless. The new company is also now firmly entrenched within the European Community. This example demonstrates that companies from any country and any region can play the transnational game. In the future I think many more transnational mergers will take place between companies that originate outside the United States, Japan, and the European Community.

Asea Brown Boveri is now well positioned for the remainder of this century and far beyond. In the decades to come, the newly freed countries of Eastern Europe and the former Soviet Union will be demanding more electrotechnology, as will the newly industrializing countries in Asia, Africa, and Latin America. North America's aging power plants, many of them inefficient and dangerously polluting, will soon need to be replaced. So will much of the continent's decaying electrical infrastructure. Worldwide concern for the environment, coupled with the company's technological leadership, promises a robust demand for pollution-control systems and for the company's clean-running trains, which get freight off atmosphere-polluting trucks.

Asea Brown Boveri's enviable position, achieved in a relatively short time, demonstrates the power of the transnational concept when all its elements are brought together. In sum, the key elements include the following:

• The pursuit and creation of broad equity ownership and market penetration — through mergers, aggressive acquisitions, or organic growth — in major markets around the world.

• The definition and development of core competencies that give the company a competitive advantage in skills. Developed over time, core competencies deserve complete organizational support and become a precious heritage that is passed from one generation of employees to the next.

• The relentless pursuit of global-*scale* advantages to achieve low-cost positions and leadership in vital business functions while considerable authority is delegated to the local level for implementing the strategy and tailoring the presentation of products and services to customers in their own cultural terms.

• Movement toward a global *scope,* in which the allocation of assets and the sources of sales are roughly the same as the proportions of the world market for the business in which the firm is engaged.

• The development of a corporate culture of mutual trust and a pattern of flexible organizational behavior in which managers continually act to improve productivity, to learn and communicate across functions and national borders, and to respond sensitively to customers.

• An organizational structure — usually a transnational flexible matrix — that serves the global-local strategy and employs multidisciplinary and multicultural teams to integrate the organizational behavior with the strategic elements of skills, scale, and scope.

• Standards of behavior and commitment at all levels, particularly the local level, that earn insider status, winning for the company the same respect and admiration enjoyed by highly esteemed local competitors.

• Responsible corporate governance that is consistent with the concept of global ownership and global citizenship.

There is one additional element—people. The emergence of truly transnational companies will make great demands on future managers and employees. Essentially, these companies will recruit people who match the company's strategic and organizational requirements. Words and phrases like *global vision, cultural sensitivity, functional expertise, adaptable to change,* and *committed to continual improvement* become as descriptive of the people employed as of the way corporations conduct their business.

For managers and employees, it is important not to dismiss these terms as slogans or merely the latest managerial jargon. They describe real attributes and real skills—qualities of mind and orientation that should be assiduously cultivated by any manager or business student who is seeking a career in a global business. And today almost all businesses are global.

A global vision obviously requires adopting a view of the entire world as a single market and sphere of corporate operations. It also requires an attitude something akin to that of a world citizen, who values all nations and cultures and excludes none. Some people find that concept fundamentally offensive, believing that it conflicts with the traditional pursuit of national interests and sounds vaguely unpatriotic. Yet, in historical terms, the very idea of a national interest is relatively new, perhaps only 250 to 300 years old, about one-tenth of recorded human history. More to the point, however, in the conditions of the late twentieth century, does anyone really believe there is room for a national interest that is not in overall harmony with the global interest?

I am most comfortable with the idea of both national citizenship and world citizenship. The two are additive and complementary, certainly not mutually exclusive, particularly in today's world. One can, and indeed should, develop an attitude of world citizenship without diminishing one's complete affection and loyalty for one's local and national identity. Moreover, cultural sensitivity begins at home. People who are best able to understand and deal with foreign cultures, in my experience, do so initially by understanding their own national origins, including their history and cultural development, as a firm basis for comparing them with other cultures.

As it happens, Americans approach the matter of cultural sensitivity from a unique vantage point. Our national origins and cultural experiences span the oceans, reaching to all the continents and regions of the Old World. Some overseas visitors are astonished to find that many elements of American culture are merely reproductions of their own. Meanwhile, we Americans believe that the cultures of our ancestors and the ancestors of our friends and neighbors, be they European, African, or Asian, belong as much to the United States as they do to the "Old Country." The result is at least the potential for an inclusive approach to matters of culture with broad tolerance and respect for the cultures of many lands. Ben Wattenberg caught this theme in *The First Universal Nation,* in which he argued that because of extremely diverse yet intertwined cultural origins, Americans are uniquely capable of embracing the world's many cultures in a relatively open manner.[20] If Wattenberg's view is correct, then it's not surprising that transnational management and organizational culture seem to have many American characteristics.

This is not to argue, however, that transnational corporations are peculiarly American phenomena or are composed primarily of American elements. To the contrary, transnational organizations are, by definition, inclusive and, above all, pursue the best and most competitive practices without regard for national origins. This approach demands people who are especially adaptable and are not particularly concerned with national origins or characteristics.

Adaptability and a global vision are best developed by living and working in different societies, learning languages, and immersing oneself in unfamiliar cultures. Of course, many Europeans and Asians, having been raised speaking more than one language, find it a much easier task than do many Americans. In fact, few American managers are fluent in a foreign language, despite the rush to globalization. Regrettably, many think that the mastery of a foreign language is unimportant.

Most aspiring managers of transnational companies will sooner or later confront the issue of living and working abroad. My own background of living and working in many places and on three continents convinces me of the value of the experience, from a personal as well as a professional point of view. The contact with unfamiliar cultures and peoples and the sense of being part of the sweep of world events can be challenging and exhilarating.

You may even find adventure on occasion, as an associate of mine did in the Philippines when we were setting up Louis Allen's international management-consulting business there in 1970. The associate was Antonio Del Rosario, a high-visibility public relations specialist who at one point was captured by the Huks, the communist insurgents in the Philippines, who took him to the mountains and held him for ransom. One night the hut in which he was being held was surrounded by government soldiers, who engaged the Huks in a firefight, killing several of them and freeing Antonio. The captain of the Huks escaped, however.

Antonio went on to detail his experiences in a book, which became the basis for a movie that was shown widely in the Philippines. In the movie version, Antonio is, of course, portrayed as a great and fearless hero, while the captain of the Huks is pictured as a blackhearted villain. The Huk captain, upon seeing the movie, grew so enraged that he sent Antonio a message demanding his death. Thereafter, whenever Antonio and I met, he was accompanied by at least two guards, one usually armed with a submachine gun and the other with a shotgun. Whenever we had lunch in a restaurant, for example, one of the guards stood at the front door and the other at the back, lending our business a bit more urgency than perhaps it needed. Not everyone finds—or wants to find— quite the degree of adventure that Antonio did, but I can assure young people who are considering a career in international business that it is rarely dull.

Of course, many young people are already preparing themselves to enter global businesses by pursuing their graduate education in several countries and languages, thereby getting a head start on their more insular colleagues. Such a head start not only provides a competitive edge, but reduces the pain of the inevitable price of a life where roots are seldom driven deep, since relocation is almost inevitable. Corporate gypsies can advance their careers, but their children can suffer from the constant moving, the anguish of making and then leaving friends, and the difficulty dealing with uncertain and varied schooling. My children, for example, have developed a strong global vision, but they also have a powerful desire to put down roots. They are not candidates for the life of the transnational employee.

Global employees must not only follow a career path that takes them to other countries, they must pursue continual training both within the company and outside it. Many leading companies no longer relegate international training to self-contained courses, but instead weave global concerns into every phase of their employees' development. General Electric, for example, has junked its long-running two-week international management course at its Management Development Institute and is now emphasizing global issues in all its executive training courses.[21] And General Electric is by no means the only one.

Perhaps no company has been as successful in developing a globally diverse cadre of managers as has Nestlé. Though the giant food company is based in Switzerland, only 3 percent of its 295,000 employees worldwide are Swiss. In most of the foreign countries in which Nestlé does business, most employees and managers are drawn from the host countries. Nestlé does have some 600 or so managers who are not from the country in which they work, but only about half of such expatriate managers are Swiss. Moreover, most expatriate managers for Nestlé remain in their posts for ten years or more, enabling them to become fluent in the language and competent in the culture. Nestlé's traditional policy of delegating considerable authority to local managers enables its management teams in each market to use fully their well-developed capacities for understanding and relating the customer needs to Nestlé's business. Nestlé's policies are so successful that most consumers around the world think of Nestlé as being a local company.

To prepare for careers in such transnational companies, business students must take advantage of the many opportunities now available to study and work abroad. The European MBA Consortium, an association of eight distinguished European graduate schools of business, encourages students from other countries to study at their member schools. Many graduate schools of business are adding foreign internships or initiating exchange programs with foreign business schools. Almost all major graduate schools of business, some with the help of corporations, are now sponsoring students who go to live and work in Eastern Europe, where they get a firsthand look at free enterprise being born, get basic experience in tough areas like the reform of manufacturing, and venture outside their narrow academic specializations.[22] The University of Pittsburgh's business school is even sending professors to teach for a while in Eastern Europe.

Programs in international business studies are also available at a number of American graduate schools, including the Lauder Institute at the Wharton School of Business, University of Pennsylvania; Thunderbird (formerly the American Graduate School of International Management) in Glendale, Arizona; the program in international business at the University of South Carolina; and the numerous courses in international business offered by New York University's Stern School of Business.[23] Other schools are adding courses in such subjects as total quality management. Perhaps what is most significant, many graduate schools of business are revamping their entire curricula to frame virtually every course in a global context. The Wharton School of Business and the graduate schools of business at Columbia University, the University of Maryland, and Southern Methodist University are just a few that no longer partition off international business in separate courses.

All these developments are healthy, if somewhat belated. Business students must seek international courses and programs, and business educators must make them more widely available. But the rise of globalism and transnational corporations makes more than purely pragmatic demands on us. A foreign language here, a course in international finance there, and even a foreign internship are all well and good, but global business itself must be placed in a larger context—the world and all its peoples. Yes, we must learn to compete globally, but to what end? What is the relation of value-added activity to the creation of true value—human, intellectual, and social?

As we hurtle toward a world that will be dominated even more by huge transnational companies that are seemingly everywhere and nowhere, such questions become increasingly urgent. Shareholders, managers, workers, customers, and entire communities struggle over the governance, obligations, and direction of these huge organizations that so directly affect their lives and livelihoods. Governments fear a loss of national sovereignty to companies that are operating beyond the capacity of any single country to regulate them. Citizens worry that such mammoth companies will degrade the environment, trample ethics, and dominate their lives in ways both visible and invisible.

Meanwhile, the context for all these questions appears to be a world that is simultaneously becoming more globally integrated and more ethnically and even tribally fragmented every day. If the center cannot hold, will transnationals rush to fill the power vacuum? Or will they, too, fall victim to rising nationalism? Who will call the tune? What will it sound like — harmonious or discordant — and to whose ears? Who gets to dance and who has to sit out, and, most important, who decides?

PART THREE

GOING CONCERNS

CHAPTER SEVEN

CALLING THE TUNE

SINCE GIANT CORPORATIONS FIRST APPEARED on the scene in the nineteenth century, their various constituencies have struggled over their control and direction. In the publicly held corporation there has always been an inherent tension between the shareholders who owned it and the managers who ran it, a division of roles that was codified by the securities laws of 1933 and 1934. Today, however, the stakes are so large and the forces at work so different from previous eras that they make a qualitative difference in the character of the conflict.

On one side stand the directors and executives of global corporations and on the other, the institutional shareholders who own most of the coporations' shares. Gone are the millions upon millions of individual shareholders and the dream of a "people's capitalism"; gone, too, are many of the cozily familiar national companies in which such investors might proudly participate. In the contemporary struggle for the soul of the corporation, the companies are so big, the stakes are so high, and the outcome is so uncertain that this formerly little-noticed and long-standing corporate debate has moved onto the front pages and into the consciousness of everyone, from fund managers, board chairmen, and CEOs to hourly workers and ordinary citizens. The issues being debated reach to the very core of corporate existence: purpose, accountability, governance, and measures of business performance—issues that ripple outward to affect virtually all of us.

What should be a mutually beneficial relationship is tainted by acrimony, suspicion, and misunderstanding. Each side accuses the other of abusing power and behaving irresponsibly, and both sides advocate reform and change. Institutional shareholders complain that some top corporate executives are beholden to no one but themselves and a few hand-picked cronies. They point to egregious examples, such as Allegheny Ludlum, whose CEO carefully selected the board members, compensated them not only with generous fees but with lucrative consulting contracts, and operated the company with a free hand. The results were a disastrous decline in the company's fortunes and the value of the shares. They cite the well-documented disparity between corporate performance and executives' salaries. They are concerned that even in seemingly well-run companies, the corporate boards of directors do not faithfully represent the primacy of the shareholders' interests. They believe that the representation of shareholders is a farce when boards are dominated by other chairmen and CEOs in a kind of self-perpetuating buddy system. Tempers rise when institutions that own substantial amounts of stock get no more information or attention than does the proverbial pensioner in sneakers who walks into a broker's office to buy a few shares. All this adds up to deep suspicion of entrenched corporate managers who operate a company for their own enrichment at the expense of the shareholders. There are enough documented cases of overcompensated executives and cozy boards of directors managing underperforming companies to lend genuine credence and support to their concerns.

Investors also point with dismay to the decisions of state courts that have upheld legislation designed to make takeovers difficult. They think that antitakeover legislation is stimulated by corporate executives who are seeking legislative shelter from hostile attacks and consider it just another example of executives' self-protection from the exigencies of the market at the expense of shareholders. They believe the market provides the ultimate discipline of corporate management and that shareholders are best served when so-called underperforming companies can attract the attention of other buyers and be sold to the highest bidder.

Corporate executives, on the other hand, worry that institutional investors with an excessive orientation to short-term returns on their investments can vote them out of office and even force the sale of the company just to realize immediate gains in the value of their portfolios. They complain that there is no way to recognize the difference between continuing shareholders who are committed to the long-term future of the corporation and speculators who take short-term positions in the stock. And they respond that under the law the retiree in sneakers has exactly the same rights to information about a corporation as do large institutions that have invested hundreds of millions of dollars in shares. They see large institutional shareholders trying to force themselves or their representatives onto corporate boards as a tactic to disrupt the management, to advantage a few shareholders at the expense of the many, and to force the management continually to give in to pressures for short-term performance at the expense of the long-term health of the enterprise.

The emergence of transnational corporations and the rise to prominence of institutional investors took place almost simultaneously, each feeding the other. As companies became first global and then transnational in response to the global imperative, they increased enormously — in sales, profits, assets, employees, and worth. The total value of the outstanding shares (usually called *market capitalization*) of many of these global behemoths sometimes exceeds the GNPs of many countries. Regardless of where transnational companies are registered — in Switzerland, Delaware, England, or Japan — their shares are traded on at least one major stock exchange and often several major stock exchanges around the world. The size of the market capitalization of transnational corporations alone mandates that the preponderance of their shares be owned by investors with equal or greater resources. The only investors that meet this criterion are institutions: for the most part, insurance companies, trust departments of major banks, mutual funds, investment funds composed of blocks of money from a variety of sources, or large pension funds.

Many financial institutions have long been investors in corporations, but the participation of pension funds, the fastest-growing component of institutional investing, is relatively new. It was only in about 1950 that GM established the first modern pension fund. Today, pension funds command vast resources. For example, the College Retirement Endowment Fund manages funds that exceed

$125 billion, and the pension fund for the employees of the state of California is about $70 billion.

In the United States, pension funds, with some $2.5 *trillion,* are now the largest source of institutional money. Public pension funds account for about $800 billion of that total.[1] And the funds often have huge amounts of money to place, sometimes as much as $1 billion a year. They hold about 40 percent of the common stock of the country's businesses and about 40 percent of the medium- and long-term debt of the nation's largest companies. As Peter Drucker put it, they are corporate America's largest owners, as well as its largest lenders.[2] Pension funds will continue to grow in size and importance through the 1990s as the vast number of baby boomers move through their prime earning years.

Institutional funds have grown so large that they now dominate the New York Stock Exchange, usually accounting for two-thirds of the daily trading volume. Only the large institutional funds have the financial capacity to absorb the shares of large companies without taking the undue risk of an overweighted portfolio. It is common to find something in the range of 70 percent of the shares of large market capitalization corporations owned by major institutional investors. In the case of SmithKline Beecham, with a total market capitalization of approximately $20 billion, about 70 percent of the shares are owned by fewer than 100 British and American institutional investors with an average share holding of $175 million.

This pattern of institutional ownership is typical of large companies in the United States and Britain. In continental Europe and Japan the pattern of ownership is different, with large commercial banks and insurance companies playing a greater role. In France, many of the largest and most influential corporations, such as Rhone-Poulenc and Thomson, SA, are owned in whole or in part by the French government. In Germany, ownership of companies has long been concentrated in the hands of powerful commercial banks. It is well known that the German banks earn far more in fees for routine bank services supplied to client companies than they do from the companies' stock dividends. In Japan, the big industrial groups, known as *keiretsu,* are coalitions of banks, leasing companies, insurers, manufacturers, suppliers, and distributors, all of whom are bound by the fact they own shares in each other. And though they do not reap big dividends from their shares, their interrelationships bring them business, which explains their bias toward growth and the difficulty of hostile takeovers. Since neither the German commercial banks nor the members of the Japanese keiretsu intend to sell the shares they hold, they have little interest in the price of shares and concentrate instead on building long-term value.

Though the ownership of companies overall in the United States and Britain is dominated by institutional shareholders, the average institution generally owns less than 1 percent of any one company's outstanding shares. Similarly, investment in a single company's shares usually is about 1 percent of the institution's total investment capital. These percentages, however, can range up to as high as 5 percent of a single company's total outstanding shares and a correspondingly higher proportion of the institution's total portfolio. The institution aims for reasonable diversity, but the ownership of shares in most large market-capitalization corporations is concentrated in the hands of fewer than 100 professionally managed institutions—even though the roster of all shareholders often exceeds 20,000.

The climate of mutual distrust came about when the two revolutions—the emergence of transnational companies and the rise of institutional investors—converged in the 1980s. Instead of embracing one another, they collided. For most of their early history, the pension funds had been content to invest in safe, low-yield instruments, such as government bonds. But by the 1980s, for demographic reasons having to do with the number of workers, the funds found themselves inundated monthly with millions of dollars that had to be invested. They were also persuaded by studies showing superior returns on investments in corporate securities, as opposed to fixed-income instruments, such as government and corporate bonds. Accordingly, they turned to the stock markets and focused their buying power on the shares of large corporations. As more shares, and therefore voting power, became concentrated in fewer hands, hostile takeovers became much easier to accomplish. Acquirers no longer had to reach millions of individual shareholders and persuade them to sell; they needed only to reach a few-score fund managers.

For their part, many fund managers got wind of the spectacular results being achieved by their more adventurous colleagues who plunged directly into financing takeovers. For example, as Sarah

Bartlett detailed, pension funds fueled the leveraged buyouts of the high-visibility takeover firm of Kohlberg Kravis Roberts (KKR) in the 1980s.[3] When KKR raised the largest fund ever—some $5.6 billion—in 1986, 55 percent of the total was supplied by just eleven state pension funds: those of Illinois, Iowa, Massachusetts, Michigan, Minnesota, Montana, New York, Oregon, Utah, Washington, and Wisconsin. According to Bartlett, it took more than sixty other institutional investors to make up the rest of the fund.[4]

Meanwhile, the managements of some companies attempted to take their companies private at preposterously low premiums, as was the case of Ross Johnson with RJR-Nabisco. Other executives sought to protect themselves from the takeover frenzy by adopting poison pills to discourage takeovers or by granting themselves golden parachutes—incredibly rich severance benefits—in the event that their companies were taken over and they were ousted. Still others paid exorbitant "greenmail" to buy back company shares that had fallen into the hands of potential acquirers, such as Carl Icahn and T. Boone Pickens.

Shareholders, especially institutional shareholders, loudly objected to such management ploys—and they became more activist. In 1984, sixty institutions with investment responsibilities totaling $250 billion formed the Council of Institutional Investors, largely in response to Texaco's and Disney's greenmail stock repurchases that year.[5] In 1986 the council promulgated a shareholder's bill of rights embodying four main principles: one share, one vote; equal and fair treatment of all shareholders; shareholders' approval of actions, such as greenmail, poison pills, and golden parachutes; and independent approval of executives' compensation and auditors.[6]

Though the feverish pace of hostile takeovers and buyouts has slowed, tensions remain, many of them rooted in the nature of fund management itself. Funds that are entrusted to institutional investors are managed by professional portfolio managers who are charged with the fiduciary duty of maintaining the value of the principal placed in their care and earning a return on the capital that meets or, even better, exceeds the standards of their investors or employers. The failure of portfolio managers to live up to their investors' expectations on a regular and sustained basis causes the investors' to withdraw the funds and place them elsewhere or to fire the portfolio managers, or often both. The results of money managers' performance are published annually, indeed often quarterly, and the managers' relative performance is routinely ranked. It is very much like a continuous race, but there are no time-outs and no one to pass the baton to. Consequently, professional money management is competitive and Darwinian; survival of the fittest is the only law.

The money managers' outlook on the rest of the world, particularly the corporate world in which they place their equity investments, tends to be similarly Darwinian. The managers smile upon companies when the price of shares rises and frown when it does not. Though many institutional money managers sincerely take a long-term view of their investments, any sudden unexpected rise or fall in the share value of shares that affects a manager's relative performance can quickly bring the law of the jungle to apply. Since the value of shares is fundamentally a product of the law of supply and demand and institutional portfolio managers tend to behave in similar ways, the price of corporate shares can swing wildly. The wild swings, in turn, represent buying or selling opportunities. Over time, however, supply and demand tend to balance out, with the price of shares representing a fair appraisal of the value of the corporation to investors.

Most institutional investors purchase shares in a corporation with a view to selling at a higher, well-defined target price. The sales generate cash for new investments and provide the means for the constant regeneration of the portfolio. The sales also book the profit on the investment, thereby scoring the final return on the investment. With the advent of programmed trading on the New York Stock Exchange, purchase and sale targets are set for various companies' shares, which allows the computer to kick out a transaction order automatically when the target prices are hit. Obviously, these programmed targets are adjusted from time to time as the prospects for individual companies are reevaluated. No individual company will outperform the market forever, so once the investment is made, the portfolio manager's decision is never *whether* to sell, but only *when* to sell and at what price. With the advent of the computer and programmed trading, the price decides the *when*. Usually, the target price is dictated by the manger's view of the current price of the shares relative to other possible investments. But other factors that are unrelated to the value of the company's shares — such as the relative performance of the manager's entire portfolio of investments — can also be decisive in determining the target price.

It's difficult even to know who owns a company on a given day. Similarly, it's difficult to know what the large institutions own, because they continually adjust their portfolios to record the best relative performance. The fundamental commitment of the institutions is to the value of the shares, which is only an imperfect barometer of the health of a corporate enterprise at any time. Since the institutions purchase the shares with every expectation of selling at a profit, they may be holders of the shares for a day, a month, a year, or even five or more years. Essentially, they are financial investors in a corporation's shares as a commodity to be bought and sold, together with the shares of many other companies.

In the aggregate all these elements describe a vigorous and healthy market. There is nothing immoral about buying and selling shares in large companies or about demanding good performance and its rigorous measurement. But the size of the funds being managed and the size of the investments being placed are introducing some new factors into the otherwise efficient market. The largest funds are so big—more than $50 billion is no longer unusual—that a 1 percent investment becomes a major portion of a corporation's weekly or even monthly trading volume. As a result, the only way to buy or sell such a huge volume of stocks without distorting the market is through a gradual, time-phased process. Gradual sales make it more difficult for large funds to buy and sell at precise price points. Consequently, these funds have to consider holding shares over a longer time than they are comfortable with and are accustomed to.

Approaching the issue from a different direction, a number of studies have documented that most money managers do not outperform the market for any but the shortest periods. Operating on the theory that if you can't beat it, join it, many large funds now invest through the purchase of broad indices of the market, such as the Standard and Poor, 500 or, in Britain, the FT 100. Known as index funds, these investments stay in the individual companies that make up the index for a long time—theoretically for as long as the institution wishes to invest in corporate equities.

For these two reasons, the large funds are reluctantly confronting the uncomfortable reality of living with their investment decisions—indeed with their investments—over longer periods. Of course, they jealously guard their prerogative to buy and sell, and they keep their fingers tightly on the trigger—as they must—to maintain their ability to improve their standing in the performance rankings. And their basic instincts and habits manifest the trading talents that brought them to the business of managing other people's money in the first place. The law of the jungle still prevails because, ultimately, it is the spread on the transaction — the profit on the trade — that determines the performance of professional money managers.

Nevertheless, the prospect of long-term ownership brings a whole new set of considerations to the institutional investor. It requires judgments about the quality of the company's management, its competitive relationships, the value of its technology, the direction of its research and development, its market share, and its global positioning more than about the relative value of the company's shares at a given moment. Long-term ownership raises the difficult question of when and how far institutional investors should assert their interests as owners to protect the value of their investments. In short, the prospect of long-term ownership takes money managers directly into the unfamiliar fields of corporate governance and corporate management.

During the period of investment in any given company, the institutional investor becomes a shareholder with all the legal rights and powers of ownership. These rights include, of course, the right to vote the shares at annual general meetings or when extraordinary decisions are required on such matters as mergers or acquisitions. As owners of substantial portions of the company's shares, they believe they have every right to take positions on matters of the corporation's governance and to judge the corporation's performance. After all, they have staked many hundreds of millions of dollars of other people's money on the company's ability to perform at an expected level. Why shouldn't they have a say in the way the business is managed, particularly if things are not going as expected and the company or, more accurately, the value of the company's shares seems to be "underperforming"? As a result, institutional investors and shareholders' organizations have become increasingly active in exerting their influence on the running of companies. Shareholders' resolutions on issues like golden parachutes and poison-pill defenses against takeovers are growing. In 1990 in the United States there were some 300 such resolutions, of which 16 passed; in 1989 there were 245, of which only 2 passed.[7]

The roster of activist pension-fund groups includes, among oth-

ers, the Florida State Board of Administration, NYCFire, NYCPo-
lice, New York City Teachers Retirement System, New York State
and Local Retirement System, California State Teachers Retirement
System, and the Teachers Insurance and Annuity Association/Col-
lege Retirement Equities Fund. Two of the most active are the California Public Employees Retirement System (Calpers), with assets
of some $70 billion, and the State of Wisconsin Investment Board,
with assets of $20 billion. Calpers alone made twelve governance
proposals in 1990 and won victories or compromises in ten of
them.[8] Among other victories, the fund persuaded GM to change its
bylaws to guarantee that a majority of the company's board would
remain outsiders. Initiatives by the fund also resulted in instituting
confidential voting by shareholders at Hercules and Inland Steel.
(Whirlpool's shareholders voted down a Calpers proposal for confidential voting.) The fund also briefly backed a disgruntled Lockheed investor's takeover bid for the company. In another case, the
fund filed suit against Occidental Petroleum over the building of a
museum to house the art collection of the company's late chairman
Armand Hammer.

Many of the institutions have banded together in associations
such as the Council of Institutional Investors, which continues to
press its case for a shareholders' bill of rights. Institutional Shareholder Partners is an advisory service for big investors, headed by
corporate gadfly Robert A. G. Monks, who, along with Nell Minow,
wrote *Power and Responsibility*, a book promoting shareholders'
rights.[9]

In the United States, institutional investors, groups of investors,
and politicians have been galvanized most recently by the issue of
executives' pay. Investors were outraged over the escalation in executives' pay and stock options despite companies' poor performance, falling profits, widespread layoffs, and in some cases huge
write-offs of shareholders' equity. Examples of huge compensation
packages became front-page news: Steve J. Ross and N. J. Nicholas,
Jr., co-chief executives of Time Warner, were reported to have made
between them $99.6 million in 1990. The 1991 salary-and-stock
package for Roberto C. Goizueta, the chairman of Coca-Cola, was
estimated to be worth more than $86 million. Graef Crystal, a for-
mer compensation consultant and now a professor at the University
of California at Berkeley, estimated that, on average, the CEOs of
America's thirty largest companies took home an estimated $3.2

million each in 1990 in salaries, bonuses, stock options, and restricted performance shares, compared with $1.1 million for the thirty top chief executives in Britain, $800,000 in France and Germany, and $525,000 in Japan.[10] The average annual compensation of the CEOs who accompanied President Bush on his ill-fated trip to Japan was $3.4 million.

According to the Securities and Exchange Commission (SEC), shareholders' proposals on executives' compensation at annual company meetings grew from 35 in 1986 to 110 in 1990.[11] Calpers, which owns more than 1.5 million shares of ITT, was so incensed by CEO Rand Araskog's compensation of $30 million over a four-year period during which the company's shares fell 10 percent that the pension fund's director demanded and got a change in the company's bylaws governing the way executives' pay is determined.

The SEC has now entered the fray on the side of shareholders. In February 1992 it sent letters to eleven corporations forbidding them from excluding executive-pay initiatives from their proxy ballots. For decades, the SEC did not allow shareholders to vote on executives' pay. (Under the securities laws, companies can ask the SEC to allow them to exclude proposals from their proxy ballots. Historically, the SEC has always considered executives' pay to be a matter of "ordinary business," which boards of directors can refuse to put to a vote by the shareholders.) The votes on executives' pay, however, will be nonbinding because such matters of governance fall under state laws, which in all fifty states currently empower boards of directors to set executives' pay. Nevertheless, by 1993 publicly traded corporations will have to provide shareholders with detailed information about executives' pay, including the criteria that boards of directors use in setting pay and comparisons of executives' compensation with changes in the price of the company's shares and dividend payouts. Congress is entertaining even tougher measures, including a proposal that would raise the taxes of any company that pays its executives more than twenty-five times the pay of its lowest paid worker.

As a result of the SEC's reversal of policy, we are likely to see many initiatives to limit executives' pay coming before a vote of the shareholders. Shareholders of Baltimore Gas & Electric, for example, planned to entertain a proposal to cap the pay of top executives at twenty times that of the average worker. A proposal before the shareholders of Grumman Corporation would suspend the management-bonus plan until the company's stock regains its 1986 level.[12] Though big institutional investors are unlikely to vote against the top management and the resolutions will be nonbinding even if they do pass, the movement to limit executives' pay is growing.

State legislatures that have passed antitakeover legislation have also drawn the ire of institutional investors, as have state courts that rarely intervene on the side of shareholders. Investors object that the "business judgment rule" is construed so broadly by the courts that boards of directors are rarely held accountable for highly questionable actions. Under the rule, courts excuse directors for their actions as long as those actions are disinterested attempts to make money for the shareholders. As with much business law, courts are reluctant to substitute their judgment for the judgment of the parties involved, so the explanations of directors encounter few judicial challenges.

The case of *Paramount Communications v. Time, Inc.* is an example. Time's board, after spending six years appraising and engineering the merger of Time with Warner Communications, chose not to submit to shareholders a last-minute, higher-price takeover bid from Paramount Communications. The Delaware Supreme Court held that the merger with Warner was motivated by purely business reasons, however good or bad those reasons might be, so Time's directors were entitled to the protection of the rule.

Summarizing the complaints of institutional investors, Roland M. Machold, the director of the Division of Investment for the state of New Jersey, wrote: "Taken collectively, changes in corporate governance, the judgements of state and federal courts, and the enactment of state laws that protect corporate interests have unbalanced the covenant that exists between investors, corporate management, and the public interest, as kept in place by the organs of government. This covenant is the cornerstone of our system of private enterprise and an essential ingredient in dynamic capital markets."[13]

To avoid acrimonious proxy battles, many companies are now conferring regularly with institutional shareholders and accepting some of their long-sought proposals, such as phasing out poison-pill takeover defenses, eliminating golden parachutes for executives in the event of a takeover, and making votes by shareholders confidential. The CEO of Sears promised to meet with representatives of Calpers twice annually. Calpers also persuaded Boise Cascade to cease counting shares not voted as no votes in tallies of proxies. Some companies have resisted the proposals of the institutional shareholders. Pfizer, United Technologies, and United Telecommunications each refused to alter their poison-pill provisions, despite the urging of the Wisconsin Investment Board, which subsequently filed proxy proposals in all three instances.[14]

As the struggle over corporate governance has heated up, much of the focus of the debate has fallen on the makeup of boards of directors. Though directors are elected by the shareholders and have a legal obligation to guard investors' interests, investors complain that boards are often packed with company executives. Furthermore, in most leading American companies and many British ones, the roles of chairman and CEO are filled by a single individual. In addition, say the critics, most outside directors are nominated by CEOs and are sometimes paid hefty fees; provided with numerous perks, such as life insurance; and in myriad ways, large and small, are made beholden to the management. When it comes to voting for directors, investors complain, shareholders are given the choice on proxy statements of either voting for the company's nominees — the number of which usually coincides with the number of vacancies — or withholding their votes.

In a widely chronicled case, Robert A. G. Monks, the president of Institutional Shareholder Partners and a vociferous critic of the way directors are chosen, bought 100 shares of Sears, Roebuck and then sought a seat on its board to dramatize the issue. When the board's nominating committee declined to accept him, he took his candidacy directly to the shareholders. Sears responded by reducing the size of its board from fifteen to ten members, to eliminate a vacancy and make it more difficult for Monks to get elected. It also refused to provide him with a list of shareholders and, according to Monks, declined to circulate material about his candidacy to Sears's employees, who own a quarter of the company's stock, unless he paid the company $300,000.[15] Needing only 25 percent of the vote to be elected, it is estimated that Monks exceeded that figure with institutional investors, who were easy to reach because they must disclose their large holdings to the SEC.[16] Among the institutions supporting him was the ever-active Calpers. But Monks was able to reach only about 40 percent of the total number of shareholders and was ultimately defeated. He vowed to try again.[17]

"I suspected it before," Monks wrote of the experience, "but now I am convinced that to have truly independent directors—who represent shareholders—change is necessary."[18] Monks argued that the SEC should expand its 1977 proposal allowing the direct nomination of directors by shareholders to see that information about such candidacies is included in proxy materials. He urged confidential voting to prevent reprisals against institutional investors, employee-shareholders, and money managers, and he would prohibit company officers from chairing board nominating committees. He also proposed that institutional investors be allowed to communicate with each other and organize, free of SEC restrictions. And he would encourage institutional investors to develop a national data base on current and potential directors and track their performance on matters of interest to shareholders.[19]

Similar sentiments have been heard in Britain, where pension funds have raised their stake in the equity capital of listed British companies' from 7 percent to 32 percent in the past twenty-five years. Overall, institutions now own some 60 percent,[20] and the corporate-governance movement has picked up steam accordingly. In 1991 alone, shareholders managed to force out top executives at a number of companies, including British Aerospace, Asda Group, TACE, Bunzl, and the food retailer Budgens. And the Institutional Shareholders Committee, which represents pension funds and insurance companies, demanded that executives' pay should be set by a company's outside directors.

British fund managers also want the offices of chairman and CEO split. The pressure has increased recently because of problems at a number of well-known British companies, such as Blue Arrow, the Midland Bank, and Dixons. Currently, there is no clear trend among British companies. Some companies, such as Vickers, Courtaulds, and Midland, are separating the roles, while others, such as Grand Metropolitan, Reed, and Marks and Spencer, are combining the roles. There are successful companies under both structures. SmithKline Beecham splits the roles.

Those who favor splitting the roles argue that it is the only means of guaranteeing the chairman's independence. Split roles also introduce a system of checks and balances, supporters say, and allow the appointment of a chairman and a CEO who have complementary skills. Opponents reply that a combined chairman-CEO ensures strong leadership and prevents stalemates between chairmen and CEOs who clash. The real danger, they say, is a weak board, not combined roles.

Institutional investors in Britain have also actively promoted the appointment of outside directors. An organization called PRO-NED (for professional nonexecutive directors) was founded in Britain in 1982 to promote the idea of independent outside directors and to help companies make such appointments. Its members include the Bank of England, the British Institute of Management, the Institutional Shareholders Committee, the Confederation of British Industry, the London Stock Exchange, and numerous other large institutions. They insist that the appointment of outside directors should not be based on patronage, and they recommend the use of professional search firms as the best way to find truly independent directors. Outside directors who are approached by a professional recruiter will know that they have been chosen on the basis of merit, not because they are in someone's pocket. And boards should have less of a tendency to continue to pick directors exactly like themselves, with the same background, education, and mind-set (not to mention the same gender, race, and age). In the United States, the Institutional Shareholders' Committee, in a "Statement of Best Practice" on the role and duties of directors, also called for independent directors and promoted the splitting of the roles of chairman and CEO, the adoption of independent compensation committees, and the full disclosure of information to shareholders of management buy-out proposals.[21]

Although pressure by institutional shareholders in continental Europe is not as widespread as it is in the United States and Britain, it is growing. In a closely watched case in Belgium, several investment funds in Wagons-Lits, the Franco-Belgian travel group, have challenged in court the terms of a bid for the company by Cobefin, a joint vehicle of Accor, a French hotel group, and Societe Generale Belgique, Belgium's largest holding company. In the Netherlands, institutional shareholders forced Nationale-Nederlanden NV to improve the terms of its merger with NMBPostbank Group NV. In Germany, shareholders of the tire maker Continental A.G. voted to end a restriction on their voting rights after management's rebuff of overtures from Pirelli, and they were instrumental in the ouster of Continental's CEO. In France, insurer Union des Assurances de Paris led the shareholders of Compagnie Financerie de Paribas in pushing aside its CEO for bungling a takeover bid for another French company. Sometimes the pressure on European companies comes from U.S.-based institutional investors, who have fewer qualms about making waves than do local institutions. For example, the U.S. mutual-fund manager Fidelity Investments has opposed management proposals put forth in the proxies of German and Dutch companies.

The situation in Europe is aggravated by the fact that many of the laws governing shareholders' rights were promulgated during the 1960s and 1970s, when the greatest fear was takeovers by American corporations. Many of the laws, in the interests of keeping national industries national, effectively eliminated the possibility of takeovers and insulated management from the legitimate demands of shareholders.

As European stock markets, responding to the global imperatives of cross-border capital flows, open up to foreign investors, such pressure by institutional shareholders is likely to increase. Beginning in 1993, with the creation of the free internal market between the European Community and the European Free Trade Association, Sweden is expected to begin allowing foreigners to purchase as many shares as they like in Swedish companies on an equal basis with Swedish shareholders.

Across Europe the forces of globalization are battering at the ramparts that protect managements from complete disclosure and accountability to shareholders. Nowhere is this more apparent than in Switzerland. Famous for secrecy and national statutes protecting banks and corporations from any non-Swiss intrusion—much less threat—the Swiss are beginning to change their ways. The large transnational Swiss companies are leading the parade to change regulations inside Switzerland and to court international investors. Their motives are not altruistic; they seek to lower the cost of their capital by tapping into the huge pool of institutional investment funds available elsewhere in Europe, the United States, and Japan. The lower cost of capital is an essential element in their transnational strategy of improving their global competitiveness.

Not all the walls against unwanted takeover bids have crumbled, however. The Swiss still have peculiar regulations that limit the number of shares a single person or entity can vote, thereby preventing an accumulation of voting shares by a single predator. But even this statute is being challenged. And with Switzerland preparing to apply for membership in the European Common Market, the pace of liberalization and integration with the world's financial markets will only increase.

The traditional pattern was broken in 1988 by the large Swiss health care company Hoffman-La Roche, when it split its shares fifty to one. Before the split, the shares had been trading at about SFr 250,000 (U.S. $20,000) each. Splitting them made the price of a share more comparable to the shares of other international health care companies that are traded in London and New York. At the same time, Hoffmann-La Roche greatly simplified its overly complex and convoluted share structure, thereby making it easier for international investors to understand what they may be buying. Since then, the company has improved the amount and quality of its financial reporting and in the fall of 1991 again split its shares.

The results are readily apparent. With many more shares in circulation and improved financial disclosure, trading activity has stepped up, creating a more accessible and liquid market for the company's shares. An active market is a prerequisite for consideration by large institutional funds. The price of shares has increased substantially. The price–earnings ratio for Hoffman-La Roche, at 26, is in the same range as that of Merck, Glaxo, and other leading global health care companies. In contrast, the shares of Hoffmann-La Roche's two neighbors in Basel, Sandoz, and Ciba-Geigy, still languish with price–earnings ratios in the low- to midteens.

Hoffman-La Roche has been quick to exploit the strategic advantages of joining other transnational companies on the world's capital markets. In April 1991, it raised U.S. $1 billion with an innovative bond issue at a rate of only 3.5 percent. A further SFr 1.03 billion was raised through a share-rights and warrant issue in October 1991. This low-cost refinancing has reduced the continuing costs of two major strategic moves that the company made in the past three years: the U.S. $2.1 billion purchase of 69 percent of Genentech and the acquisition of Aspro-Nicholas, a European over-the-counter medicine business for U.S. $821 million.

The benefits of a transnational financial strategy have not been lost on the other big Swiss companies. Nestlé is widely expected to split its shares, which now sell at about SFr 9,000 (about U.S. $5,000). Meanwhile, the three big Swiss banks – Union Bank of Switzerland, Swiss Bank Corporation, and Credit Suisse – have revealed details of their hitherto hidden reserves. "We have to come up to the expectations of well-informed international investors," Hans Geiger, a member of the executive Board of Credit Suisse, told the *Financial Times*.[22]

A number of Swiss companies, including Ciba-Geigy, Asea Brown Boveri, and Sandoz, as well as Hoffmann-La Roche and Nestlé, have now opened their share registers to foreign investors. These companies are leading the effort to become more open and accessible to improve their competitiveness. The executives of these and other leading Swiss companies know that to maintain and improve their competitive positions in the world market, it is no longer enough to be Swiss.[23]

As transparency (a term commonly employed in Europe to describe openness and full disclosure) and accessibility attract investments from large institutional shareholders, the Swiss companies are being drawn into the unfamiliar arena of greater accountability to their demanding non-Swiss shareholders. Barriers to takeovers in Switzerland are being dropped as disclosures improve. The consequence there, as it is everywhere else, is improved competitiveness and greater accountability to shareholders.

The eagerness with which transnationals seek to gain access to institutional capital and the corresponding assertion of shareholders' rights by the institutions have raised anew some fundamental questions about the nature of the corporation: What is ownership? What is the true measure of corporate performance? What is governance, and what is management? To whom is the corporation accountable? To put it another way, all these issues may be boiled down to a single question: In whose interest is the corporation to be run?

These important questions are not new, of course. They apply to all publicly held and traded corporations. In recent years, however, they have taken on a new urgency as a result of the megamergers and hostile takeovers that punctuated the end of the eighties and particularly because of the immense size and global influence of many transnational corporations.

Of all the issues in the current debate, the question of ownership may appear the simplest—especially to shareholders—but like many seemingly transparent ideas, it is loaded with unexamined assumptions, many of them historically conditioned. The concept of corporate ownership goes back to the early days of the Industrial Revolution, when steam and mechanical power spawned a host of manufacturing enterprises in Europe and the New World. The owners were usually the founders of the enterprise, and its assets were primarily material—land, buildings, and equipment. The owner-founders conceived the business; built the factories; hired the people; and, of course, provided the initial capital. They literally paid the piper and called the tune.

As enterprises required additional capital for expansion, they sold shares to investors who joined the founders as principal shareholders and often participated in planning the company's overall direction. These owners were stewards for the future of the enterprise and the welfare of its various constituents. When times were tough, they were expected to dig deeper to come up with the necessary capital to see the company through. With their capital and often their personal efforts at stake, they were committed to the enterprise. Indeed, in a real sense, they were tied irrevocably to its destiny. In return for that commitment, they had the right to make the crucial decisions that determined the company's future—whether to merge, acquire, sell, expand, contract, liquidate, and so on. These ownership practices and the concepts embodied in them are the foundation of the legal status of corporations and the rights of the owners in Britain, the United States, and most other Western countries.

Yet, as we know, things are different today. The enterprises are huge, and the profile of their shareholders changes continually. Amid the constantly shifting tides of stock transactions, the autopilot of programmed trading, and the Darwinian laws of high-pressure fund management, continuity of ownership, to say nothing of commitment and stewardship, is difficult to discern. Yet with the ownership of shares in a British or an American company comes instant power and responsibility. Every share carries a vote, regardless of how long the share has been held. All votes are equal. For many large corporations, fateful decisions put to the vote of shareholders are determined by fewer than 100 owners, even though the total number of all shareholders is counted in the tens of thousands. As Charles Handy pointed out, and as every corporate chairman knows, every company is up for sale every day.[24] The large institutions, managed by professionals with a trader's mentality, hold the votes. It should be no surprise that many CEOs spend more time with financial analysts and institutional money managers than with their employees and staff. Some CEOs behave as if it is more important to keep their large shareholders, rather than the company's customers and workers, happy.

Yet, it seems wrong to equate speculation in the value of a company's shares with ownership in the traditional sense. In today's world, shares are purchased so they can be sold. Indeed, the sooner the target price is reached and the shares are sold, the happier the money manager tends to be. The same institutional investor usually owns shares in major competitors in the same industry, a hedge on corporate performance that falls well short of the commitment that characterized owners of an earlier age. Some institutional investors further hedge their investment by selling short, so they can profit even if the value of shares falls. But the biggest difference between owners of an earlier era and many of the shareholders today is in the duration of their ownership. Should an investor who purchased the shares three months ago with an eye to a quick profit on the transaction have the same rights and powers as a shareholder of ten years or more?

Many corporate executives, and I am certainly a member of this camp, believe that the high-performance trading environment and the degree to which management is beholden to relatively few large institutional shareholders have been major contributors to the tendency of corporate executives to place too much emphasis on short-term profit performance, sometimes to the exclusion of long-term strategies and crucial investments in technology and organization.

The long period of crucial research that led to Tagamet dramatically illustrates the necessity of long-term investments. James Black, a British pharmacologist, was hired by Smith Kline & French in 1963 and installed at its Research Institute in Welwyn Garden City, England. He had been thinking for some time about the problem of histamine, which is ubiquitous in the human body and, among other things, stimulates the secretion of gastric acid that leads to ulcers. Traditional antihistamines were ineffective in the treatment of ulcers. So Black theorized that there must be more than one histamine receptor and that a histamine antagonist that was specifically designed to latch onto such receptors was called for, a hypothesis he brought with him when he joined the company. During the late 1960s, however, powerful elements in the company, focusing on short-term performance, wanted to shut down the Research Institute. Fortunately, wiser heads prevailed, and Black was allowed to continue his research. Finally, in 1973, almost five years after the effort to close the institute and ten years after he had come on board, he verified his hypothesis and synthesized a number of selective compounds that interfered with the histamine-induced secretion of gastric acid. In November 1976, Tagamet, the first histamine 2 receptor antagonist was introduced in Britain for the treatment of severe ulcers; nine months later, it was introduced in the United States. For a short-term investor, a thirteen-year period is an eternity; in pharmaceutical research and development, it's common.

Had short-term thinking prevailed, there would have been no Tagamet, at least from SmithKline. In terms of financial value, Tagamet became the first billion-dollar drug, and the value of Smith-Kline's shares quintupled within six years. More important, it relieved the suffering of millions of people the world over. As the first medication that was narrowly targeted at a specific receptor, it ushered in the era of "rationally designed" drugs, which are much safer and more effective than conventional medicines, and are now major components of the treatment of many serious diseases. In those terms, the value of the original research is nearly incalculable.

In today's environment, fund managers may be reluctant to stay the course for such long-term investments. In fact, a company's new investments in technology or a promising business may depress the company's stock, creating a situation in which the price of shares understates the company's value, leading to a takeover bid. In the airline business, for example, we have now seen the long-term damage done to Trans World Airlines and Continental by Carl Icahn and Frank Lorenzo in the name of maximizing shareholder value.

American and British corporate executives have long been criticized for their tendency to manage for the short term. In today's high-pressure environment with an exclusive focus on the price of stocks, that tendency has been further exaggerated and sometimes taken to absurd lengths. In February 1991, the board of General Dynamics Corporation, the number two defense contractor in the United States, adopted a controversial executive bonus plan tied directly to the price of the company's stock.[25] Adopted under pressure from the company's largest shareholders, the plan grants each of the company's top twenty-five executives huge bonuses every time the stock price rises ten dollars and stays at that level for ten consecutive trading days. The first such gain, in May 1991, won the executives a bonus equal to one year's salary. All ten-dollar gains thereafter have brought bonuses at double the annual salary.

In September 1991 the company's chairman, former astronaut William Anders, pledged publicly to return "excess cash" to shareholders, an announcement that immediately boosted the price of the company's shares to the next ten-dollar plateau, where it remained for the next ten trading days, triggering bonuses of double the annual salary. The pledge of returning "excess cash," depending upon how "excess" is defined, could mean refusing to invest for the future and selling off assets. Further, brief gains in the stock price may not be synonymous with the executives' good overall performance, even in other crucial financial areas. In fact, the definition of performance has been narrowed to performance of the price of shares.

Critics of American management's short-term outlook often say that many executives manage only from quarter to quarter; the General Dynamics plan shortens the focus to a mere ten days. Critics also contend that the combination of the bonus plan and returning "excess cash" is a formula for the eventual liquidation of the company, a prospect that today's transient owners cannot be concerned about.

In a discussion of the issue of the duration of ownership, a large institutional investor asked me under what circumstances a large shareholder would merit consideration for a seat on the board of directors. I replied that provided a significant investor was willing to commit irrevocably to continuing ownership in the company over a long period, say ten years, a seat on the board could certainly be considered. The conversation promptly ended on that note. It was clear to me that this institutional investor wanted the rights of ownership without relinquishing the prerogative to sell at any time for any reason.

On an even more philosophical level, I can't help but wonder if it is in the interests of society that the rights and powers of corporate ownership—that control the fate of tens of thousands of people and enormous technological prowess because of the intellect of many employees—can be bought and sold as if they were only commodities or a collection of inanimate buildings and machines? Should the motives of a dozen or so professional money mangers determine the fate of employees who have dedicated a lifetime to the corporation? The rights and powers of shareholders seem out of all proportion to the realities of large complex organizations. No other large collection of people in democratic societies would subject themselves to such distant and arbitrary—yet fateful—decisions.

These considerations are generating a variety of proposals to reform corporate ownership while maintaining the role of the stock markets as arbiters of corporate value. One proposal is that there should be two classes of shares: A shares, which would be actively traded but would not carry the rights and powers of ownership, and B shares, which, after a period of qualification, would become voting shares and could be held by other stakeholders, such as employees and communities. How such shares would be apportioned seems to be a difficult question to answer. So is the probable effect on trading, with the B shares no doubt selling at a significant discount to the more readily exchangeable, purely financial A shares.

Another more practical proposal is to make all capital gains subject to taxation, including the gains of pension funds, charitable endowments, and the like, but to graduate the rate of taxation on the sale by the length of time the shares have been held. For example, the gains on shares held for ten years or more would be free of tax; those held for less than one year would be taxed at a higher rate than earned or ordinary income. Ownership for periods of one to ten years would be taxed at rates that would gradually fall with time. Such a change might have a deleterious effect on stockbrokers and trading volume, but would certainly redefine the time span of ownership and would check the dangerous tendency to overemphasize short-term profits and short-term transactions.

Everyone will readily agree that profits are necessary for the generation of future working capital and for the long-term health and vitality of the enterprise. Everyone will also certainly agree that investors deserve a return on their investments in the form of dividends and the appreciated value of their equity. Profits are a vital ingredient in the success of a business. But the true purpose of a business is to manufacture and sell high-quality products and services to a growing number of pleased and happy customers. Profits are a means of achieving the true purpose of the enterprise, and, at least until a better index is found, they are the best measure of vitality. Nevertheless, we should not confuse the end with the means.

Another reform that is bringing corporate management closer to shareholders is a change in the way senior executives are being compensated. Traditionally, an executive of a large international company is compensated by a mix of a salary, an annual bonus, and long-term incentives that are usually paid through stock options. The executive's salary is established by monitoring a profile, often international, of the salary ranges of a panel of other companies. A key element, usually overlooked in public discussions of the pay of top executives, is that a CEO's salary range is not only based on a competitive analysis, but must provide room to reward and motivate the next two levels of managers, who in most cases are the driving forces for growth and, of course, are the source of the next generation of top executives. The yearly bonus is normally based on the company's annual performance against targets set by the board of directors. The targets are invariably bottom line, usually earnings per share, and bonuses range from zero to 150 percent of the executive's annual salary. The tying of the annual bonus to earnings per share increases the pressure on top executives to strive hard to improve the yearly — indeed, usually quarterly — growth of profits, ostensibly to keep the shareholders happy.

Long-term incentives are added to the mix to ensure that executives do not sacrifice the long term merely to earn an annual bonus. One common incentive is to grant the executive the option to purchase the company's shares at a fixed price, which is established by the market price on the date of issuance, usually for ten years. Executives risk no capital and taxes are not payable on the gains until the options have been exercised and the shares are actually purchased. Therefore, the value of the shares, assuming that the price of the shares increases, accumulates tax free until that time. Since the annual salary and bonuses are taxed as ordinary income, most senior executives regard long-term stock options as their primary vehicle for increasing their personal wealth. In that sense, options fulfill the principal purpose of motivating top executives to think and make decisions for the long-term interests of the company. More than any other factor in the compensation package, stock options align the top managers with the interests of long-term, continuing shareholders.

The weakness in the mix of salary, bonuses, and ten-year stock options is that the compensation is usually quite often not related to the actual performance of the company. Bonus awards are paid against targets proposed by the management, and unless the board is truly vigilant, the targets can reflect the company's mediocre performance. Furthermore, stock options are often made either valuable or of little value by the upward or downward movement of the stock market as a whole, regardless of the actual competitive performance of the company. Institutional shareholders understand all these considerations and are naturally angry when they see their investments producing little or no relative return while the top corporate managers seem to be doing very well. For the same reasons, conscientious boards of directors and senior executives are seeking better ways to measure and reward the creation of real economic value.

A concept that is gaining currency in large corporations is the establishment of performance measures that consider the combined impact of the contribution of profits and balance-sheet investments over time. Essentially, this approach changes the measure of performance from the growth in earnings per share to consistently earned profits at levels that are significantly higher than the cost of capital to the corporation. In other words, the new approach measures and rewards an economic view of value creation, rather than an accounting view of short-term profitability.

An example of this kind of thinking is found in the 1991 annual report of the Quaker Oats Company. Quaker Oats is measuring the creation of value in a way that integrates value-added profits from an investor's point of view with a manager's desire to create products and services that satisfy customers. Its 1991 annual report to the shareholders states:

THE INVESTORS' PERSPECTIVE

Investors expect to be compensated for the risk they accept when they invest in a stock. The higher the risk, the higher the expected return. From a shareholder's viewpoint, value is created when a company's total return — dividends and stock appreciation — meets or exceeds their expected return.

This expectation of performance is embodied in our first financial objective: To provide total shareholder returns that exceed the cost of equity and the S&P 500 over time.

THE COMPANY'S PERSPECTIVE

In fiscal 1991, we adopted a concept called "Controllable Earnings" as our primary financial performance measure. Controllable earnings give us a tool to measure economic value creation. This new system will enhance our ability to set and track progress against business goals consistent with shareholder value maximization.

Adjusted Operating Income - Capital Usage Charge = Controllable Earnings

> SENIOR MANAGERS ARE FOCUSED ON OPPORTUNITIES TO:
> * grow economically profitable businesses
> * increase the rate of return on capital
> * reduce investments in uneconomical businesses (those returning less than our costs of capital).[26]

I believe Quaker Oats is on the right track, but the real point is its development of a rational system of measuring the company's performance that can be explained to all the shareholders. Similar principles have been adopted by other well-known American companies, including AT&T, Berkshire Hathaway, Emerson Electric Company, and Beckman Instruments, to name a few. Such rational standards, clearly communicated, should align the managers of the company with the investors to a much greater degree than is often the case.

With the greater uniformity of standards in international financial markets; increasingly similar accounting standards; and clearly communicated, rational measurements of corporate performance and related techniques for rewarding corporate executives accordingly, there is reason to hope that the tension between large investors and corporate management will begin to ease. However, time is critical. Quaker Oats's first financial objective is to produce returns to shareholders that exceed the cost of equity and the S&P 500 *over time*. But what is an acceptable time frame for computing a company's performance — and acceptable to whom?

Indeed, the conflicting interests of all the stakeholders in a corporation may be understood in terms of their different time horizons. The time horizon of big institutional shareholders, as I noted, may be quite short, whereas the top managers' tend to be much longer, since the executives want to expand the business, increase their power and prestige, and guarantee their own security. Customers, especially those for big-ticket and high-technology goods and services, have the longest time horizon. When they buy a computer, a gas-fired turbine, telecommunications equipment, or an automobile, they are buying more than a product. Increasingly, they see themselves as buying after-purchase services as well—warranties, maintenance, and possible upgrades—and they want a stable company to ensure that those services will be available in the future. Because of this growing "software" component, the producer-customer relationship is becoming increasingly permanent. In a real sense, a purchase decision today is an investment decision entailing a long-term mutual commitment.

From the perspective of a moment or a day, these various time horizons appear hopelessly at odds. Yet over time, the interests of all parties converge, and the corporation becomes an enormous engine for the productive use of physical, human, and intellectual assets in the creation of value for the society at large, as well as for the company's employees and investors. But only a commonly held concept of time—one that resists the temptations of the short term and the complacency of the long term—will harmonize these competing interests. It must be the final plank in the bridge that will unite the managers and investors, the company and its customers. The development of a common view of time sounds like a metaphysical abstraction, but it needn't be. If companies can arrive at rational measures of performance, as those such as Quaker Oats are doing, then they can also arrive at rational measures of time.

The responsibility for bringing together the interests of the various constituencies served by the corporation ultimately rests with the board of directors. The board must see that the interests of all parties are served in a way that creates real value. It must also assure that the management fulfills its responsibility to the investors, as well as to the customers and employees. Most important perhaps, the board must understand that time is the fourth dimension of management and ensure the convergence of the various interests being served. These issues are the real stuff of corporate governance. The managers operate the company, recruit and train an organization of people, and develop and deploy the intellectual assets of the company. The board of directors, in governing the company, guarantees that the interests of the important constituencies—or stakeholders—are appropriately balanced and that true value for all concerned is created over time. The authority constituted by the board is the power to hire and fire the managers.

With that power as the ultimate sanction, the board reviews and approves strategies and plans, establishes long-range direction and policies, evaluates results, decides on the basic allocation of resources, and compensates the managers and employees with an eye to their performance.

Perhaps the most extraordinary recent example of a corporate board shouldering its responsibility was the shakeup of GM, carried out largely by outside directors on April 6, 1992. The shakeup was extraordinary because GM's board has historically acted as a rubber stamp for the management. Nevertheless, following the largest losses in American corporate history, including some $7 billion in North America, the board demoted the president and the company's chief financial officer; removed Chairman Robert Stempel from his post as head of the powerful executive committee of the board; and handed over the reins to an outside director, John G. Smale, retired chairman and CEO of Procter & Gamble. (When Smale ran Procter & Gamble, he was known for eliminating hierarchical organizational structures and replacing them with cross-functional teams that included everyone from production workers to executives.[27] And during his nine-year tenure as CEO, he moved the company into new markets around the world, competed successfully in Japan, and doubled the company's earnings.) In another move that was little noticed but highly significant, the directors also eliminated two directorships held by GM executives, giving the eleven outside directors even greater weight on the now fifteen-member board.

The role of the managers and corporate governance by the board of directors are basically the same for all publicly held corporations, regardless of their size or global scale. There are, however, several dimensions of complexity that apply primarily to transnational companies. First, because of their size, they are, more than most other companies, owned by large institutional investors, who, as I have detailed, place special demands on their investments. Second, the transnational nature of the corporation requires that the regions of the world being served have some real measure of representation.

Investors of all types and sizes, particularly institutional investors, want to be assured of the active governance of a company by boards comprised largely of independent directors who are capable of exercising their duties to the highest professional standards. Increasingly, the majority of members of such boards are drawn from outside the management of the company, so they are independent directors in fact as well as in name. The investors also insist that committees of these boards be composed entirely of independent directors who establish compensation for the top executives and review with the outside auditors the financial statements of the companies on a regular basis. In line with the demand for greater independence and professionalism at the board level, there is a growing movement in Britain to separate the roles of the chairman and CEO. Such a separation more clearly demarcates the important differences between corporate governance and operating management.

In the days of multinational companies, international matters were often represented by an "international advisory board," composed of prominent people from a variety of countries in which a company did business. This board met with a company's managers once or twice a year, often in one of the world's great watering spots, to discuss major international trends. Although this type of board was of value, it had no authority or inclination to take on matters of corporate governance. Its charter was, as its name states, strictly advisory. It was also handicapped by its members' limited knowledge of the company's business, which necessarily limited their advice to general matters.

With the advent of transnational companies, these international advisory boards are giving way to regular boards of directors that include representatives from different parts of the world. These board members must travel long distances to attend board meetings on a regular basis, but they are constituted with full authority and soon become familiar with all the details of the company's businesses. They participate in the decisions of governance and bring to boardroom debates the perspectives and experiences of their varied national and cultural experiences. Since globality is central to the strategic purpose of large transnational corporations, broad international representation on the board is a vital ingredient to a company's long-term success. ICI, of Britain, was one of the first large companies to move in this direction, with representatives from the United States, Germany, and Japan elected to its main board more than five years ago.

SmithKline Beecham deliberately recruited independent directors from France and Germany to complement its original group of

American and British directors, and it is committed to further internationalization of the board. It has also shrunk the board from twenty members to sixteen, eliminating in the process three directorships held by company executives. Outside directors now hold nine of the sixteen directorships. Furthermore, the independent directors have been assigned to two-member teams, with two nationalities represented on each. The teams are charged with spending at least two days per year learning an important business sector on their own without any filtration by the chairman, the CEO, or the corporate staff. Team members really get into the bowels of the business. For example, Sir Robert Clarke, the retired chairman of the British merchant bank Hill Samuels who serves as vice-chairman of the board of SmithKline Beecham, spent an entire day in Montgomery County, Pennsylvania, with one of the company's salesmen of animal health products, calling on veterinarians. When he returned at the end of the day, his face was wreathed in smiles; he and his partner had sold $2,400 worth of products. These teams of binational, independent directors have achieved some positive results. In addition to learning the company's business in many countries, they have also helped bring the board closer together across cultural boundaries, and they have helped interpret the transnational nature of the board and the business to middle managers and employees. And, perhaps most important, they advance the board's goal of exercising the kind of informed, impartial, and multicultural oversight that best protects the interests of all stakeholders in the corporation.

Throughout the 150 years or so of corporate history, there have been attempts, at least nominally, to take everyone's interests into account. During the phenomenal post–World War II boom in the United States, when American corporations enjoyed such unchallenged success that they were able to accommodate all parties without apparent strain, a philosophy of stewardship developed among many prominent CEOs. These CEOS saw themselves as wise custodians of the interests of all the competing constituencies of the corporation: shareholders, employees, and customers. At its worst, the midcentury philosophy of stewardship amounted to little more than a paternalistic and occasionally self-righteous management that assumed that it alone knew what was best for all concerned. In defense of this view, however, it should be said that such CEOs at least made some attempt to consider workers, customers, and communities, even if, on occasion, they shortchanged shareholders.

A backlash was bound to develop, and it did, when hard times, global competition, the ascendancy of institutional investors, and a new generation of financial buccaneers began to place enormous strains on corporations. Against the often-complacent stewardship model was raised the war cry of "maximizing shareholder value." And so, as I have described, corporations have been playing out a new drama of these clashing interests for the past decade or more. But, as I have also noted, there are hopeful signs that the pendulum is swinging back toward a more balanced position. The recent trend toward closing the breach between shareholders and executives represents a fundamental shift in the philosophy of the past decade—maximizing shareholder value—to a more broadly economic conception of value that incorporates the interests of everyone.

I am not proposing a return to the often self-serving stewardship model of the postwar period. Boards of directors, reformed along many of the lines suggested by institutional investors and broadened internationally to represent the transnational world, are far more evenhanded than the executives who simply called the shots, confident that they knew what was best for everyone. More to the point, such boards are to be guided by a philosophy of creating economic value, not by a cloudy notion of serving the greater good. The idea is not to exclude the greater good, but to acknowledge that the greater good is truly served only when there are equitable ways of arriving at an agreement on what it is and rational standards for measuring it.

But even if such reforms resolve the struggle inside the corporation, what of the struggle outside it? Nations and their governments must now contend with transnational corporations that are often bigger than they are and that operate far beyond the capacity of any one country to oversee. From tax policies to environmental questions to labor issues, transnationals, as the term suggests, present unique challenges in a world that is organized along nationalist lines. As global economics collides with local politics, neither will emerge unchanged—and so I now turn from governance to government.

Chapter Eight

THE SOVEREIGN COMPANY?

IF A GREAT MANY COMPANIES now stand at the transnational cross-roads, so do most countries. These countries are also faced with the choice of participating fully in the global trading system or falling hopelessly behind in competitiveness and prosperity. No one wants to be left behind, yet many governmental officials around the world hesitate, temporize, and remain standing at the crossroads paralyzed with anxiety. In a world of obvious economic interdependence, they worry that nation-states, including the most powerful, are losing their sovereignty. In the world's capitals, there is a growing feeling that the power of the nation state to control its own destiny and influence events is on the wane. Not only do these politicians and civil servants seem hesitant about defining the national interest as it applies to the strategy and behavior of transnational corporations, but they sense that national authority alone no longer provides many answers to the major problems appearing on national agendas.

Consider the agenda:

1. *Industrial growth and competitiveness.* This item is first on the agenda because the global imperative is bringing the strongest competitive forces to bear in most vital industrial sectors.

2. *National security.* National security is increasingly a matter of collective action, as was clearly demonstrated in 1991 by the war in the Persian Gulf, in which the United States supplied most of the forces but took action only after lining up a coalition of eighteen active allies and obtaining limited authority from the United Nations, as well as from the U.S. Congress.

3. *Illegal Drugs.* This global phenomenon can be tackled only by concerted international action directed at eradicating both the supply and the demand of illegal drugs.

4. *Crime.* Crime is related to illegal drugs because of the symbiotic nature of crime and the international supply of drugs and financing of the drug trade.

5. *AIDS.* AIDS is a global scourge of increasing ferocity against which there are no national barriers and that is further draining the already-depleted coffers of many national health care systems.

6. *Monetary policy.* Monetary policy is increasingly dictated by international comparisons that, in turn, govern interest rates and exchange rates and, in the case of the United States, the funding of the national debt.

7. *Environmental issues.* The depletion of the ozone layer, acid rain, and the pollution of the oceans are matters of profound concern to people throughout the world and can be addressed only on an international level.

A few items on this agenda, like acid rain, can also be tackled on a regional basis, as in North America or Europe, but most require entirely global approaches. Since the use of military force by nation-states is becoming less and less germane to an agenda that consists primarily of economic and social priorities, countries must approach most of the items on their agenda on a collaborative basis. As they do so—sometimes willingly, sometimes reluctantly—they fear that their cherished national prerogatives and power will steadily erode.

The presumed loss of sovereignty is taking place on two fronts simultaneously: first, to international and supranational bodies like

GATT, The Group of Seven, the European Commission, the International Monetary Fund, and regional trading blocs, and second, to transnational companies that operate beyond the capacity of any one country to oversee or control. The two phenomena, of course, reinforce each other: Global trade means global economic interdependence that requires international rules and cooperation, and such cooperation toward freer world trade means more opportunities for global companies and thus more global interdependence.

The tremendous growth in international commerce, which has fueled the expansion of global companies, has occurred under the umbrella of GATT, an international organization that began operating in 1948. GATT's Articles of Agreement pledge its 108 member countries to foster international trade. From 1947 through 1979, a series of negotiations, called "rounds," aimed to reduce tariffs among the member nations and to reduce or eliminate national subsidies of primary export products.

These regular GATT rounds led to a vast increase in international trading in manufactured goods. It then required an accident of history to put in place a powerful and complementary global financial system. The rise of OPEC (Organization of Petroleum Exporting Countries) in the 1970s required an international mechanism for recirculating the enormous profits reaped primarily by Saudi Arabia and its neighbors. With no place to spend or invest their sudden profits, the oil moguls of the Middle East stimulated the integration of a vast global network that connected the money centers of Europe, North America, and Japan. Originally oriented toward so-called petrodollars, meaning the hard currency earned by the OPEC nations, the global network continued to flourish long after OPEC declined.

In the 1980s, the process of globalization was completed through direct foreign investments in plants and equipment and organizational expansion, augmented by cross-border mergers and acquisitions. Meanwhile, GATT members gradually agreed to move beyond tangible barriers to trade and began to consider less visible obstacles, such as regulatory procedures and structural impediments to access to each other's markets. With the current highly contentious Uruguay Round of negotiations, which began in Punta del Este in 1986 and continues in Geneva, the opening of services (especially financial services), the protection of intellectual property, and the elimination of agricultural subsidies have been added to GATT's agenda for liberalizing the world's current $4.3 trillion in annual trade.

Similarly, much of the original impetus for the European Economic Community came from the desire to open trade among the member nations. Many matters of law and policy—from tariffs to technical specifications for products to regulatory rules—all of which were formerly the province of national governments, are now referred for decision to the European Commission in Brussels. But the drive toward union is not confined to the economic sphere. Since the first Treaty of Rome established the European Economic Community in 1957 with six members, the European Community has been moving toward political union as well. In 1975, members agreed on the direct election of a European Parliament, albeit with limited powers. In 1985 the first European passports were issued. In 1986, in perhaps the most significant ceding of national authority, the European Community adopted a procedure that allows most proposals to be passed by a weighted majority vote, rather than by the unanimous consent of all member countries. And in 1991 the twelve-member nations agreed on a treaty to establish common foreign and defense policies and a single currency by the end of the century. Though the treaty has been thrown into confusion by the refusal of Danish voters to ratify it in a referendum on June 2, 1992, the drive for political union is likely to continue.

European governments aren't the only ones wrestling with issues of sovereignty. In the United States, for example, the issue of national sovereignty in international trade has been fought most recently over "fast-track" procedures for the approval of trade bills. Since 1974 such procedures have required Congress to accept or reject foreign trade bills without amendment after the president has submitted them for congressional approval. The procedures were originally adopted after Congress rejected parts of trade agreements in 1968, which led to a six-year period in which most U.S. trading partners refused to negotiate until they could be assured that trade bills would not be amended unilaterally by Congress.

In 1991, when these fast-track procedures came up for renewal, an intense debate took place. Opponents of fast-track rules argued that they cede too much authority to the executive branch of government and, by extension, to the trade representatives of foreign countries. They further contended that fast-track procedures allow no debate on portions of trade treaties that may contravene local and state environmental and safety laws (often deemed invisible trade barriers when they vary widely in strictness from country to country). "With so much at stake," wrote Ralph Nader, "Americans should not subordinate their rights to have their Congressional representatives evaluate all of an extensive proposal that affects national, state and local health and safety standards, in addition to conventional matters of tariffs."[1] Proponents of the fast-track procedures, however, warned that scuttling them would also likely scuttle the Uruguay Round of GATT; the proposed free-trade agreement with Mexico; and the Enterprise for the Americas initiative, which envisions free-trade agreements with many Latin American countries.

Although the ceding of national authority to supranational bodies has been more or less voluntary, it has been difficult for many countries to accept and hard for their citizens to understand, and it is still far from an accomplished fact even in areas that demand concerted, multilateral action. The perilous condition of the Uruguay Round, which is teetering on the verge of collapse, demonstrates the fragility of these emerging global arrangements. The harmony of the European Community has been threatened by Britain's refusal to join the other eleven members in common social and labor policies, its reluctance to give up the pound in favor of a common European currency, and its resistance to a strengthened "federal" European structure that could overrule Britain on important defense or security policies.

Only a series of artful and somewhat hazy compromises, the consequences of which will not be clear for some years to come, managed to bring the historic treaty negotiations at Maastricht to a successful conclusion in December of 1991. But Britain steadfastly maintains the right of its Parliament to decide on monetary union, if and when it becomes a reality, and insists that it could not be signed away by the prime minister. Many Germans, too, despite their long-standing support of a European union, did not like the idea of giving up the mark in favor of a single European currency. According to public opinion polls released on the eve of the Maastricht agreement, some 71 percent of the Germans wanted the decision on a single currency postponed.[2] The Social Democrats, who control the upper house of the German legislature, complained that Chancellor Helmut Kohl should have insisted on increased democratic powers for the European Parliament to watch over the European central bank that will control the new currency. In France, opposition to the treaty cuts across ideological lines, embracing elements of the extreme Left, the extreme Right, and most shades of opinion in between. The opposition was summarized by the conservative writer Alain Peyrefitte this way: "No diplomatic instrument has ever had such an irreversible impact on our national sovereignty."[3] Furthermore, as the ambitious treaty on European union was being thrashed out inside the Maastricht town hall, angry Dutch and Belgian farmers, opposed to the ending of agricultural subsidies that may come with union, fought with police outside. But by far the most direct and effective expression of opposition to the treaty has been its rejection by Danish voters, who were said to fear that their country would be swallowed up by a federal Europe. Though the negative Danish vote will not delay the coming of the single market, it does throw the issues of monetary and political union into confusion because the treaty must be ratified unanimously and because Denmark cannot vote on it again unless it is changed.

As the Danish referendum illustrates, the ceding of authority to supranational bodies has at least been painstakingly negotiated in full view of the public, which in the democracies can take out its displeasure in the voting booth. And though the yielding of some sovereignty causes anxiety and reasonable people disagree about its wisdom, it is at least being pursued on the grounds that, in the long run, it is in the national interest. The anxiety over transnationals reaches to a deeper level. Unplanned by policymakers and unforeseen by the public, transnationals seem to have emerged almost overnight. Elected by no one and seemingly operating beyond the regulatory capacity of any single nation, transnationals raise the specter of an unanticipated and certainly involuntary loss of sovereignty. What is most troubling, they do not appear to be bound to any particular nation and therefore do not operate in concert with any identifiable national interest.

Thus many people now wonder if companies have become sovereign while nation-states are gradually seeing their ability to guide their own destinies gradually seeping away. Do the interests of transnationals transcend those of the countries in which they operate? If the identity of such companies is not national, where does the companies' allegiance lie? To answer such questions—and to address, if not allay, the fears that prompt them—it is necessary to understand how identity and allegiance really operate for transnationals and, perhaps more important, to understand the national interest clearly as it applies to corporate enterprise.

Those who are concerned about corporate allegiance to the national interest tend to view international commerce as a "zero-sum game," in which each transaction has a winner and a loser. They believe that the sum of international transactions identifies and quantifies national winners and losers and that a gain by one participant means a corresponding loss for some other participant. But commerce and industry are not that simple. The whole purpose of free enterprise is to create value, not to redistribute and reshuffle a finite amount of wealth endlessly. When value is created — as, for example, when a new medication improves health and shortens hospital stays, thereby keeping people productive and reducing the drain on health care systems — wealth is tangibly increased. The producer of the medication profits, of course, but so do the people and societies who use it. It is a "win-win," rather than a "win-lose" situation.

Similarly, international commerce is not a matter of reshuffling a finite amount of wealth among countries. For example, many developing countries have recently awarded contracts to global telecommunications companies to provide cellular telephone systems. Cellular systems will allow such nations to skip the costly and laborious process of hard-wiring their entire countries — it requires only about seven months to install a cellular system, but ten to twenty years to install a land-line system of the same size[4] — and will quickly provide them with the capacity for digital communications on which so much commerce depends today. And these nations will further profit from the transfer of advanced technological knowledge to their societies at the lowest current price. So regardless of whether the global telecommunications companies repatriate the resulting profits or reinvest them somewhere else, everybody wins.

Granted, these companies have no allegiance, in the traditional sense, to any of these countries. They do, however, have a strong desire to perform competitively and to the highest global standards of value, quality, and service. Meanwhile, the allegiance of purely national companies is often based on little more than a fondness for a protected domestic market, which may, for a time, provide comfortable business conditions and preserve some jobs, but which, in the long run, leads to a loss of competitiveness and the very erosion of national wealth such protection is supposed to prevent.

Furthermore, global commerce is immensely complicated. Throughout the world, day and night, a vast, incomprehensible number of connected and unconnected transactions takes place continuously. These transactions are impossible to quantify comprehensively, not only because they are so numerous and complex, but because economic activity involves human beings pursuing interests and goals that are rooted in motives that defy a rational analysis in terms of "economic man."

Unfortunately, economists at universities have reinforced the simplistic notion of commerce as a zero-sum game by teaching that economics can be analyzed by applying sophisticated mathematical models similar to those used in calculating the paths of the celestial bodies in the universe. By now, it must be apparent that no one has come up with the right mathematical formulas. It's no wonder. A far more descriptive conceptual model of a nation's or, indeed the world's, economy would be much closer to the incalculable diversity and fertility of nature than to astrophysics. Yet, the simplistic zero-sum concept dominates popular rhetoric and commentary, particularly regarding international trade and national interest.

This is not to suggest, however, that there is no such thing as national interest. Indeed, there must always be national interest even if it is not well articulated and equally cannot be directly applied to the conduct of international trade and commerce. The clearest contemporary example of the application of national interest to corporate purpose and international conduct is Japan. There is no doubt that following the devastation of World War II, Japan formulated and put into effect a clear national policy of rebuilding an industrial infrastructure and gaining competitive equilibrium with Europe and North America while introducing a modern democratic political system. The national government promulgated policies that were designed to protect nascent industries, encourage savings and investment, and provide high-quality education to Japan's only significant natural resource, her people. Industry focused on building an internationally competitive production capability and exporting enough value-added high-quality products at least to cover the nation's foreign-exchange requirements for the importation of essential raw materials, energy, and food.

Every Japanese citizen and every industrial company was expected to contribute to the national goals, and nothing was allowed to impede or contradict the pursuit of the clearly stated national interest. In describing their overarching and enduring corporate goals, most significant Japanese companies adopted "national company policies" pledging their efforts to contribute to the national interest, that until recently, specifically included increasingly strong exports.

A clear and well-understood set of national goals and the enlistment of every citizen and business in the pursuit of them has served Japan well. The success of the Japanese "miracle" is obvious and has become a source of envy and resentment throughout Europe and the United States. A great many people outside Japan think Japanese corporations have become too successful and that the companies pursuing national company policies are predators that are unfairly exploiting the international trading system. What is generally not remembered is that the reconstruction of the Japanese and German economies following World War II was part of the clearly stated American and European national interests as well. The Allies eagerly sought to help rebuild the industrial and financial structures of their former enemies for humanitarian reasons and as forward bulwarks in the policy to contain the Soviet Union. The policy of reconstructing the economies of Japan and Germany has not only helped their people, it has greatly assisted the economies of the Allied nations by providing strong markets and by strengthening the international trading system. The collapse of communism alone has justified the effort. But the success of the international trading system as an engine for producing wealth for people everywhere, particularly the former allied nations of North America and Western Europe, has been the real triumph.

Now, almost fifty years since the war ended, the winds of change are again blowing and with gathering force. People are disturbed and confused. Citizens wonder where their national interests lie, particularly with respect to the international trading system. Should international trade and investment defenses be raised or lowered? Should nations continue to build an open global system with clear and fair rules? Should the multilateral international system that has been constructed around the GATT agreements over the past thirty years be further developed, or should it be abandoned in favor of inward-looking national or regional policies? Should we jettison the multilateral approach manifested in GATT and seek instead bilateral agreements country by country? What are others doing, and what do their people really think? Are we being unfairly exploited and unfairly criticized?

These questions are being raised in all societies. Increasingly, they appear in the daily newspapers and television broadcasts in the United States, Europe, Japan, and elsewhere, and they are strikingly similar in content and tone. The most disturbing thing about this universal phenomenon is that these questions are not being addressed by political leaders anywhere. Indeed, the politicians seem more confused and uncertain than do their citizens. Even in Europe, rushed to put the single market fully in place by the end of 1992, no one led the community boldly forward because most of the national leaders faced elections dominated by local issues.[5]

The world stands at a watershed. The success of the Japanese tempts many people to want to copy Japan's frankly nationalistic orientation or, at the least, to use their counties' trade policies to retaliate against Japan's international export strategy. In fact, in many countries, the resentment against this single country threatens to poison attitudes toward free trade in general. In such an atmosphere, the idea of national interest becomes equated with protectionism, while free trade comes to be seen as giving away the country.

Meanwhile, transnational companies are providing perhaps the strongest single counterforce against the repeated questioning of the open international trading system and the attraction of a narrow and self-defeating definition of national interest. The orientation of transnationals is clearly global, and these companies define the interests being served more and more in terms of a global society. Moreover, their activities across borders are premised on the notion that international trade is not a zero-sum game. The results prove it. Large transnational companies with roots in the Western economies of Europe and North America have been in the vanguard of this movement. But the key to the movement's ultimate success will be the leadership provided by the main Japanese companies. Some of these successful Japanese companies have already joined the global movement. And there is reason to believe that the imperatives of the global marketplace will eventually draw in other Japanese companies and with them, the Japanese government itself.

As a member of a team of top SmithKline Beecham managers who were recently delegated to study the management techniques of high-performing Japanese companies, I was interested to see the

changes in thinking as well as in doing since I lived and worked in
Japan twenty-five years ago. A significant change in two such companies, Canon and NEC, is that their national company policies
have been restated to take on a distinctly global view. Canon, adher-
ing to what it calls its "International Creed," puts it this way:

> Canon, striving to become a premier international company, seeks to
> serve society and mankind worldwide through the following individ-
> ual and collective efforts of all its members:
>
> To help build a better world, contributing to the prosperity and happi-
> ness of peoples of every nation, through the wealth created by the
> development of the world's most advanced technologies and highest
> quality products.
>
> To contribute to the advancement of communities of which Canon is a
> constituent part by demonstrating exemplary corporate citizenship
> through responding to consumer needs, creating rewarding employ-
> ment, and promoting industrial cooperation.
>
> To provide opportunities for all those employed as members of the
> Canon family group to attain self-fulfillment through their work, by
> which they can contribute to the common welfare and human
> progress. All members of the Canon family group, as responsible citi-
> zens, contribute to the good of their respective communities.
>
> To contribute to harmony and cooperation among peoples by fostering
> free trade and international exchange through the conduct of rational
> and responsible global business policies based on broad, long-term
> vision.[6]

The major change represented by this statement is, of course,
the strong commitment to a global society and, by implication, the
withdrawal of any commitment to exports that exclusively benefit
Japan. In the place usually reserved for stating the commitment to a
nationalistic export strategy, there is a pledge to provide rewarding
employment and to advance the communities of which Canon is a
"constituent part." When I asked exactly what these words should
be understood to mean, I was told that as a result of a new corporate strategy directed personally by Canon's chairman, the com-

pany's new policy is to spread production and therefore employment and to provide community support in the global markets the
company serves. Canon's new statement of purpose is a direct
result of this change in strategies.

NEC has replaced its national company policy with a similar
global policy. Both Canon and NEC now believe that their overall
obligations are to the people of the world. The obligations apply not
just to the quality of products and technology, but to global employment and investment. These two leading companies have defined
their destinies in terms of the global market and correspondingly
have redefined their responsibilities in terms of the societies they
serve around the world.

Over the years, in my regular, at least annual, trips to Japan, I
have noted in conversations with friends subtle shifts in awareness
of Japan's new place in the world. But only recently have I been able
to observe some genuine changes in behavior. As a director and
then the chairman of the U.S.-Japan Business Council, a private
organization of Japanese and American businessmen charged with
improving economic and business relations between the two countries, I have found that most of the official dialogue has reflected the
strident tones of our national governments. The recent SmithKline
Beecham study group, however, provided a unique perspective
because we studied official company documents in preparation for
our visit, spent an entire day with the senior managers of the companies, and — most important — concentrated only on companies
performing at a high competitive level. In short, we intensively
studied some of the most outstanding companies. It is not surprising that these high-performing companies are in the vanguard with
respect to corporate strategy. The essence of the change among
these companies is their turning away from their "national company policies" and the neomercantilist goals supporting a narrow
national interest and embracing a global orientation that redefines
national interest as a full partnership in the global trading system.

Further evidence of the change in the direction of Japanese corporate goals and practices was a remarkable speech delivered by
Akio Morita, chairman of Sony Corporation and vice chairman of
the Keidanren (the Japanese Federation of Economic Organizations)
in Honolulu on January 3, 1992.[7] Entitled "A New Paradigm for
True Partnership," Morita's speech promised "some new thinking
about how Japan can play a more meaningful and constructive role

on the global stage." Arguing that the "crucial burden of change" lies with Japan, which he said, "is in desperate need of a new philosophy of management; a new paradigm for competitiveness; a new sense of self," Morita put Japan's nationalistic trade policies in the historical context of the postwar experience:

> For the past 45 years Japan has thought of itself as a rebuilding nation with a duty to focus solely on its own self interests in molding a newly democratic, free market society. The end of the war gave birth to a new Japan; and the policies of the government, the practices of business, and the assistance of the United States were all aimed at nurturing this new infant member of the global community.

It is this unusual nation-building experience, of course, that present-day Japan bashers have conveniently overlooked. Nevertheless, Morita boldly declared that "those days are over, and the old ways of doing things can no longer apply." Using an oblique metaphor of golfers' handicaps (which are designed to even the competition among players with different levels of ability), Morita conceded that Japan had used such handicapping "to play its own version of the free trade game, to obviously successful results." But it is just such outdated practices, he said, that "prevent Japan from being able to join the leading economies of Europe and North America in true global partnership."

Much of the success of Japanese industries has been achieved on the backs of employees, who are paid comparatively less than European and American employees for longer hours. Moreover, said Morita, in an effort to win a market share before all other considerations, Japanese companies take slimmer profit margins and pay stockholders smaller dividends than the shareholders of American and European corporations would tolerate. All these competitive practices, deeply rooted in the highly competitive domestic Japanese market, have allowed Japanese companies to compete "viciously" on price, but at some cost to their international image. As Morita stated:

> This competitive approach, fully accepted as necessary by society, made Japanese industry strong. But it does not translate well overseas. For it is precisely this philosophy of competitiveness which also leads to multilateral trade friction.

Though none of these highly competitive practices technically violates the rules of competition, Morita noted, they surely fail "to embrace the spirit of competition found in the United States and Europe."

Should anyone doubt that Japan's business philosophy provokes resentment, they need only look at the case of Japanese automobile "transplants" in Europe, where many European officials have strongly resisted accepting the Japanese cars made in Europe as being European. "The reasons for this," said Morita, "must go beyond the issues of local content and location of home headquarters because companies like Ford do not seem to have similar problems. So I concluded that it must be due to Japan's peculiar business philosophy."

Most striking, Morita said that Japan must do nothing less than "reinvent itself" if it is to be a part of the global economy and "blend with the prevailing attitudes and practices of international business." "Global responsibility and leadership," he noted, "does not come without first making a strong commitment to being a contributing, global team player."

I have quoted Morita's speech at such length because I believe it is an early indicator, along with the redirection of the goals of leading Japanese companies, of a real shift in Japanese attitudes toward global trade and a redefinition of Japanese national interest. The fact that his speech and a corresponding magazine article by him in *Bungei Shunju*, a leading Japanese weekly, have attracted a great deal of criticism in Japan does not detract from their importance. On the contrary, Morita has always been ahead of his time, a trait that was instrumental in the creation of Sony.

In this context, Morita's speech will be seen as something of a watershed in Japan's view of itself and its place in the world. It is particularly remarkable because during the past decade, Morita has been an articulate critic of Western management and business practices in public and in private. He does not shy away from speaking his mind in a direct fashion and in a manner that is not always as polite as most of his countrymen are reputed to be.

Looking back over the past thirty years, in which I worked, lived, traveled, and in various ways did business in Japan, I realize that I have been witness to a historic transformation. Obviously, Japan's economic success has been incredible and unprecedented, but I am thinking of an even more profound change. The people of

Japan, especially the generation of leaders who are currently in their fifties and early sixties and are now taking the reins of business and governmental power, have completed the emotional and attitudinal transition to Western democratic and economic values that was set in motion by the Meiji reformation 140 years ago. Only thirty years ago, with the launch of Contac in Japan, I was the first Western businessman whom most of the company's wholesale and retail customers had actually encountered. Now such personal experiences are commonplace. With such experiences and on the back of its outstanding economic performance, Japan is taking its place in the world, and the Japanese people are doing so without abandoning their national and ethnic cultural heritage. Their success in completing this transition to a new role is being watched carefully and closely by all the emerging democracies of Asia.

However, no one should think that statements like Morita's or a more global outlook by Japanese companies are purely altruistic. Enlightened leaders in Japan recognize that much of their success has been due to their selfish exploitation of the global trading system in ways that will no longer be permitted. They worry about protectionism and deeply fear outright ostracism from the global community of trading nations. As Kenneth S. Courtis, a senior strategist and economist at Deutsche Bank Capital Markets (Asia) in Tokyo, put it, "Japan is on the threshold of greatness. But it can't run a $1 trillion current account surplus this decade without incurring huge problems."[8]

Conversely, many Japanese leaders know they have much to gain by becoming full-fledged, accredited members of the global system. But these changes in philosophy and commitment also demonstrate the strong attraction of the global marketplace itself. No company of any size and status, no matter how successful, can afford to stand aside from the imperatives of the global market, nor can it ignore the real obligations and responsibility to a global society that come with a true transnational status. So whether their national leaders want them to or not, such companies will be drawn ineluctably into transnationalism in every sense of the word. They will be compelled to take equal account of all the nations and communities in which they operate. They will take care not to engage in nationalistic trade practices that alienate host governments or, more important, their customers in those nations. (Were it not for the enlightened practices of Honda and other Japanese automakers and the lingering memories many American consumers have of the poor-quality domestic cars foisted on the public in recent years, I think there would have been a serious consumer backlash against the Japanese car companies in the United States, rather than the abortive "Buy American" campaign.)

The apparently neutral behavior of transnationals may confound notions of a narrow national interest, but in the long run, by strengthening the global trading system, which is the real engine of the creation of wealth around the world, transnationalism contributes to a more prosperous and more just world economic order, and such an order is in the interests of all nations. It is no accident that a man of Morita's experience, talent, and global outlook is far ahead of his country's political leaders. Most politicians around the world seem to be lurching from poll to poll, unable or unwilling to provide inspired leadership and to articulate new national goals. Indeed, many of the world's political leaders appear to be floundering between the Scylla of outright protectionism, often disguised as "regionalism," and the Charybdis of an open, laissez faire global trading system. Consequently, it is difficult to understand what the national interests of the United States and other major trading nations are as they apply to major corporations that are competing globally.

In my view, the change taking place in Japan only serves to underline the need for the further development of the global economic system. Full-fledged participation in the global system is unavoidable. A retreat from it is probably impossible, but even if it were possible, it would only doom the citizens of any country that did so to permanent second-class status. This lesson has been painfully learned by the former members of the communist bloc and by most of the nations of South America and Southeast Asia, which for decades isolated their economies and their businesses from the rest of the world. Political demagogues like Pat Buchanan in the United States; Edith Cresson, the recently deposed prime minister of France; and Shintaro Ishihara in Japan can still appeal to nationalist and protectionist sentiments and make life difficult for their political opponents. But I doubt that many responsible citizens of any country want to turn the clock back to the days of competing nations. An even worse prospect is competing regional economic groups, clustered around the tripolar economic superpowers, Japan, Europe, and the United States. If the world turns from a global interdependent economy toward regional blocs, companies may cease to be the major competitors on a global playing field; instead, the game will be taken over by regional blocs. With these stark alternatives in view, the course of national interest seems clear: a commitment to full participation in the global trading system and a willingness by all participants to formulate clear rules for making the system as open, objective, and fair as possible.

In considering the relationship of national interest to global economic interdependence, we must consider the notion that global military conflict is being replaced by global commercial and industrial competition. I don't mean to suggest that the level of violence and military action in the world is subsiding; quite the contrary. About fifty armed conflicts are raging in the world right now. The difference is that these conflicts are not caused by ideological competition and are not being waged on a global scale or being backed by global adversaries, as was the case for most of this century. Rather, these conflicts are localized and reflect primarily the resurgence of ethnic and cultural identities—a revival of tribalism under the umbrella of economic interdependence—a key feature of the emerging world to which I return in the final chapter.

Much of today's *global* tension is between competing forms of capitalism, and transnational companies are in the front line. A national policy of economic isolation is no more likely to succeed than isolationist foreign policies did in the 1930s. A decision not to participate now will merely postpone the engagement and cause those who enter the struggle late to do so from an even weaker position.

If countries are unable to articulate their national interest as it applies to the global enterprise and if their national agendas are crowded with items requiring international agreement and collective action, what is left for them as nation-states? Are nations obsolete? Are they being squeezed out by supranational bodies that assume the necessary authority to solve social and economic problems and by transnational corporations that are operating on a global scale? In the context of global interdependence, what national policies are required to keep a nation competitive with other members of the system and to enable it to share equally in economic growth?

It is well beyond the scope of this book and beyond the ability of this writer to answer all these important questions. But perhaps it is

worth turning around the question about transnational corporations serving the national interest. In another paradox of the
transnational world, the national interest is best served by policies
that are international in orientation. Surely a national priority is
effective participation in a global economy. Since transnationals are
now the chief means for the creation of international wealth,
nations may well ask themselves what they can do to attract, retain,
and encourage transnational corporations. Most will conclude that
it is in their national interest to create a hospitable environment for
such companies.

Let me be clear about what I am *not* saying. I am not arguing
that governments shouldn't regulate industries, promulgate trade
policies, or zealously guard the interests of the people they are
sworn to serve. That's unrealistic, as well as undemocratic. Nations
and policymakers certainly do have a function to perform. Trade
agreements don't negotiate themselves; commerce is not, contrary
to Adam Smith, always magically self-regulating; and wronged citizens acting individually in the face of giant corporations have little
hope of success. The idea then is not to do away with policies and
politicians, but to come up with the right policies. It is not a matter
of jettisoning the notion of national interest, but of seeing it clearly
in the context of today's realities.

What national policies serve the national interest in an interdependent world? The overarching policy must be a national commitment to *full participation in the multilateral global trading and investment system.* History is replete with examples of nations that have
withdrawn from the postwar global economic system in favor of
statist policies that focus inward. Some of the nations that made
that choice, such as the Soviet Union, India, and Brazil, have been
large and, in traditional economic terms, deemed to be self-
sufficient. The results have been uniformly disastrous at least, in
part, because these countries' inward policies were inhospitable to
transnational corporations. Nothing less than a national commitment to global economic interdependence is called for.

The multilateral nature of the global trading system must also
be recognized. The United States has constructed a North American
Free Trade Agreement with Canada and Mexico for each of which it
is the major trading partner. The agreement is a positive and welcome development as long as these countries remain part of the
global trading system and subject to its rules. Since the United

States conducts 70 percent of its trade with partners other than Canada and Mexico, this agreement cannot be a substitute for the vigorous complex of the multilateral system.

A commitment to the global trading system carries with it a firm commitment to allow an open field to all competitors. Only free competition produces strong businesses capable of holding their own in the global marketplace. The protection of mature or noncompetitive industries has merely prolonged the pain and deceived employees and shareholders. France provides probably the best current example of how state protection through national-ization and preferential treatment of so-called strategic companies has led to noncompetitiveness. France's desperate attempt over two decades to maintain a national computer company has produced a series of ill-fated joint ventures and strategic alliances with Honey-well, Siemens-Nixdorf, and IBM that have served only to keep the French capability below the threshold of true international competi-tiveness.

Given the highly integrated global system of companies, suppli-ers, and markets, narrow nationalistic policies often backfire any-way. The U.S. government, for example, imposed a tariff on flat-panel display screens for notebook computers to protect American makers of the screens from Japanese competitors. But Apple and IBM needed the more advanced Japanese screens to stay competi-tive, so, to avoid the crippling tariff, they moved the production of their portables outside the United States. In sum, the tariff did little to help American makers of the screens, harmed two major Ameri-can computer makers, and caused manufacturing jobs to leave the United States.

The American steel industry offers an even more ironic example of failed protectionism. For years, the largest U.S. steel companies have sought and won tariff protection from the U.S. government against foreign competitors, especially the Japanese. Meanwhile, smaller American steel companies, such as Birmingham Steel, Nucor, and New Jersey Steel, were investing in production abroad, developing a state-of-the-art steel-making technology at home, and providing ownership stakes and productivity bonuses to their workers. As a result, these upstart companies can now produce steel more efficiently and cheaply than can their Japanese competi-tors, who cannot afford to scrap the huge investments tied up in aging equipment on prohibitively expensive Japanese land.[9] And the large U.S. steel companies, after enjoying years of protectionism, are not only little better off against their Japanese competitors, but they seriously lag behind their innovative domestic competitors.

The lesson should be clear: Protectionism, closed markets, and discriminatory regulations rarely produce the expected results. A free and open market remains the best means of allocating resources and making rational decisions, though it may be far from perfect. As Winston Churchill said of democracy, it "is the worst form of government except all those other forms that have been tried."[10] Anything short of a free-market economy repels serious transnational investments. An open market includes, as Switzerland and Sweden have learned, the freedom for investors from anywhere in the world to purchase listed company shares and to invest directly in domestic companies.

There is an argument for providing some shelter to nascent industries, such as superconductors and biotechnology, that could spawn new industrial sectors. These industrial greenhouses, however, should be constructed so they are transparent and open, with explicit time limits.

We live at a time when rapid and unpredictable change is the order of the day. But business likes stability. Political stability, especially when achieved by working democratic institutions, is, of course, desirable, but what is really required to attract investment are *stable fiscal, monetary, and tax policies.* In the United States, the tax policy has changed regularly, every two or three years, regardless of the party in power. Each change not only alters the rules but piles complexity on top of existing layers of complexity. Moreover, the tax policy is no longer a matter of providing revenue for the government; it has become a curious mix of social and industrial policies that do not encourage economic growth, but merely add great expense because of their complexity and often disastrous and unintended commercial consequences. The only thing that can be counted on in the U.S. tax policy is that it will undoubtedly change and change often.

Not only should policies be stable, but the rules and regulations in which they are embodied must be clear and transparent. The *clarity and transparency* of government-imposed rules and regulations, which are essential to international competition, have become major guidelines for the European Commission's construction of the new Europe after 1992. On the other end of the global scale is

Japan, which has few clear rules of commerce and industrial policy, but relies istead on confidential "administrative guidance," which breeds favoritism and corruption and is a major barrier to serious non-Japanese competition. The scandals in the Japanese securities market, which led to the fall of the prime minister in 1991, had such strong political repercussions because the practice of compensating large investors for their trading losses is widely believed to have occurred with the knowledge, support, and secret "administrative guidance" of the powerful Ministry of Finance. In any case, American officials have been lobbying the Japanese government to issue all regulatory guidelines publicly in writing and to apply them equally to all companies.[11]

Foremost among stable, clear, and transparent policies must be the *protection of intellectual property.* Certainly, companies that develop innovative products desire and deserve adequate protection of patents and copyrights. There can be no compromises with a sound legal system. The absence of the protection of intellectual property is tantamount to a death sentence for technologically intensive industries. Such protection is as important as is the protection of other forms of personal property, and countries that fail to provide it are likely to become outcasts in the world trading community.

Sound national policies with an internationalist cast may also extend to matters whose relevance to international competitiveness is not always readily apparent. Chief among them is an educational policy. Japan, perhaps more than any other country, has understood that a fundamental resource for international competitiveness is an *educated population.* Lacking raw materials, indigenous energy sources, and arable land, Japan realized that its only natural resource was its people. So, following World War II, it put in place a sound national education program that provides every citizen with a first-class education through high school. The results, of course, have been spectacular; Japan has risen to eminence in high-tech industries and has reinvigorated mature industries, such as automobiles, in great part by bringing to bear a highly educated work force. As the twentieth century ends, it must be clear that highly educated people are the essential ingredient in an advanced industrial society. No nation can hope to improve its circumstances without making a sustained world-class investment in its children.

The pharmaceutical industry offers excellent examples of the effects, both intended and unintended, of national policies that bear on transnationals. Again, I don't intend any special pleading. I use the pharmaceutical industry as an illustration because it is the industry I know best and because it is fully global.

Although the primary aim of the drug-approval process is to ensure safe and effective medicines, unnecessarily slow drug-approval procedures often harm a nation's competitiveness, even though they are partially intended to have the opposite effect. (Such procedures also harm patients who may be in desperate need of a new medication, a situation that has become increasingly common as scientific advances have allowed drug companies to put more of their efforts into discovering treatments for chronic and catas-trophic diseases.) The review time for the twenty new drugs that were approved in the United States in 1988, by the Food and Drug Administration (FDA), averaged about thirty-one months, com-pared with about fifteen months for any of the same drugs that were first approved in foreign markets.[12] In other words, it took more than twice as long for the same drugs to win approval in the United States. As a result, most companies first seek approval of their new drugs in countries other than the United States. But slow approval procedures have the unwanted side effect of harming domestic producers, who derive most of their profits in the home market, unlike many foreign companies operating there. More effi-cient and more uniform review-and-approval regulations allow transnationals to roll out global products more quickly to recover their enormous costs and, in the process, eliminate competitive dis-advantages for purely national companies. In fact, it is often the size of the domestic market that initially provides national companies with the critical mass to make the global leap. In any case, more uni-form standards benefit everyone—consumers everywhere and national companies and transnationals alike.

In 1991–92 the Council on Competitiveness, chaired by Vice President Quayle, recognized the implications for public welfare and the competitive strength of the American pharmaceutical industry of excessive regulations and bureaucratic delays by the FDA. For the first time in thirty years, and despite strong opposi-tion from FDA officials, the council made real progress toward streamlining the American process of reviewing and approving new drugs.

Price controls on prescription drugs are another area of national policy that bears examining in international perspective. A number of countries have implemented price controls or cost-containment measures at the national level. In Japan the government sets high prices for new pharmaceutical products and systematically reduces them five years after their introduction. Most European countries also practice some form of price control. Among the most severe is France, which has the lowest drug prices in Europe, but, because of volume prescribing, one of the highest overall drug bills. Not coincidentally, France also has the worst record of pharmaceutical innovations among major developed countries.

Germany has adopted the concept of therapeutic clustering, in which drugs with similar indications are grouped for the purposes of reimbursement by health insurers. Though this practice has reduced drug prices in Germany by approximately 25–40 percent, the system groups drugs regardless of whether they are new or old, traditional or innovative, protected by patents or not and thus removes the incentives for companies to be innovative and undercuts the intent of market exclusivity conferred by the protection of intellectual property. The temporary decrease in revenues that results from such controls is expected to weaken seriously the German pharmaceutical industry's investment in research and development and thus competitiveness in the long run.

The United States is one of the few countries that does not exert some form of price control on prescription drugs. Many observers believe that the absence of price controls is at least partially responsible for the fact that nine of the top twenty pharmaceutical firms worldwide are based in the United States. According to a study by the U.S. International Trade Commission, the American industry leads the world in innovation: a majority of the globally successful pharmaceutical products introduced from 1975 to 1989 were developed by U.S.-based companies.[13] (And the commission rigorously defined innovative companies as "those which develop new chemical entities . . . through extensive R&D programs and market them as brand-name ethical preparations."[14]) Because American companies can operate with a relatively free hand on pricing, the study reported, they have routinely plowed about 17 percent of their sales back into research and development—"approximately three times the level allocated by the remainder of the chemical and related-industries sector."[15] Ironically, just as the issue of price controls on pharmaceutical products is being debated for the first time, the

European Commission has issued a draft directive recommending the abolition of all price controls and eliminating administered pricing practices on pharmaceutical products.

Switzerland, the United Kingdom, and Germany also have strong pharmaceutical industries. The strength of all these national industries was achieved by their early expansion beyond national borders. Among the top eighty pharmaceutical companies in the world in 1989, U.S.-based companies accounted for 40 percent of the global sales, German-based companies accounted for 31 percent, British-based companies accounted for 25 percent, and Swiss-based companies accounted for 21%.[16] On the other hand, the industries of France and Japan have, until recently, concentrated on their sizable domestic markets. (Japan is the second largest pharmaceutical market in the world after the United States, and France is the third largest market in Western Europe.) As a result, the Japanese and French industries have not yet developed the extensive research and development and marketing structure that the American and some Western European companies have.

If leading companies, by virtue of going global, strengthen a nation's industry, then it is in the interest of that nation to develop policies that encourage such companies, which return benefits in the form of taxes (on profits as well as on shareholders' dividends), increased investment, technology development, and the manufacture of high-quality products. A country's tax policy is a particularly thorny issue for government officials in this regard. Periodically, tax authorities challenge the ability of technologically intensive companies, such as pharmaceutical producers, to write off all research and development expenses conducted in that country against nationally made profits. They assert that since the benefits of research and development accrue to the world, only a portion of the expense should be deductible from taxes in the country in which the work was done. Though these challenges are raised only occasionally, if they became a matter of policy, they would make a hopeless muddle of all current international tax treaties and would drive more research and development out of these countries. Surely this is a consequence that few would consider to be in the national interest.

The adequate protection of intellectual property rights is of obvious concern to pharmaceutical companies. Though many countries are now strengthening their laws in this regard, piracy continues to cost the pharmaceutical industry hundreds of millions of dollars worldwide each year. But beyond simple piracy lie more subtle and complicated intellectual-property issues. For example, as regulatory approval times have lengthened for new drugs, the effective life of the patents for these drugs has shortened by that amount. In the early 1960s, the average effective life of a pharmaceutical patent in the United States was about fifteen years; today it is about ten years and ten months.[17] Meanwhile, it is estimated that the time required for a new drug to recoup the costs of its research and development is about nineteen years.[18] Recently, however, the United States, Japan, and the European Community have developed patent-restoration laws or market-exclusivity policies that offer some relief. In the case of the Japanese, however, there remain some areas of concern. During delays in the granting of patents for foreign firms, Japanese firms may sell the pharmaceuticals domestically. Further, Japan often grants narrow patents to foreign pharmaceuticals, which forces foreign companies into cross-licensing with Japanese firms and reduces the profits for the companies that originated the products.

Canada's patent system, the weakest of any industrialized nation, presents an even more striking example of a nationalistic policy that is not in the best interests of the country. For most of the 1980s, Canada allowed the compulsory licensing of pharmaceutical products for a token royalty. In effect, the Canadian practice amounted to the expropriation of private property (in this case, intellectual property). The purpose was to lower the cost of drugs, which it may have accomplished to a moderate degree, but the unintended side effect was to drive the global pharmaceutical companies out of the country. Research laboratories, offices, and factories closed, including a new state-of-the-art Smith Kline & French factory outside Toronto. All pharmaceutical research and development ceased, and Canada became a pariah in the eyes of global, research-based pharmaceutical companies. In effect, Canada removed itself from the global economy, at least as far as pharmaceutical products are concerned. There are prospects for change, however. Assuming the successful conclusion of the Uruguay Round of GATT negotiations, the intellectual-property provisions will require Canada once again to respect pharmaceutical patents and rejoin the multilateral global trading and investment system.

As these examples show, national interest will increasingly come to be redefined in the context of global interests. Clearly, the status of nations and even the traditional concept of national sovereignty is changing in a world that is growing steadily more interdependent. As countries cede their authority to supranational bodies and make their domestic climate more hospitable to transnationals, they seem to lose sovereignty, but, in the long run, they gain wealth for their own people and contribute to a more stable and just economic order around the world. In other words, they improve their national competitiveness through a retreat from nationalism, protectionism, and militarism. The few surviving international outlaws—Cuba, North Korea, Libya, and Iraq—demonstrate the folly of national policies that are out of step with the rest of the world.

The alternative to a rule-based multilateralism, embodied in supranational institutions like GATT, is a return to the old power-based system that in this century alone has produced two world wars and the prolonged Cold War period of unprecedented tension, hostility, and danger. It may be hard to swallow in some national capitals, but just like corporations, nations must define their vision, strategy, and goals in ways that are compatible with a global society. Every bit as much as corporations, nation-states and political leaders must confront the global imperative and choose whether to retreat or to embrace the future.

CHAPTER NINE

TRIBES AND
TRANSNATIONALS

THE ORIGIN OF THIS BOOK, or more accurately, the stimulus that caused me to consider writing a book about large global companies, was the appearance of a cover story in *Business Week* in 1989 entitled "Stateless Corporations."[1] The article argued that large transnational companies were becoming corporations without a national identity or affiliation—that they were "untethered"—and suggested that as a consequence, they were no longer capable of being held accountable for their actions. I promptly fired off a short letter of rebuttal to the editor, which was printed in a subsequent issue. Long letters to the editor never get printed in their entirety, but some topics do require more than 100 words. A friend suggested that if a well-informed and responsible journal of the global business scene could arrive at such conclusions, there might be a need for a thorough examination and explanation of what transnational companies really are and implications they pose for the countries in which they operate. Hence the conception of this book. Now I want to conclude my exploration of transnationals as I began it in that brief letter to the editor: by looking at the serious issues raised by these so-called stateless companies that concern us all as citizens in societies, not just as consumers in markets.

Stateless means, of course, without nationality. But in a strict sense, large transnational corporations do possess a nationality. Every corporation must be registered somewhere. I cannot think of a major corporation that does not have its headquarters unit domiciled in a major city and nation. Certainly, in a legal sense, then, transnational companies are anchored by state or national registrations and by their headquarters. But that is not really the point. The concern of the article in *Business Week* was that transnational corporations have become so large and so important in many nations throughout the world that they are somehow free from normal corporate obligations and responsibilities in any country.

In my brief reply, I argued that transnational corporations are, in fact, "many stated," that is, they must respect their obligations to all nations in which they do business. Not only must they observe the laws and accept the responsibilities imposed by the many countries in which they operate, but they must measure up to the highest standards among the nations in which they do business and apply those standards globally.

Though countries around the world differ in the rigor of their laws and standards governing corporate behavior, global corporations are invariably held accountable to the standards of the most stringent country and tend to operate on those principles in all countries where they do business. Thus, the common denominator in transnational corporate behavior from country to country is usually the *highest* common denominator, not the lowest. Companies operate at the highest level of responsibility for the simple reason that they cannot afford to be seen to be performing with double standards. Nor should a society accept double standards from corporations any more readily than it does from other large institutions.

Examples abound of transnational companies being held to the highest global standards. The United States, for example, insists that transnational corporations go to extraordinary lengths to make certain that their far-flung operations do not engage in corporate bribery, especially in countries where bribery is commonplace. To take another example—again drawn from the United States, which generally maintains some of the toughest standards in the world—there has existed for more than twenty years a legal requirement, only recently repealed, that pharmaceutical products exported from the United States had to carry exactly the same labeling as that approved by the FDA, despite the fact that every country has its

own health authorities and regulations for labeling pharmaceuticals. Indeed, the same regulation prohibited the export of any pharmaceutical product that had not yet been approved by the FDA,
for decades the slowest pharmaceutical-regulatory agency in the
world.

In general, the countries with the most stringent standards of
corporate behavior are the United States, the countries of Western
Europe, and Japan—as it happens, the three indispensable markets
for a genuinely transnational strategy. Apart from the immorality
of, say, bribing foreign officials, there is a real danger that such
behavior could jeopardize an offending company's status in one of
those key areas of the world. Though such behavior occasionally
occurs, most companies are rational enough not to want to take that
risk. And the bribe, though it may occur outside the key global markets, can nevertheless have serious repercussions for the company
there. Thus the highest standards increasingly become applied the
world over, even in countries that don't particularly welcome them.

Nevertheless, on rereading the article in *Business Week,* I believe
the writers reflect a deeper if less-well-articulated concern about
transnationals—and that is the profound ambivalence, even fear,
we may feel about a world dominated by large, global corporations,
whose leaders are remote, often unknown, and not elected in any
real sense. As consumers, of course, most of us are happy to buy the
products of transnational companies when we think they represent
good value. Many of us feel generally pleased that the firms producing these products and services are doing so for people all
around the world. But at the same time, as citizens, we are vaguely
uneasy about the size and relative distance of these industrial and
commercial giants.

People normally function on several different levels. In our purchasing and consuming modes, we can applaud the advances
brought about by keen global competition. We are delighted to have
choices and purchasing opportunities that previous generations
never dreamed possible. On a higher plane, however, when we consider the larger interests of our communities and the society at
large, another set of questions and concerns arises. Are these wonderful products being created and produced at some larger but hidden cost to ourselves, our friends and neighbors, and our planet?
Can large, remote corporations with such huge global resources and
concentrated technical and economic power be trusted to do the

right thing? Won't the avid competition that brings us better value also threaten to destroy companies and whole industries at home that are unable to match the resources of major global competitors? As these giant international companies grow larger and ever more dominant in their industries on a global basis, will they suffocate entrepreneurial innovation and snuff out opportunities for small local companies? Above all, how can we as citizens measure whether the broader interests of our society are being observed and respected?

A generation ago, in considering these questions, most of us would have replied that our national government was primarily responsible for providing the answers and the assurances we were seeking. We relied on the federal government to set the standards and do the measuring. We believed it should be both the judge and jury in regulating industry and commerce for the greater good of the society at large. Today, the role of government is far less clear. For one thing, we have had a generation of disappointing experiences with large central governments. Governments in many countries have proved themselves poor managers of the assets entrusted to their care. Most of the European industries that were nationalized in the 1950s and 1960s and performed so poorly have now been privatized, usually with dramatically improved results. Many of those that remain in state hands—the German telecommunications monopoly, for example—are scheduled to be sold to public shareholders as soon as they become competitive, in itself a telling admission. The world's greatest experiment with management by government in what was the Soviet Union literally collapsed under the weight of its own bureaucracy and moral corruption. The experience with state socialism casts great doubts on the intellectual integrity of central governments.

Even in the democratic society of the United States, the worst and least forthcoming polluter of the environment is the federal government, in its operation of facilities that produce nuclear weapons. And there is no apparent remedy. There are no capital reserves against such liabilities, as is required of private-sector corporations. There are no audits by independent accounting firms, as is also required of publicly held corporations. There do not appear to be any contingency plans or programs for remedial action. In short, the government seems inept in looking after its own environmental responsibilities.

At the local level, many communities are also struggling to manage their obligations, but they often do so in ways that are incompatible with the broad interests of society. Garbage is still being loaded onto barges in New York City and London for dumping into the oceans offshore. Is it any surprise that beaches 100 miles away are polluted with waste? Municipal effluent is being pumped directly into the English channel and North Sea by cities and towns in the United Kingdom. The Mediterranean is becoming a dead sea as a result of the pollution issuing from the many towns and villages along its shores.

Just as there is serious concern about the deleterious effects of short managerial time horizons in industry and the financial markets, there is also serious doubt about the ability of any government to look beyond the next election and to take decisions beyond the narrow interests of an entrenched bureaucracy. At the same time, the agenda of citizens' concerns is growing and reaching well beyond any single country's borders. In most societies, the list is topped by environmental concerns, ranging from global issues, such as pollution of the oceans and global warming, to local issues, such as the quality of the air and drinking water. AIDS, drugs, crime, and terrorism also figure prominently among the major concerns shared by people everywhere. Yet as I discussed in the previous chapter, solutions to these issues are well beyond the reach of any national government.

Governments simply no longer seem able to provide many of the answers or the assurances we seek. Consequently, concerns about the actions of transnational companies take on an even greater urgency and evoke greater anxiety. We are being asked to take too much on faith if we are to rely entirely on the wisdom and civic responsibility of boards of directors always to reconcile shareholders' demands for profits with the needs of society. And somehow the "invisible hand" described by Adam Smith 200 years ago has always failed to inspire much confidence that it can really ensure that the right things will get done in the right way by those in pursuit of personal gain.

Taking the nearly universal concern about the environment, we may look at what is actually happening. For good and obvious reasons, most anxiety about the environment has been directed at the activities of large corporations. Now many of those corporations are growing larger and, increasingly, global and transnational. Is the

emergence of these global behemoths cause for even greater ecological worry, or are there signs of change in the way such companies
regard their responsibility for the environment? Once again, there
aren't any easy answers, but perhaps I can identify a few patterns or
straws in the wind that will contribute to an understanding of the
events that are unfolding in a world of fading national governments
and growing transnational companies, global interdependence, and
supranational bodies.

Nowhere does the probable pattern for the future—and the anxiety it arouses and answers it provides—appear more clearly than
in recent experiences with the GATT agreements. It is under the
umbrella of the GATT rules for global trade that the tremendous
growth in international commerce has taken place, which, in turn,
has fueled the expansion of global companies. GATT writes rules
for international trade. It does not directly concern itself with protecting the global environment or other concerns of society. It does,
however, apply some principles that indirectly affect the way
nations, industries, and individual companies behave with respect
to the environment. Chief among those principles is nondiscrimination in international trade. Any national policy or practice that
applies equally and evenly to both domestic and foreign producers
is likely to get the green light from GATT; national policies that dis-
criminate against foreign producers are not. For example, when
Thailand attempted to ban imported tobacco products, a GATT
panel decreed that if all tobacco products, foreign *and* domestic,
were banned then there would be no problem. But in targeting
imported cigarettes only, Thailand was found to be in violation of
the GATT rules. The same reasoning was brought to bear when
Canada attempted to stop exports of salmon fished from Canadian
waters on the grounds that salmon were overfished. GATT asked
why Canada had not moved to limit domestic consumption as well.

GATT subjects national environmental policies to the same lit-
mus test of nondiscrimination. For example, when the United States
attempted to ban imports of tuna from Mexico because Mexican
tuna boats were killing more dolphins in the eastern Pacific than
American fishing regulations allow, GATT ruled in January 1992
that no nation could use the leverage of trade to force its environmental views on another country.[2] This decision outraged American environmentalists and wildlife advocates, who had hoped to
use the leverage of trade with the United States and access to the

huge American market as a bargaining chip in bilateral negotiations to improve environmental practices in less-developed countries. But the GATT decision pointed out that a broad international agreement that set agreed-on standards for fishing practices, including the protection of dolphins in all oceans, could be enforced by international trade sanctions. Such an agreement would require general international support, especially from Russia and Japan, the nations with large, oceanic fishing fleets, but would then be enforced widely throughout the world and apply to fishing fleets from all countries. Meanwhile, unilateral action utilizing trade embargoes to enforce one nation's views of positive environmental standards of conduct on another won't be allowed.

In a report written for GATT by Jagdish Bhagwati, a professor of economics at Columbia University, states however, there is a strong argument that, in the long run, open trade policies and global competition are most likely to serve global environmental interests.[3] According to Bhagwati, environmentalists have a stake in free trade. For example, he suggested that open borders in agricultural commerce would encourage the most efficient use of environmentally threatening pesticides and herbicides. Farmers in Europe, subsidized to grow high-cost grain, use about ten times the quantity of fertilizers and pesticides for each bushel of wheat grown as do their counterparts in Argentina and Australia. The elimination of Europe's agricultural subsidies and protective tariffs would greatly reduce the cost of grain to European consumers. Equally important, it would improve the environment by considerably reducing the consumption of the more expensive grain grown in countries that allow the use of large amounts of harmful fertilizers and pesticides.

The Bhagwati report also argued that positive environmental effects result from economic growth stimulated by the open international trading system. The case was bolstered by a study conducted by two Princeton University economists, Gene Grossman and Alan Krueger.[4] Using data from the World Health Organization to compare levels of sulphur dioxide pollution in the air of cities in forty-one countries around the world over a twelve year period, Grossman and Krueger found the worst pollution in cities where the inhabitants are classified as moderately poor. Extremely poor cities are not as dirty as those that were beginning to climb the economic ladder. However, when the per capita income rises to about $5,000, a curious phenomenon occurs. The air becomes cleaner. "The reason is simple," Grossman wrote: "Attention to environmental issues is a luxury poor countries cannot afford."[5]   But when a country's GNP approaches a level about equal to that of Mexico or Malaysia, the turnabout begins. Then societies can afford to trap dirty emissions and switch to cleaner fuels and more complete combustion.

Grossman and Krueger drew some interesting conclusions regarding a free trade agreement with Mexico. First, more liberalized trade is likely to generate the kind of income growth in Mexico that will lead to cleaner air. Second, liberalized trade "may well increase Mexican specialization in sectors that cause less than average amounts of environmental damage." These researchers also found that pollution-abatement costs in the United States are not a significant factor in explaining the pattern of bilateral trade or of the activity of the so-called *maquiladoras* (predominantly foreign-owned firms located in Mexico near the U.S. border that produce largely for export to the United States under a Mexican policy that allows the duty-free import of foreign components for assembly and re-export).[6]

Help in the battle to improve the quality of the air without sacrificing economic vitality is on the way from another unexpected direction. The advanced technology used to improve both thrust and fuel efficiency in large aircraft jet engines is now being applied to the production of electric power. Large jet turbines producing about 500,000 kilowatts per hour are now the most efficient means of producing electricity. They are fueled by natural gas, which is cheaper and more abundant than oil and burns more cleanly than all other fossil fuels, especially coal. There are large deposits of natural gas in the North Sea, the central plains of the United States, and elsewhere in reasonable proximity to areas that demand large amounts of electric power. The advanced engines are the first means of generating hydrocarbon-fueled electric power in which the output of electricity totals more than 50 percent of the energy consumed to produce it. All other electric power plants using fossil fuels — coal, diesel, and even natural gas — produce less (often significantly less) than 50 percent of the energy that is consumed. Natural gas-powered jet turbines are relatively small units, are easy to install, and can be dropped into the electric-power grid in strategic places without requiring the construction of huge new power-generating plants.

These new power generators are being produced and sold by

three global companies: GEC Alsthom, Siemens, and Asea Brown Boveri. Each of these three large competitors has put together an international consortium of collaborating companies. The three competitive consortia are now bidding against each other for contracts all around the world. The intense worldwide competition among them has improved the design and engineering and lowered the cost of gas-fired jet turbines. Now, almost all new requirements for producing electric power are specifying natural gas-fired jet turbines. The demand will continue to grow as aging power plants in Europe and the United States are replaced with these more efficient and more environmentally friendly units. Greater efficiency will lower the cost while improving the quality of the air. Acid rain, primarily a product of electric power plants fired by coal with a high sulpher content, will be significantly reduced.

As new jet turbines using natural gas come on stream, the industrial casualty will likely be coal, particularly the deep-vein mines from which relatively high-cost coal with a high sulphur content comes. The British Coal Board, a nationalized company responsible for operating British mines, recently told a select committee of the House of Commons that competition from low-cost, lower-sulphur-content, open-pit-mined coal from Australia and Columbia and high-efficiency gas-powered jet turbines may spell the loss of most contracts from Britain's privatized power-generating utilities.

Before the privatization of the electric-power utilities in the mid-1980s, the nationalized power company CEGB (Central Electricity Generating Board) and the British Coal Board had a cozy contract. The CEGB paid higher than market prices for coal, thereby keeping the mines open. The excess costs were passed on to the British consumers of power, who in effect were required to subsidize employment in the mines and the use of coal with a high sulphur content, with all its damaging effects to the air and its role in acid rain. Now the new publicly held utility companies, PowerGen and National Power, must confront the hard realities of the marketplace and answer for their actions directly to their customers and shareholders. Of course, the power companies now insist on buying from whomever they choose to achieve the best productivity and economies. The resulting withdrawal of business from the British Coal Board could mean a decrease in the number of coal pits from sixty-five to ten, accompanied by reductions in the work force from 57,300 to 12,000 people by the end of the decade.

The decline of coal mining as an industrial force has been under way for some time. During the bitter miners' strike in the mid-1980s, Arthur Scargill, head of the miners' union, said that the British Coal Board planned to shut seventy mines and eliminate 70,000 jobs. In fact, it has since closed 105 pits and cut 112,000 jobs. In 1980 200,000 men were working the mines. By the year 2000, one generation later, the number could be as low as 10,000. As David Bowen and Mary Fagan concluded in an article on the crisis facing the coal industry, "British Coal seems in serious danger of losing its status as a major British corporation and one of the oldest industries in Britain could be moving toward the end of its natural life."[7] Despite the fact that deep-vein coal mining is one of the most dangerous and debilitating occupations and the product is a serious contributor to air pollution, this displacement is seen in Britain as a major political issue in the struggle between the Labour party and the Conservatives. As I have said, there are no easy answers when social and industrial change are involved, but there can be no doubt that the environment is the beneficiary of the decline in coal mining and that the technology transferred from the aircraft industry to the generation of power by the major global competitors is a major factor in the shift to more efficient and cleaner electric power.

Other good environmental omens are emanating from large global manufacturing companies, which have known for some time that building in high quality not only makes a better and more reliable product, but reduces costs. Managers also know that factories whose workers have excellent safety records are invariably the most productive and efficient. And lately managers are learning that the strict adherence to environmentally sound practices also lowers costs. Correcting manufacturing defects is costly. Accidents cost money. Correcting environmental mistakes is immensely expensive, and the possible liabilities associated with environmental problems are truly frightening.

Large corporations that expect to be in business for a long time now realize that it is very much in the interests of all concerned, including their shareholders, to be punctilious in observating the best environmental practices. In fact, before the Earth Summit in Rio de Janeiro in the summer of 1992, a group of forty-eight executives of international companies issued a report stating that good environmental practices and good business practices go hand in hand.[8] The roster of participants included the CEOs of Chevron,

Alcoa, Du Pont, Johnson Wax, Nippon Steel, Mitsubishi, Nissan, Volkswagen, and Royal Dutch Shell. Hoping to influence governments and businesses to adopt sounder environmental policies, the group asserted that in the future the most successful companies will be those that achieve ecological efficiency, which, they said, generates higher profits because it produces less waste and uses resources more economically.[9] And the group joined environmentalists in urging that the prices of goods and services be gradually adjusted to take into account their environmental costs. There is nothing saintly or even altruistic about this position. It is simply good business practice for those with a long-term view.

Environmental activists, on the other hand, are coming to recognize that often the best chance for protecting endangered ecological systems is cooperative work with large, well-financed corporations. As this realization dawns and as corporations recognize that environmental sensitivity is sound business, the relationship between the two camps is changing from antagonism and deep mutual suspicion to open communication and selective cooperation. A case in point is the exploration of the upper reaches of the Amazon Basin for oil. Many oil companies are working along the eastern foothills of the Ecuadoran and Peruvian Andes in search of oil. One of these companies is ARCO Oriente, a subsidiary of Atlantic Richfield Corporation (of which, it should be said, I am an outside director).

ARCO Oriente is exploring the Ecuadoran section of the Amazon rain forest. In undertaking the project, the company employed a team of environmental consultants to assist in the preservation of the unique and invaluable ecology of the rain forest. The environmentalists insisted that all transportation be by means of helicopter, so that roads would not be cut through the forest. Roads are not only destructive in their own right, they also open the virgin forest to bands of migrant farmers who employ slash-and-burn techniques from which the primordial forest never recovers. The environmentalists also advised careful consultation with the local tribes about which trees should be cut and which should be left untouched for use by future generations. Working with the exploration and production team, the environmentalists have discovered and catalogued eighteen previously unknown plant specimens. The Nature Conservancy, the Natural Resources Defense Council, and other environmental groups have concluded that the only way the Amazon rain forest can be protected is through work with large, responsible companies, such as ARCO, which have strong balance sheets, a culture of corporate integrity, and the foresight to undertake development in a responsible fashion.

The alternative to such cooperation is not "no development." National governments want development, and their populations want the work and the wealth-creating opportunities it brings. It is impossible to fence off large tracts containing important natural resources by regulation or other means. Inevitably, some group, often less responsible, will come forward eagerly to take on the job, but usually with fewer financial resources and less interest in the long-term future than have large, financially secure companies.

Of course, there will be accidents and mistakes. There will be bad decisions and, occasionally, there will be motives that are less than pure. We have only to look back over the past few years to remember the horrendous mistakes of the Exxon Valdez, the Union Carbide Bohpal explosion, and the Ciba-Geigy Rhine spill, to mention just a few of the more notorious ones. But in each case, the companies involved paid dearly in both monetary terms and in lost public esteem. All executives know that their jobs are on the line and their companies are put at great risk when episodes of such magnitude occur. The risk is more than any rational person wants to take.

But of course environmental degradation does not take place merely through occasional and highly visible catastrophes. Far more frequently, it results from cumulative, day-to-day activities — automobile emissions, the poor use of land, dumping pollutants in the ocean, and so on. The daily operations of some companies and even entire industries may also contribute to the daily toll. As they do so, resentment against them may accumulate as well. In 1988, the chemical industry was reeling from decades of environmental damage and negative public opinion to the point that it became the second-most-disliked industry after tobacco. The loss of public trust was so pervasive that the very survival of the industry seemed, at times, in doubt. As Union Carbide chairman Robert Kennedy put it, the chemical industry "needed a way to reverse the tide of public outrage."[10]

Following a period of intense self-examination, the leading companies in the chemical industry concluded that the answer lay not in a new public relations initiative, but in a *change in industrial behavior.* Beginning in Canada, the chemical industry worked to develop a new culture under the banner of Responsible Care, an initiative designed to improve the responsible management of chemicals and to increase the member companies' accountability to society.[11] The initiative was adopted in September 1989 by the U.S. Chemical Manufacturers Association, representing the major American chemical companies. The Responsible Care initiative is now spreading to Europe. Britain, France, and the Netherlands adopted the code in 1989, and other European countries are considering doing so. Adherence to its code is now a requirement for membership in the Chemicals Manufacturers Association in Canada and the United States and will soon be required by Britain's Chemical Industry Association.

The program commits the companies to the proper stewardship of their products from their inception to their disposal. It sets goals for improving the companies' performance and it requires the involvement of outsiders, including consumer and environmental activists who are critical of the industry. Significantly, responsibility lies with each individual company, not some remote trade association that is designed to deflect public criticism.

The Responsible Care program consists of five key elements:

1. A set of guiding principles that address health, safety, and environmental quality.

2. Six codes of management practices that detail methods for implementing the guiding principles in six specific areas of management: community awareness and emergency responses, the prevention of pollution, safe processing techniques, distribution, the stewardship of products, and the health and safety of workers.

3. A public advisory panel consisting of informed citizens and community leaders who identify public concerns and review the codes of management practices.

4. Specific standards for performance audits and self-evaluations by members.

5. Executive leadership groups that meet periodically to discuss their progress and share their experiences in implementing the codes.

Implementation, of course, is the key. Recognizing the public's skepticism, the industry adopted the slogan "Don't Trust Us, Track Us," and, more important, acted on it. According to the manager of a Du Pont plant, Du Pont "already had a lot of the Responsible Care Program elements in place, but tended to have an approach—almost subconsciously—that hadn't included the public. Things have now changed dramatically, thanks to the program."[12] One small measure of this new openness may be seen on a huge sign posted outside the plant for all to see: It lists the goals for reducing waste and emissions and the plant's progress toward achieving them.

Du Pont also had to tackle the problem of achieving consistent organizational behavior across its diverse product lines and in the many countries in which it operates. It has since developed detailed evaluation criteria and benchmarks against which to measure the continual improvement of performance for each step in the self-evaluation standards worldwide. With a significant cultural change in progress in the chemical industry, it is not surprising that Du Pont voluntarily proposed a phase-out of ozone-destroying chemicals—CFCs—long before the federal government in the United States established regulations calling for the eventual cessation of their production.

I don't mean to suggest that suddenly, as if by magic, large corporations have been visited by angels of goodness and that everything will be fine in the future. On the contrary. But the realization is dawning in corporate board rooms that environmental problems in the production and use of products can no longer be considered to be problems that can be passed on to society or the purchaser. Indeed, most corporate officials now accept the principle that "the polluter pays" when it comes to cleaning up environmental damage.

More positively, many now believe that they are responsible for preventing pollution in the first place and that it is not only good public relations, but good business, to do so. As Michael Porter argued, the nations with the toughest environmental standards often lead the world in exports of the very products affected by the regulations.[13] And regulations that focus on the outcomes, rather than the methods, of pollution abatement often lead companies to reengineer their technology in ways that reduce not only pollution but their production costs.

It is fortunate that forward-looking global companies are now shouldering their environmental responsibilities because it has become clear that neither governments nor citizens' groups alone can do the job. Indeed, governments are at least as much a contributor to the problem as they are a source of solutions. And the only thing the larger society, acting through the government, can do is to lash out to punish apparent offenders. Moreover, common sense and courts of law combine to absolve purchasers of polluting products from responsibility. That leaves the responsibility squarely with the industrial producers. Those with the largest market shares—in most industries they are large global competitors—must take the initiative to create business and cultural change, as the chemical industry is doing. And if the chemical industry, historically one of the worst environmental polluters, has seen the light, then there is reason for some optimism.

Another concern often expressed about the emergence of large global companies is that their very size and global stature will stifle effective competition and inhibit future innovations. In large, mature industries, such as automobiles, aluminum production, and paper products, this may indeed be true. Beset by relatively slow growth and a mature technology, these industries often suffer from excess capacity. Consolidation, usually through mergers and acquisitions, is generally the consequence, which certainly eliminates many of the midsize players. But in most industries, including some large ones, such as computers, airframes, household appliances, and steel, there are obvious industry dynamics that provide new ideas, new entrants, and intense competition. And in most industries, many new small companies are springing up on an almost daily basis to add fresh ideas and technology to the rich stew of competition. The new-company phenomenon seems particularly strong in the United States, where the venture-capital industry is well developed, but there are enough examples in Europe and Japan to make the case that it is becoming a global trend.

In my field, health care products, the spirit of innovation and entrepreneurship has never been stronger, especially in biotechnology. As a field of commercial endeavor, biotechnology is only ten years old. In the United States the infant biotechnology industry has already achieved a critical mass. There are close to fifty publicly held new biotechnology-based pharmaceutical companies.[14]   In 1980, Genentech became the first biotechnology company to sell stock to the public, raising some $35 million that year, and in 1991 the biotechnology industry raised $3.4 billion in eighty-eight separate stock offerings.[15] The top twenty companies have a combined market capitalization of about $20 billion. And worldwide sales of biotech-related drugs, vaccines, and tests now top $4 billion annually.[16]

Observers agree that the industry is poised for rapid growth during the 1990s. By some estimates, total biotechnology revenues will increase sevenfold to reach $40 billion by the turn of the century.[17] So far five products from the biotechnology industry have won FDA approval. But the tide is rising. As I write, eight new products from these young companies are expected to receive approval soon. And more than 100 biotech drugs are currently in clinical trials.[18]

This tremendous explosion of entreprenuership and innovation began when scientists learned how to replicate and manipulate natural proteins found in plants, animals, and humans. Recombinant DNA or gene-splicing technology allows researchers to study how diseases work and then develop bioengineered drugs to fight them. Among the most promising and innovative of these new technologies is "antisense," a technique in which a DNA-like molecule is tailored to attach itself to a corresponding piece of DNA or RNA in cells and to disable its ability to produce harmful proteins, thus short-circuiting the kinds of processes that lie at the heart of cancer and AIDS. Other promising bioengineering techniques are being pursued in chemical synthesis, bacteriology, cell transplant and gene therapy, and numerous other fields. Bioengineered drugs are currently being used to treat hepatitis, dwarfism in children, anemia, and a host of other ills. Ten different categories of new drugs are also currently in development to treat autoimmune disorders, such as rheumatoid arthritis and multiple sclerosis.[19] And in laboratories, crop plants are being genetically engineered to resist pests, and microbes are being developed to consume toxic wastes.[20]

Far from killing off innovation and entrepreneurship, globalization in the health care industry has helped stimulate them. The potential financial return on a successful global product has helped attract venture capital to these bold biotech start-ups. The possibility of spreading risk over global markets emboldens these companies to pursue the costly research and development efforts required to bring a new treatment to market. And, perhaps most important, the global business climate, coupled with the worldwide explosion of biological sciences—itself partly a result of global integration— allows these companies to pursue cutting-edge treatments for the most devastating scourges of humankind.

But innovations by tiny companies operating in the shadow of giant global competitors are not restricted to the health care field. Taking just one example, electronic flat-panel displays use liquid-crystal technology that was developed and popularized about twenty years ago. These liquid-crystal display panels—LCD panels, as they are called—are ubiquitous. Laptop computer screens; hand-held calculators and video games; home appliances; digital watches; and many other instruments, appliances, and promotional displays use LCD technology. Manufacturers are located mostly in the Pacific Rim, and well-known Japanese companies, such as Sharp, Hitachi, and Toshiba, lead the market. Serious American and European competitors were driven out years ago. It is hard to think of a market that is more tightly dominated by intensely competitive, extremely competent manufacturing companies than LCDs.

Yet recently a new technology, called Polyvision, has appeared that threatens to make large-size, thin-film transistor liquid crystal displays (TFT-LCDs) obsolete. The new Polyvision displays are inexpensive and relatively simple to manufacture, compared to the TFT-LCDs. Unlike most LCD panels, the new displays operate well in all lighting conditions and offer much better contrast than conventional large-size LCDs. Most important, Polyvision is rugged; it can withstand the wide swings in humidity and temperature that conventional displays cannot. And Polyvision is much easier to manufacture: it is made in twenty steps compared to sixty or so different steps involved in the production of TFT-LCD panels.

Polyvision was developed in a French laboratory by a division of the New York City–based Alpine Group. The small company, with revenues of only $6.3 million in its most recent full fiscal year, is staking its very existence on the new technology. According to Robert E. Calem, the Alpine Group has already attracted the attention of McDonnell Douglas and Corning.[21] Both companies are working on applications of Polyvision, and in September 1991, two leading French investment banks acquired a 10 percent stake in Alpine Polyvision.

Limited processing runs have been carried out in Massy, France, and a large-scale production facility has just been completed in

Wallingford, Connecticut. The first product using Polyvision displays is likely to be large-area signage where other electronic display technologies cannot compete with the "printed page" look of Polyvision. A host of other electronic products will follow, including high-contrast panel displays, retail marketing signboards, bank-rate boards, and other large-area sign applications. Meanwhile, McDonnell Douglas has been working since 1989 to apply the Polyvision technology in cockpit displays in aircraft. Corning France, a subsidiary of Corning, Inc., is working on a rear-view mirror using Polyvision technology that will sense the bright light from the high beams of an automobile approaching from the rear and automatically darken, reducing irritating and dangerous glare.

Polyvision has all the appearances of reality. It promises to dislocate an entire industry in which a handful of Japanese companies operating on a global basis from low-cost factories in the Pacific Rim have achieved dominance. Ironically, even this novel development is the product of cross-border work in France and the United States, in this case by a small entrepreneurial company.

Beyond worries about the emergence of transnationals harming the environment or stifling innovation lie even darker fears of criminal negligence and lawlessness by giant corporations operating like vast criminal enterprises. We do not live in a perfect world, after all, and corporations are no more paragons of virtue than are the rest of us. The debacle of the Bank of Credit and Commerce International (BCCI), perhaps more than any other corporate scandal of recent years, makes such fears seem frighteningly justified. This international banking operation not only defrauded tens of thousands of small depositors, but for many years operated outside the law in other ways, laundering drug money, financing illegal arms deals, and buying off politicians in many of the world's capitals. Yet BCCI was subject to the same banking regulations and examinations in such countries as Britain, the United States, and Canada as were all the major money-center banks that finance the international trading system. The executives, and allegedly the major shareholders, cleverly exploited the international financial system by using less-regulated locations, such as Luxembourg and the Cayman Islands. The fact that their illicit activities could go undetected for so many years lends some credence to concerns about lawless activity on a global scale.

Yet, it is fair to say that the BCCI scandal is the exception, though we may not think so if we believe the unending stream of melodramatic television and Hollywood movies in which global companies are routinely depicted as behaving like BCCI's latter-day pirates. I don't mean to minimize the magnitude of BCCI's lawlessness, but excessive concentration on such isolated and spectacular cases deflects attention from the more difficult and unclear ethical questions raised by the more mundane day-to-day operations of transnationals around the world.

I can think of no more vexing case in that regard than the long-running controversy over the marketing of packaged infant formula in less-developed countries by Nestlé, American Home Products, and other producers. I choose this example precisely because it is so controversial and because it still has not been brought to a conclusion that satisfies everyone. Even so, I think it not only raises the issues in their most challenging form, but illustrates the mechanism by which transnationals are held accountable, despite the erosion of national sovereignty around the world and the growth of far-flung global companies.

Critics of Nestlé and other global companies that sell similar products argue that the aggressive marketing of baby formula in less-developed countries discourages breast feeding, while health authorities now agree that breast feeding of newborns is the best practice. Discouraging breast feeding in less-developed countries is especially pernicious, critics say, because poor mothers dilute the relatively costly formula to stretch it, which leads to malnutrition and, in countries with contaminated water, higher rates of infant mortality. Nevertheless, even critics agree that the use of baby formulas is helpful for mothers who cannot breast feed or can do so only partially or who themselves are not well nourished.

Beginning in the early 1970s, activist groups—notably Action for Corporate Accountability and International Baby Food Action Network—lobbied against the marketing practices of the formula manufacturers. Over the years, the controversy has been marked by a series of boycotts of the companies that agreed to comply with the activists' demands and then were accused of breaching some of their agreements. In 1981, the World Health Organization and UNICEF worked out the Infant Formula Marketing Code, which sets guidelines for marketing infant formulas. In 1984, Nestlé voluntarily agreed to comply with the code, and the first boycott ended. However, the boycott was renewed in 1988 because the manufacturers were providing free samples of formulas to hospitals in less-developed countries, a practice that Nestlé and the other companies ceased in 1991. Today, the controversy continues over the issue of whether the companies are operating strictly within the limits of the marketing code.

My purpose is not to judge the merits of this particular case, but to point out some interesting features of the way in which it has unfolded and what it means for concerned citizens in a world of transnational corporations. First, concerns about infant formula were first raised by activists in developed countries (Action for Corporate Accountability is based in Minneapolis)—not in the less-developed countries themselves. In other words, the standards applied to corporate behavior in the less-developed countries are those of the most advanced and highly developed countries, where safeguards and standards are highest and where most of the debate originates. In this example, the standards of Minneapolis and those generally of the developed world are becoming universal case by case. Whether Nestlé and other companies were right or wrong, they have had to confront those concerns and standards and attempt to meet them in all countries in which they operate.

The criticism of corporate behavior has been directed to transnational companies, not local producers. Local producers are, of course, impervious to criticism from geographically and culturally distant activists. Global companies, by contrast, are often extremely sensitive to such criticism, not wishing to offend people anywhere, especially in the world's largest markets.

The very size and visibility of global companies makes them obvious objects of attention by concerned citizens and regulatory agencies. And the presence of global companies everywhere makes them accessible anywhere. An activist in Minneapolis who is concerned about conditions in less-developed countries can easily lobby and engage global companies and hardly has to leave home, much less travel to distant nations.

The intervention of the World Health Organization and UNICEF underscores the increasing globalization of the highest standards, the increasing importance of supranational bodies, and the effectiveness of citizen action on global issues. The activist groups may not yet be entirely happy with the outcome, but they certainly cannot say they have been ignored or defeated. And the infant formula companies, which may think that many of the criticisms are unjustified, certainly would not deny that they have to adjust their behavior to satisfy citizens everywhere, not just in the countries in question. Like athletes playing for the world championship, corporations must play to the highest standards of the world league. It goes with the territory.

Finally, beyond all the foregoing concerns about the effect of transnationals on our lives, lies perhaps the broadest and most unsettling anxiety: the fear of general economic exploitation and the domination of people around the world by these giant, octopuslike corporations. We are all familiar with the view that sees economic and cultural imperialism as the underlying dynamic of global trade and global companies. There is no question that global companies bring the countries of the world closer, but it should be equally clear in this newly multilateral world that such companies are not operating outward from centers of imperial might. In fact, it is their very globality and transnational status that disconnects them from the old nationalist power politics. Moreover, as a result of freer trade and the rise of global companies, there are numerous competing centers of economic activity around the world, many of them located in countries that were considered to be in great economic difficulty not so long ago.

What is different today, of course, is that the flows of trade and finance that have always characterized world trade have been augmented by flows of technology and investment. Far from increasing domination, such exchanges give people a greater capacity to resist domination through the wealth that is created, the technology and knowledge that are transferred, and the general improvement in living conditions. A recent study by two economists for the OECD—a group of twenty-four industrialized nations that are devoted to promoting economic growth in both advanced and less-advanced countries—argued that the removal of global trade barriers would bring *annual* economic gains of $475 billion to OECD member-states and $220 billion to developing and former communist countries.[22] As David D. Hale, chief economist for Kemper Financial Companies pointed out, the more than thirty stock markets, capitalized at more than $500 billion, that now operate in the developing world will make these countries less dependent on bank lending and will enable them to attract the huge savings pools controlled by institutional investors, such as the pension funds of North America.[23]

The transfer of advanced technology to developing countries has enabled many of them to become major competitors in industries that were previously thought to be the exclusive province of major industrial nations. South Korea now competes in automobile manufacturing and the production of computers. India is developing a thriving computer software industry. And Japan, now the second largest economy in the world and an early beneficiary of technology transfer following World War II, came to dominate many high value-added industries, and is now perhaps the most important source of new technology in the world.

But the benefits of technology transfer are not confined to developing countries. Major industrial nations also reap great benefits from the technology that flows into their already technology-rich countries. The Japanese automakers' transplant factories have brought advanced manufacturing techniques to the United States and, as a result, increased the efficiency and productivity of American companies that have been forced to face the realities of life-and-death competition. In the four years that Toyota has been building cars in Georgetown, Kentucky, many thousands of American manufacturing executives have visited the plant to learn Toyota's advanced production techniques. In 1991 alone, more than 20,000 American executives made the trip.[24] In steel manufacturing, Japanese techniques of plant automation, computerization, production control, processing, and surface coating have revitalized the American industry, allowing it once again to compete on price and quality around the world. The transfer of Japanese technology has also benefited such important American industries as automobiles, machine tools, and electronics. It's a tough way to go to school, but most executives would agree that the heat of competition and the fight for survival are the best, and perhaps the only, ways to bring about significant improvement in corporate performance.

And it is not only technology that global businesses transfer to developed and less-developed countries, but knowledge in general, both of particular disciplines and of better ways of doing business. Moreover, the transfer of knowledge leads to higher—and increasingly world-class—educational standards everywhere. With the emergence of industries that require an educated populace, countries have an incentive, indeed a duty, to invest in their educational systems. And the graduates of these educational systems have a market in which to sell their skills.

By almost any measure — monetary or non-monetary — the globalization of trade and the transfer of technology over the past twenty-five years have improved the quality of life for billions of people, especially the 2.4 billion inhabitants of countries the World Bank classifies as "low-income economies."[25] While the advanced industrial nations grew by an average of 2.4 percent from 1965 to 1985, Indonesia enjoyed a 4.8 percent annual growth rate; Brazil and Malaysia, a rate of more than 4 percent; and the Four Little Dragons (Hong Kong, Singapore, South Korea, and Taiwan), a rate of 6 percent or better.[26] During the same period, the developing countries raised their world share of manufactured exports from 7.3 percent to more than 17 percent.[27] South Korea rose out of poverty faster than almost any country in history, its living standards rising tenfold since 1950.[28] Nonmonetary standards of wealth are also rising. In the "low-income economies" people now live eleven to thirteen years longer than they did in 1965. Ten percent of college-age Indians, Brazilians, and Turks enroll in college, a figure just a shade under the percentage achieved in Britain, Italy, and Japan in 1965. In Thailand 23 percent of college-age citizens sign up for higher education, and in South Korea the figure is 26 percent, up from just 6 percent in 1965.[29]

But even if increasing global integration through the medium of transnational corporations has not brought old-style economic exploitation, what of cultural domination? Are we rushing headlong toward one homogeneous world in which the onslaught of global products, technologies, and standards utterly effaces national, regional, and ethnic differences? What's to become of the individual's cherished cultural heritage, overshadowed by transnational corporations and increasingly important supranational bodies, from policy groups to trade blocs to multistate federations like the European Community?

As I have been suggesting throughout, the other face of global integration is a corresponding rise in nationalist, ethnic, and cultural diversity. This diversity shows itself as a kind of clamorous tribalism and cultural fervor that many thought had disappeared into the history books. From the breakup of Yugoslavia to the threatened disintegration of Canada, the evidence is everywhere. The former Soviet Union has fragmented into states that are drawn largely along old nationalist and linguistic lines. Nation-states are growing smaller and tending to become more synonymous with ethnic and linguistic groups. The reunification of Germany, though an instance of a state growing larger, is nevertheless a confirmation of the latter tendency. Scottish and Welsh nationalism and cultural pride are powerful new centrifugal forces in the United Kingdom. In continental Europe, long-simmering nationalist sentiments among Basques, Corsicans, Catalonians, Lombardians, and the Flemish and Walloons have been given new impetus by the events in Yugoslavia—so much so, in fact, that many nervous European governments (with the notable exception of Germany) favored preserving Yugoslavian unity.

Of all the paradoxes in the transnational world, this is perhaps the greatest and most profound: Cross-border flows of trade and investments through global companies are not only the chief agents of global integration, they become the chief reason that ethnic and national groups are able to assert themselves with such renewed vigor. It is the prospect of a more united Europe that led something like 70 percent of the Scots to vote in favor of parties advocating devolution or outright independence. With 60 percent of Scotland's manufactured exports now going to Europe, compared with a mere 20 percent only fifteen years ago, and a big financial services industry, an independent Scotland would have an outward-looking, well-balanced economy. Perhaps the new dynamic is best captured by the Scottish National Party's slogan, "Independence within Europe."

Similarly, in Quebec it is the free-trade agreement with the United States and the province's strength in cross-border commerce that allows Quebec to consider seceding from Canada. Nearly half Quebec's trade is with foreign countries, primarily the United States. With a land area 2 1/2 times the size of Texas, vast natural resources, and a growing industrial base in high value-added businesses like aerospace, electronics, telecommunications, and biotechnology, the province is already a formidable economic entity. Though the drive for independence has been slowed somewhat by the recession gripping all of Canada and the second thoughts of some key Quebec business leaders, it is worth remembering that just ten years ago even the idea of separation enjoyed no support among the very business people who are now carefully weighing its merits.

The resurgence of various regions, nationalities, and ethnic groups around the world has been fueled in each case by particular historical, political, and cultural conditions. The breakup of Yugoslavia, an extreme example, appears to be animated by ancient ethnic rivalries and animosities, while Scottish nationalism is marked by a desire for political participation and cultural identity. I don't mean to equate the two situations or to minimize their differences. My point, however, is that nationalist and ethnic resurgence itself, whatever the motivation, becomes much more possible, even realistic, as a result of the globalization of trade. Global interdependence and the multilateral diversification of economic well-being go far toward removing the economic sanctions that nation-states previously applied to restive regional or ethnic groups within their borders. Once merely a gleam in the eye of a few committed nationalists and ethnic champions, such tribalism, in the hothouse atmosphere of increasing globalization, has become a viable alternative among an ever larger number of peoples.

Many observers see great danger in this new nationalist and ethnic fervor, likening it to the volatile conditions that led to World War I, which, after all, was touched off by events in the Balkans. But, today, the fierce fighting in Yugoslavia is largely the exception among the newly freed countries of Eastern Europe and, indeed, among the new nations of the old Soviet Union. With the end of the Cold War, perhaps the more salient comparison is to the terms of the peace treaty following World War I, when Woodrow Wilson strongly encouraged nationalism, believing, in effect, that each language group should have its own nation. Of that disastrous period, Eric F. Goldman, my teacher at Princeton University, wrote: "A world in the throes of an enormously stimulated nationalism had little inclination to make peace without victory, to reduce armaments, to cut down tariffs, or to consider colonies in the genuine spirit of the mandate system."[30] What is different today is that it is precisely the lowering of tariffs and the gradual dismantling of other overt mechanisms that inhibit global trade that have permitted the new tribalism to flourish in the first place. So many groups are now ready to go their own way precisely because they have somewhere to go economically—into the global trading system—and it is along the path of transnational companies and cross-border enterprises that they will get there.

Of course, global economic integration will not proceed at a uniform pace everywhere. Conditions for the countries emerging from the former Soviet Union are likely to be bleak for many years to come, and in Yugoslavia fierce tribalism has already led to tragedy. Nevertheless, I think that there is reason to hope that in the long run and for most of the world's peoples the new tribalism won't lead to the old violence. That hope lies in the pull of international trade and the sinew of transnational enterprise, which are encouraging the rise of a middle ground between the old-style, power-driven nation-state and new-style, potentially explosive ethnic fervor. This middle ground is appearing in areas of regional economic integration now taking shape not only across borders but across linguistic and ethnic groups. Evolving more or less naturally from globalization, these communities of economic interest do not operate like classic nation-states, and they tend to lead to the accommodation of ethnic and national differences.

Nowhere is this phenomenon more strikingly evident than in the American Northwest and the Canadian provinces of British Columbia and Alberta. The economic destiny of this entire region—stretching from Alaska through the two Canadian provinces and down into Washington, Oregon, Montana, and Idaho—is strongly linked to the countries of the Pacific, especially Japan. Boeing, based in Seattle, sells jetliners to Japan and other Asian nations. Wheat grown in the area ends up as noodles sold throughout Asia. Wood from the forests goes to build homes in Tokyo. Moreover, the links among the American states and Canadian provinces are so strong and the regional economy is so coherent that the entire area now promotes itself to the world as a single economic unit known as Cascadia (after the Cascade Mountains).

The consequences are interesting. For example, while much of the rest of the United States was bashing Japan following some widely published, impolitic remarks about the American work ethic by two prominent Japanese politicians, many of the people in Cascadia refused to take part, worrying that the hostility would bring on protectionist legislation that would impair their vigorous trade with Japan. And in the case of the proposed purchase of the Seattle Mariners baseball team by Japanese investors, there was an outpouring of local public support, including a rare page-one editorial in the *Seattle Times*. Cast as an open letter to baseball commissioner Fay Vincent, the editorial asked, "What would possibly keep you from letting Seattle not only keep its baseball team, but grow and flourish with it?"[31] The newspaper, like many of the region's citizens, saw the investment in the Mariners merely as a further strengthening of the region's ties with Asia. Thus, this cross-border community of economic interest undermines, on the one hand, some of the worst tendencies of the nation-state, such as protectionism, and on the other hand, some of the worst tendencies of tribalism, such as racism and xenophobia.

Similar communities of economic interest are arising in other parts of the world. Northern Italy sees its economic future as more dependent on Germany and Switzerland than on Rome or Sicily. With the breakthrough in talks between the South African Nationalist Party and the African National Congress and the hurried withdrawal of Soviet influence, the former frontline states are talking openly about a Southern Africa Trade Zone. The newly independent state of Namibia, governed by the fiercely antiwhite, anti-South Africa, left-wing leaders of the South West Africa People's Organization, has already tied its currency to the South African rand. Many European countries—most notably France, Italy, and Belgium—while ceding their authority upward to the European Commission are also ceding it downward to newly instituted regional structures within their own borders. And the best-organized regions have been engaging in successful interregional cooperation, such as the "Four Motors" project involving Baden-Württemburg in Germany, Rhône-Alpes in France, Catalonia in Spain, and Lombardy in Italy. Connected by fiber-optic cable, they cooperate on research, the exchange of technology, economic development, and cultural exchanges.[32]

Some observers have seen in these developments a return to a kind of fifteenth-century condition of "regional semi-states, where political sovereignty is inchoate and rival areas compete for economic power."[33] But I think this comparison, like the comparisons of today's world with those immediately preceding and following World War I, overlooks the contribution of transnational companies in the rise of such regions and, most important, in providing the connecting fibers among them. Today's economic regions are neither connected by lines of conquest nor separated by mutually exclusive self-interests. Rather, they are intertwined, though loosely, in a skein of cross-border investments, technology transfer, instant communication, and the creation of wealth carried on around the world daily by transnational companies. In a world that is increasingly economically integrated in this way, countries, regions, and citizens are not likely to be held together by the numbing, soul-destroying reach of imperial conquest or to drift inexorably apart on the tides of tribal exclusivity. Most important, they are less likely to resort to the violence that lies at the end of either of those roads.

Indeed, it is this complementary double movement—the simultaneous push and pull of the global and the local—that both gives the emerging transnational world its paradoxical character and marks it at every level of consideration. As I have tried to show throughout this book, the transnational world resists understanding in purely global or in purely local terms. That is why, in summary, my conclusions about it may most succinctly and accurately be stated as a series of paradoxes, apparent contradictions, and counterintuitive propositions. As should be clear by now, some of these conclusions describe already accomplished, if little-understood, facts. Others point to conditions that are just now taking shape. Still others point to the future. But all of them promise a new world for consumers, employees, companies, countries, and citizens alike.

FOR CONSUMERS IN THE TRANSNATIONAL WORLD

- The quality of products will improve even as costs decline and the number of competitors shrinks.
- Tastes will converge internationally even as the demand for individually customized products grows.
- People will use more and more foreign products that are designed and produced locally.
- Customers will behave toward products more like long-term investors even as investors purchase shares on a transaction-oriented, one-shot basis.

FOR MANAGERS AND EMPLOYEES

- A highly focused global company will provide highly diversified individualized career paths.
- Pursuing a global strategy will mean conceptualizing globally but living and working locally.
- Managing a single corporate culture will mean tolerating and channeling a diversity of national and ethnic cultures.

• Forging bigger operations will mean creating leaner, more horizontal organizational structures.

• As a company grows more global, decision making authority and responsibility will be delegated lower in the organization and more locally.

• As a company grows larger, its hierarchy and command structure will diminish while mutual trust and collegiality will flourish.

• As a company competes more fiercely, its top executives will pay more attention to the quality-of-life issues and workload of managers and other employees.

FOR COMPANIES

• Time horizons for ownership and planning will lengthen while reaction time to markets will grow shorter.

• Economies of scale will have to be ever greater, so advantage can be gained in ever more segmented markets.

• The identity of the transnational will appear uniform worldwide even as the cultures in which it operates increase in number and diversity.

• Cross-border joint ventures and strategic alliances will ultimately lead to more, not fewer, cross-border mergers.

FOR COUNTRIES

• An integrating global market means disintegrating empires.

• Successful regulations will be those that deregulate the movement of people, capital, and goods across borders.

• Determining the national identity of a transnational company will be based on the location of its assets, not on the citizenship of its owners or managers.

• The wealth of a nation will be in direct proportion to the nation's international attractiveness.

• Improved national competitiveness will require turning away from nationalism.

FOR CITIZENS OF THE WORLD

• The continued blurring of national boundaries stimulated by economic interdependence will mean a rise in cultural, ethnic, and tribal diversity.

• The decline of corporate accountability to any one country will mean a rise in the ethical standards of corporate behavior in all countries.

• The transfer of common technology, improved productivity, and higher educational standards to people around the world by giant transnational corporations will mean that individuals will become more, not less, capable of resisting domination.

It may seem curious that this point in history is best summarized as a series of paradoxes. After all, we expect the affairs of humankind to be described clearly and in ways that help us examine distinct patterns of events. It is hard to understand why our age should appear to be so different, so paradoxical. No doubt, there is a rhythm in the affairs of people, just as there is a rhythm in natural events, but the human rhythms are complicated by many wavelengths and confound the longing for mathematical regularity.

As we approach the end of this century, I believe we are making a major transition from one pattern of national and international relationships to a new and still-fragile and indistinct form. It is as if the pages of history are shifting into a new template, just as the shifting of the Earth's great tectonic plates causes continents to move, mountains to rise and fall, and oceans to engulf what was once the high ground. For people living near a fault line, the process is especially jarring, as the shifts occur and new shapes emerge.

Over the past fifty years or so, we rushed into a new set of relationships that have united the world in countless ways. The international reality enjoyed by the relatively few English gentlemen at the turn of the century described by John Maynard Keynes has reappeared as the present reality for hundreds of millions of men and women around the world. Our lives now intertwine in ways never thought possible and ways so myriad and subtle that we don't even feel or understand their effects. Such a complex of global relationships was never envisioned or legislated. It wasn't promulgated or even advertised. But it happened—and without many of us who were deeply involved in the process knowing what was actually occurring.

The global corporation has been a major beneficiary of this historic change. Stimulated by the positive moves to lower trade barriers following World War II, the transnational corporation has now moved into the vanguard and has become an instrument of global transformation. Evolving from an export-oriented international posture to the multinational phase and lately to the transnational stage, large global corporations are outpacing the traditional nation-state and its political processes. Transnational corporations have become more than major engines for the creation of wealth. Through a great global embrace that is bringing people, economies, and cultures together, transnationals have become the single most important force in advancing global interdependence.

As citizens, we are hard put to say where all this is taking us and what these new patterns mean. But we can be sure that the tectonic plates of history have shifted. We feel the tremors. We hear the rumblings. We see the ground change under our feet. And as we look with a mixture of uncertainty and hope on the new world coming into being, we must take care that this global embrace that is drawing the peoples of the world together does not become either suffocating or closed. It must crush no one and exclude no one; rather, it should bring us all together in bonds of prosperity and mutual respect. That is a world we can welcome with open arms.

Notes

CHAPTER ONE: THE GLOBAL MALL

1. "Reebok Rebounds With the Pump," *New York Times,* June 7, 1991, D-6.

2. Roger Cohen, "For Coke, World Is Its Oyster," *New York Times,* November 21, 1991, D-1.

3. Ibid., D-5.

4. Doron P. Levin, "Honda Sets U.S. Exports To France," *New York Times,* September 16, 1991, D-1.

5. David E. Sanger, "Japanese Cars Stronger in Weak U.S. Economy," *New York Times,* September 4, 1991, D-1, D-3.

6. Gregory A. Patterson, "Foreign or Domestic? Car Firms Play Games with the Categories," *Wall Street Journal,* November 11, 1991, A-6.

7. Jack Lesar, "Toyota Takes Pot Shot at Chrysler," United Press International, February 7, 1992.

8. Ibid.

9. Richard I. Kirkland, Jr., "Entering a New Age of Boundless Competition." *Fortune,* March 14, 1988, 40.

10. "World Trade Growth Sputters," *Wall Street Journal,* March 18, 1992, A-10.

11. John Maynard Keynes, *The Economic Consequences of the Peace* (New York: Harcourt, Brace & Howe, 1920), 11–12.

12. Kirkland, "Entering a New Age of Boundless Competition," 42.

13. William B. Johnston, "Global Work Force 2000: The New World Labor Market," *Harvard Business Review* (March–April 1991), vol. 69, no. 2, 116.

14. Marcia Parker, "Global Allocator Termed New Powerhouse," *Pensions & Investments,* October 29, 1990, 35.

15. Jonathan Fuerbringer, "A.D.R.'s Multiply in the Rush to Diversify Abroad," *New York Times,* September 8, 1991, III-15.

16. Diana B. Henriques, "In World Markets, Loose Regulation," *New York Times,* July 23, 1991, D-1.

17. Tim Golden, "Scanning the Sky Over Mexico's Parade," *New York Times,* August 5, 1991, D-1, D-4.

18. Robert B. Reich, "Who Is Them?" *Harvard Business Review,* (March–April 1991), vol. 69, no. 2, 84.

19. Richard W. Stevenson, "Will Aerospace Be the Next Casualty?" *New York Times,* March 15, 1992, III-6.

20. Steven Greenhouse, "There's No Stopping Europe's Airbus Now," *New York Times,* June 23, 1991, III-1.

21. Stuart Elliott, "If All Else Fails, Try Plain English," *New York Times,* August 30, 1991, D-1.

22. Ibid.

23. David A. Aaker, "Guarding the Power of a Brand Name," *New York Times,* December 1, 1991, III-13.

24. Peter Passell, "Car Wars: More Bad News," *New York Times,* June 26, 1991, D-2.

25. "The Stateless Corporation," *Business Week,* May 14, 1990, 99.

26. Joel Havemann, "European Car Market Hits the Road in Fits and Starts," *Los Angeles Times,* May 5, 1992, H-3.

27. Ferdinand Protzman, "A Clash of Views on Daimler-Benz," *New York Times,* June 12, 1991, D-10.

28. Graham Bannock, R. E. Baxter, and Evan Davis, *The Penguin Dictionary of Economics,* 4th ed. (London: Penguin Books, 1987), 282.

29. Louis Uchitelle, "Global Strategies vs. National Ties," *New York Times,* March 26, 1990, D-2.

30. Jeremy Main, "How To Go Global — And Why," *Fortune,* August 28, 1989, 72.

31. "The Stateless Corporation," *Business Week,* May 14, 1990, 103.

32. Robert B. Reich, "The Myth of 'Made in the U.S.A,'" *Wall Street Journal*, July 5, 1991, A-6.

33. Charles R. Morris, *The Coming Global Boom* (New York: Bantam Books, 1990), 155.

34. Reich, "Who Is Them?", 84.

35. T. Levitt, "The Globalization of Markets," *Harvard Business Review*, May–June 1983, vol. 61, no. 3, 92–102.

36. Keith Bradsher, "Telephone Services: A Growing Form of 'Foreign Aid,'" *New York Times*, October 21, 1990, III-5.

37. George Melloan, "Phone Technology Is Opening Up New Worlds," *Wall Street Journal Europe*, October 15, 1991, 11.

38. John Plender, "Life After Debt in Latin America," *Financial Times*, March 2, 1992, 16.

39. Keith Bradsher, "In Mexico, Fears of Free Trade Melt," *New York Times*, September 22, 1991, III-5.

40. Ibid.

41. For all statistics on Venezuela, see James Brooke, "Venezuela Is Surging Again After a Period of Difficulties," *New York Times*, September 16, 1991, D-1.

42. James Brooke, "Investors in Venezuela Are Confident," *New York Times*, February 13, 1992, D-6.

43. Keith Bradsher, "India Approves Ventures with Americans," *New York Times*, September 26, 1991, D-10.

44. Sheryl Wu Dunn, "As China's Economy Thrives, the Public Sector Flounders," *New York Times*, December 18, 1991, A-14.

45. G. Bruce Knecht, "Portugal Is Transformed for Border-Free Trading," *New York Times*, March 12, 1992, D-2.

46. *Wall Street Journal*, ad prepared by Spring, O'Brien, Tolson, & Co.

47. J. Howells, "The Globalisation of Research and Development: A New Era of Change?" *Science and Public Policy* 17 (October 1990), 275.

48. George Melloan, "Global Manufacturing Is an Intricate Game," *Wall Street Journal*, November 29, 1988, A-23.

49. "The Stateless Corporation," *Business Week*, May 14, 1990, 101.

50. John Markoff, "Hyundai to Move Its PC Unit to U.S.," *New York Times*, April 20, 1992, D-3.

CHAPTER TWO: THE TRANSNATIONAL CROSSROADS

1. Andrew Pollack, "Technology Without Borders Raises Big Questions for U.S.," *New York Times*, January 1, 1992, 48.

2. Michael Porter, *Competitive Advantage: Creating and Sustaining Superior Performance* (New York: Free Press, 1985), 320.

3. David E. Sanger, "Costs May Be Too High For All-American Chips," *New York Times*, January 1, 1992, 48.

4. Ibid.

5. Barnaby J. Feder, "Southwestern Bell's Moves Pay Off," *New York Times*, November 16, 1992, D-1.

6. Kevin K. Jones and Walter E. Shill, "Allying for Advantage," *McKinsey Quarterly*, 1991, no. 3, 80.

7. William Dawkins, "Alliance Drives a Smooth Course," *Financial Times*, November 19, 1991, 27.

8. Ibid.

9. Ibid.

10. Robert B. Reich, "The Myth of 'Made in the U.S.A.'" *Wall Street Journal*, July 5, 1991, A-6.

11. Damon Darlin and Joseph B. White, "GM and Daewoo Are Set to End Korean Venture," *Wall Street Journal Asia*, January 16, 1992, 8.

12. Ibid.

13. Alan Cane, "Hard Times for European Hardware," *Financial Times*, October 4, 1991, 25.

14. Ibid.

15. Ferdinand Protzman, "Costly German Lesson: Pirelli's Failed Takeover," *New York Times*, December 3, 1991, D-2.

16. Ibid.

17. Steven Greenhouse, "French Merger to Create A New Electronics Giant," *New York Times*, December 19, 1991, D-2.

18. Ibid.

19. Clifford J. Levy, "The Growing Gelt in Others' Words," *New York Times*, October 20, 1991, III-5.

20. John J. Keller, "Telecommunications Carriers Ready to Reap Bonanza of Operating Global Data Networks," *Wall Street Journal Europe*, March 11, 1992, 7.

21. Ken Wells, "British Air Seeks to Combat Competitors From Abroad by Getting Foothold in U.S.," *Wall Street Journal*, October 29, 1991, A-18.

22. Richard W. Stevenson, "Gain for McDonnell Douglas Raises Fears of U.S. Loss," *New York Times*, November 11, 1991, D-1.

Chapter Three: Under the Mushrooms

1. Randall Rothenberg, "Time-Warner Bid for Global Marketing," *New York Times*, March 6, 1989, D-11.

2. Ibid.

3. Yuri Radzievsky, "Multi-Lingual Marketing Campaigns: How To Speak Your Customers' Language," *Financier 15* (May 1991), 26.

4. Ibid, 27.

5. Ibid.

6. Edwin McDowell, "Coleman Is Glowing Overseas," *New York Times*, December 9, 1991, D-1. The Coleman examples that follow are McDowell's.

7. Matt Rothman, "Can Apple Sustain Its Drive Into Japan's Computer Market?" *New York Times*, January 5, 1992, III-9.

8. The Chiclets and Pillsbury examples are taken from John S. Hill and Richard R. Still, "Adapting Products to LCD Tastes," *Harvard Business Review* (March–April 1984), vol. 62, no. 2, 95.

9. Ibid.

10. Ibid.

11. Stephanie Strom, "U.S. Garment Makers Come Home," *New York Times*, October 8, 1991, D-1.

12. Eben Shapiro, "Overseas Sizzle for McDonald's," *New York Times*, April 17, 1992, D-4.

13. Louis Uchitelle, "Only the Bosses Are American," *New York Times*, July 24, 1989, D-1.

14. Doron P. Levin, "Too American for Its Own Good?" *New York Times*, October 27, 1991, III-6.

15. Harry Jupiter, "Fujitsu's All-American Strategy," *San Francisco Examiner and Chronicle*, Sunday, December 15, 1991, E-3.

16. Ferdinand Protzman, "Greetings from Fortress Germany," *New York Times*, August 18, 1991, III-1.

17. William Taylor, "The Logic of Global Business: An Interview with ABB's Percy Barnevik," *Harvard Business Review* (March–April 1991), vol. 69, no. 2, 94.

18. Milton Moskowitz, Robert Levering, and Michael Katz, *Everybody's Business: A Field Guide to the 400 Leading Companies in America* (New York: Doubleday Currency, 1990), 248, 236.

19. Christopher Lorenz, "The Birth of a 'Transnational,'" *McKinsey Quarterly*, Autumn 1989, 72–93.

20. Clifford Geertz, "Common Sense as a Cultural System," *Local Knowledge: Further Essays in Interpretive Anthropology* (New York: Basic Books, 1983), 73–93.

CHAPTER FOUR: THE WORLD UPSIDE DOWN

1. See, for example, Christopher A. Bartlett and Sumantra Ghoshal, "Managing Across Borders, New Strategic Requirements," *Sloan Management Review 7* (Summer 1987), 7–17.

2. Michael E. Porter, *Competitive Advantage* (New York: Free Press, 1985), 72.

3. Scott McMurray, "U.S. Chemical Firms Keep Export Edge," *Wall Street Journal Europe,* February 6, 1992, 7.

4. Keith Bradsher, "U.S. and China Reach Accord on Copying," *New York Times,* January 17, 1992, D-1.

5. Milt Freudenheim, "Keeping the Pipeline Filled at Merck," *New York Times,* February 16, 1992, III-1.

6. Milt Freudenheim, "Quarterly Profit Up by 20% At Bristol-Myers Squibb," *New York Times,* January 17, 1992, D-4.

7. Toshiro Fujiwara, "Management Innovations in Production and Quality at Nippon Steel Corporation" (Speech presented at the Second Global Conference on Management Innovation, London, December 1991).

8. Doron P. Levin, "Cutbacks Alone Won't Reverse Decline of G.M., Experts Say," *New York Times,* December 23, 1991, D-5.

9. Michael J. Lacktorin, "Transnationalism: Fitting Japan Into Your Transnational Strategy." (Business Series, Bulletin 129, Tokyo: Sophia University Institute of Comparative Culture, 1990), 28. The examples of changes at Unilever that follow are his.

CHAPTER FIVE: THE SOFTWARE OF BUSINESS

1. New York: Oxford University Press, 1975, 11–13.

2. "Tylenol's 'Miracle' Comeback," *Time,* October 17, 1983, 67.

3. Ibid.

4. "Can Perrier Purify Its Reputation?" *Business Week,* February 26, 1990, 45.

5. See, for example, "What's Ailing Big Blue?" *Business Week,* June 17, 1991, 24.

6. Robert McGough, "Behind the Alliance," *San Francisco Examiner,* December 15, 1991, E-16.

7. Quoted in Doron P. Levin, "Cutbacks Alone Won't Reverse Decline of G.M., Experts Say," *New York Times,* December 23, 1991, D-5.

8. Ibid.

9. Joseph Weber, "A Big Company That Works," *Business Week,* May 4, 1992, 126.

10. John Holusha, "A Softer 'Neutron Jack' at G.E.," *New York Times,* March 4, 1992, D-1. Subsequent quotations of Welch and Edward Hood are from this article.

11. Quoted in Holusha, "A Softer 'Neutron Jack' at G.E.," D-1.

12. Levin, "Cutbacks Alone Won't Reverse Decline of G.M., Experts Say," D-5.

13. "Isuzu Names American to No. 2 Post," *Washington Post,* December 4, 1991, F-1.

14. John Holusha, "Pushing the Envelope at Boeing," *New York Times,* November 10, 1991, III-1.

15. Though my emphasis differs somewhat, the Dow example comes from Roderick E. White and Thomas A. Poynter, "Organizing for World-wide Advantage," in *Managing the Global Firm,* ed. Christopher A. Bartlett, Yves Doz, and Gunnar Hedlund (New York: Routledge, 1990), 100–101.

CHAPTER SIX: MELODIOUS ARCHITECTURE

1. Louis A. Allen, *Professional Management* (New York: McGraw-Hill Book Co., 1973), 54.

2. Peter Drucker, *Concept of the Corporation* (New York: Harper & Row), 1946.

3. Details of the NEC program are taken from Shin-ichi Itoh, "NEC Meets the Challenge of the 90s through Time-based Strategy: Implementing Strategic IE" (Speech delivered at the Second Global Conference on Management Innovation, London, December 2–4, 1991), Shin-ichi Itoh is executive vice president, NEC Corporation.

4. W. Edwards Deming, *Quality, Productivity, and Competitive*

Position (Cambridge, Massachusetts Institute of Technology, 1982).

5. Quoted in Andrew Lorenz, "Rover Drives for Japanese Working Practices," *London Sunday Times,* April 5, 1992, 7.

6. Quoted in ibid.

7. Percy Barnevik, "Report from Asea's Extraordinary Shareholders' Meeting on November 11, 1987," 4–5.

8. Ibid., 10.

9. See, for example, ibid., 9–10.

10. William Taylor, "The Logic of Global Business: An Interview with ABB's Percy Barnevik." *Harvard Business Review* (March–April 1991), vol. 69, no. 2, 91.

11. Ibid.

12. Ibid.

13. Ibid., 92.

14. Ibid., 92–93.

15. Ibid., 96.

16. Percy Barnevik, "Report from Asea's Extraordinary Shareholders' Meeting on November 11, 1987," 6.

17. The discussion of Asea Brown Boveri's structure is heavily indebted to "The Organizing Logic of ABB," *Harvard Business Review* (March–April 1991), vol. 69, no. 2, 93, and to the company's literature.

18. Roger Cohen, "The Very Model of Efficiency," *New York Times,* March 2, 1992, D-8.

19. Ibid., D-1.

20. Ben Wattenberg, *The First Universal Nation: Leading Indicators and Ideas About the Surge of America in the 1990s* (New York: Free Press, 1991).

21. Claudia H. Deutsch, "Global Issues in Every Classroom," *New York Times,* August 25, 1991, III-25.

22. Elizabeth M. Fowler, "East Europe Latest Lure For M.B.A.'s," *New York Times,* June 4, 1991, D-19.

23. Elizabeth M. Fowler, "Customized Management Training," *New York Times,* June 18, 1991, D-11.

CHAPTER SEVEN: CALLING THE TUNE

1. Sarah Bartlett, "Gambling with the Big Boys," *New York Times Magazine,* May 5, 1991, 57.

2. Peter F. Drucker, "Reckoning with the Pension Fund Revolution," *Harvard Business Review* (March–April 1991), vol. 69, no.2, 106.

3. Bartlett, "Gambling With the Big Boys," 69. See also Bartlett, *The Money Machine: How KKR Manufactured Power and Profits* (New York: Warner Books, 1991) from which the article was adapted.

4. Bartlett, "Gambling With the Big Boys," 69.

5. Roland M. Machold, "The American Corporation and the Institutional Investor: Are There Lessons from Abroad?" *Columbia Business Law Review* (1988), no.3, 751.

6. Ibid., 752.

7. Mary Billard, "Grit Those Teeth, It's Annual Meeting Time," *New York Times*, May 5, 1991, IV-25.

8. Richard W. Stephenson, "Battling for Shareholder Rights," *New York Times*, June 6, 1991, D-1.

9. Robert Monks and Nell Minow, *Power and Responsibility* (New York: HarperCollins, 1991).

10. Steve Lohr, "Recession Puts a Harsh Spotlight on Hefty Pay of Top Executives," *New York Times*, January 20, 1992, D-8.

11. Stephen Labaton, "Companies Told to Let Holders Vote on Pay," *New York Times*, February 14, 1992, D-5.

12. Kevin G. Salwen, "The SEC Undergoes a Conversion in Crusade Against Executive Pay," *Wall Street Journal*, February 13, 1992, A-1.

13. Machold, "The American Corporation and the Institutional Investor," 755.

14. Leslie Wayne, "Seeking to Stay Out of Proxy Battles," *New York Times*, April 8, 1991, D-4.

15. Robert A. G. Monks, "The Oxymoron in the Boardroom," *New York Times*, May 5, 1991, IV-13.

16. Eric N. Berg, "Dissident Sears Holder Fails to Win Board Seat," *New York Times*, May 10, 1991, D-1.

17. Ibid.

18. Monks, "The Oxymoron in the Board Room," IV-13.

19. Ibid.

20. "The Private Shareholder," *Financial Times*, October 18, 1990, 20.

21. Institutional Shareholders' Committee, "The Role and Duties of Directors—A Statement of Best Practice" (n.d., released April 18, 1991).

22. Ian Roger, "Stepping Out on to a Wider Stage," *Financial Times*, February 6, 1992, 15.

23. Ibid.

24. Charles Handy, "A Company Possessed," *Director,* June 1990, 27.

25. Richard W. Stevenson, "Top Officers Rewarded at General Dynamics," *New York Times,* October 9, 1991, D-4.

26. *1991 Annual Report* (Chicago: Quaker Oats Company, 1991).

27. Doron P. Levin, "The Rubber-Stamp Era Comes to a Close at G.M." *New York Times,* April 8, 1992, D-19.

CHAPTER EIGHT: THE SOVEREIGN COMPANY?

1. Letter to the editor, *New York Times,* April 26, 1991, A-28.

2. Ferdinand Protzman, "Germans Are Rallying Round the Mark," *New York Times,* December 7, 1991, 38.

3. Quoted in Alan Riding, "Europe Is Getting Jittery About Arranged Union," *New York Times,* April 19, 1992, I-8.

4. George Melloan, "Phone Technology Is Opening Up New Worlds," *Wall Street Journal Europe,* October 15, 1991, 11.

5. Craig R. Whitney, "It's 1992, and No One Is Leading Europe's March to Unity," *New York Times,* March 29, 1992, IV-5.

6. *Introduction to the Company* (Tokyo: Canon, n.d.), 4.

7. Akio Morita, "A New Paradigm for True Partnership," January 3, 1992.

8. Quoted in Robert Neff, "Japan Takes a Good Look at Itself," *Business Week,* February 17, 1992, 18.

9. Richard Preston, "Lean, Mean, and American," *New York Times,* January 14, 1992, A-23.

10. Winston Churchill, speech to the House of Commons, November 11, 1947.

11. James Sterngold, "Regulation, Japan Style," *New York Times,* September 9, 1991, D-2.

12. *Global Competitiveness of U.S. Advanced-Technology Manufacturing Industries: Pharmaceuticals* (report to the Committee on Finance, United States Senate, (USITC Publication 2437), September 1991, 8.

13. Ibid., 2.

14. Ibid.

15. Ibid.

16. Ibid., 3.

17. Ibid., 9.

18. Ibid.

CHAPTER NINE: TRIBES AND TRANSNATIONALS

1. *Business Week,* May 14, 1990, 98.

2. James Brooke, "America—Environmental Dictator?" *New York Times,* May 3, 1992, III-7.

3. Peter Passell, "Tuna and Trade: Whose Rules?" *New York Times,* February 19, 1992, D-2.

4. Gene M. Grossman and Alan B. Krueger, *Environmental Impacts of a North American Free Trade Agreement* (Discussion Papers in Economics), rev. ed. (Princeton, N.J.: Woodrow Wilson School, Princeton University, February 1992).

5. Gene Grossman, "In Poor Regions, Environmental Law . . ." *New York Times,* March 1, 1992, III-11.

6. Grossman and Krueger, *Environmental Impacts of a North American Free Trade Agreement,* 35–36.

7. David Bowen and Mary Fagan, "Coal Faces the Final Crisis," *The Independent,* March 8, 1992, 6. Figures on employment in coal mining are also taken from this article.

8. Marlise Simons, "Ecological Plea from Executives," *New York Times,* May 8, 1992, D-10.

9. Ibid., D-1.

10. "Industry Codes and Charters: An Overview," Burson-Marsteller, March 6, 1992, 4.

11. Ibid., 5.

12. Ibid., 7.

13. Michael E. Porter, "Environmental Rules Stimulate Innovation; They Don't Stifle It." *Scientific American* 264 (April 1991), 168.

14. Dan Piraro, Chronicle Features, reprinted in "Biotechnology Industry Quarterly Report," *Smith Barney Research,* January 27, 1992, 1.

15. David Stipp and Udaya Gupta, "For Biotech, Pure Genius Isn't Enough," *Wall Street Journal,* February 24, 1992, Bl.

16. "Biotech: America's Dream Machine," *Business Week,* March 2, 1992, 67.

17. Stipp and Gupta, "For Biotech, Pure Genius Isn't Enough."

18. Ibid.

19. Ibid.

20. Ibid.

21. Robert E. Calem, "Polyvision Nips at the Heels of LCD," *New York Times,* March 1, 1992, III-7. My discussion of Polyvision is

indebted to this article and to interviews with company officials.

22. Peter Norman, "Time to Find a Free Trade Vision in the Crystal Ball," *Financial Times*, April 21, 1992, 15.

23. David D. Hale, "The Coming Golden Age of Capitalism," *Wall Street Journal*, November 7, 1991, A-14.

24. Doron P. Levin, "Toyota Plant in Kentucky Is Font of Ideas for U.S.," *New York Times*, May 5, 1992, A-1.

25. Statistics on monetary and nonmonetary improvement in the quality of life are from Richard I. Kirkland, Jr., "Entering the New Age Of Boundless Competition," *Fortune*, March 14, 1988, 42–43.

26. Ibid., 46. Growth as measured by the per capita GNP. At a 4 percent annual rate, the per capita GNP doubles in just eighteen years.

27. Ibid.

28. Sylvia Nasar, "Industrial Policy the Korean Way," *New York Times*, July 12, 1991, D-2.

29. Richard I. Kirkland, Jr., "Entering a New Age of Borderless Competition," *Fortune*, March 14, 42–43.

30. Eric F. Goldman, *Rendezvous with Destiny* (New York: Alfred A. Knopf, 1952), 272.

31. Quoted in Timothy Egan, "Mariner Fans Angered by Vincent's Response," *New York Times*, January 25, 1992, 33.

32. Neal Acherson, "The New Europe," *The Independent*, February 9, 1992, 31.

33. "Europa, Europa," *The New Republic*, May 4, 1991, 7.

INDEX